PREGNANT PASSION

Society of Biblical Literature

Semeia Studies

Number 44

PREGNANT PASSION
GENDER, SEX, AND VIOLENCE IN THE BIBLE

PREGNANT PASSION

GENDER, SEX, AND VIOLENCE IN THE BIBLE

Edited by
Cheryl A. Kirk-Duggan

Society of Biblical Literature
Atlanta

PREGNANT PASSION

GENDER, SEX, AND VIOLENCE IN THE BIBLE

Library of Congress Cataloging-in-Publication Data

Pregnant passion : gender, sex, and violence in the Bible / edited by Cheryl A. Kirk-Duggan.
     p. cm. — (Society of Biblical Literature Semeia studies ; no. 44)
    Includes bibliographical references.
    ISBN 1-58983-074-1 (pbk. : alk. paper)
    1. Sex role—Biblical teaching. 2. Sex—Biblical teaching. 3. Violence—Biblical teaching. 4. Bible—Criticism, interpretation, etc. I. Kirk-Duggan, Cheryl A. II. Series: Semeia studies ; no. 44.
    BS680.S5P74 2003b
    220.6—dc21
                             2003001743

11 10 09 08 07 06 05 04 03   5 4 3 2 1

Printed in the United States of America on acid-free, recycled paper
conforming to ANSI/NISO Z39.48-1992 (R1997) and ISO 9706:1994
standards for paper permanence.

CONTENTS

PART 1: PASSION, POWER, AND RELATIONAL CONFLICT

PART 2: LEGAL AND REGULATORY MATTERS

PART 3: TYPES, STEREOTYPES, AND ARCHETYPES

ABBREVIATIONS

AB	Anchor Bible
ABD	*Anchor Bible Dictionary.* Edited by D. N. Freedman. 6 vols. New York: Doubleday, 1992.
Bib	*Biblica*
BibInt	*Biblical Interpretation*
BRev	*Bible Review*
BTB	*Biblical Theology Bulletin*
CBQ	*Catholic Biblical Quarterly*
ExpTim	*Expository Times*
FCB	Feminist Companion to the Bible
IDBSupp	*Interpreter's Dictionary of the Bible: Supplementary Volume.* Edited by K. Crim. Nashville: Abingdon, 1976.
IEJ	*Israel Exploration Journal*
Int	*Interpretation*
JBL	*Journal of Biblical Literature*
JBQ	*Jewish Bible Quarterly*
JETS	*Journal of the Evangelical Theological Society*
JFSR	*Journal of Feminist Studies in Religion*
JR	*Journal of Religion*
JSNT	*Journal for the Study of the New Testament*
JSOT	*Journal for the Study of the Old Testament*
JSOTSup	Journal for the Study of the Old Testament Supplement Series
LCBI	Literary Currents in Biblical Interpretation
NAC	New American Commentary
NEchtB	Neue Echter Bibel
NIB	*The New Interpreter's Bible*
NICOT	New International Commentary on the Old Testament
OBT	Overtures to Biblical Theology
OTE	*Old Testament Essays*
OTL	Old Testament Library
RB	*Revue biblique*
RTR	*Reformed Theological Review*
SBLDS	Society of Biblical Literature Dissertation Series
SBT	Studies in Biblical Theology

SJOT	*Scandinavian Journal of the Old Testament*
SJT	*Scottish Journal of Theology*
StPatr	Studia patristica
TBT	*The Bible Today*
USQR	*Union Seminary Quarterly Review*
VT	*Vetus Testamentum*
WBC	Word Biblical Commentary
WW	*Word and World*
ZAW	*Zeitschrift für die alttestamentliche Wissenschaft*

INTRODUCTION—PREGNANT PASSION:
GENDER, SEX, AND VIOLENCE IN THE BIBLE

Cheryl A. Kirk-Duggan
Graduate Theological Union

In the beginning, God created life out of chaos and humanity out of dust. With the introduction of the *adamah* creature, Eve, and their offspring—gender, sexuality, and violence emerge. Sacred and secular texts about sex and violence are *pregnant:* heavy with emotional and religious implications; heavy in that many tend to misread or ignore these texts. Our focus in this work on pregnant passion is not about issues concerning conception, the process of physical childbearing, or midwifery. When a text is pregnant it is ripe, laden, and full of ideas, a fertile plain upon which a community and now we as scholars can explore, exegete, interrogate, and analyze toward discerning messages of life's bitter and sweet realities. Such a mindset, which becomes an excursion through history, literary, and aesthetic analysis, embraces passion. Thus, the first part of the title for this volume, "Pregnant Passion" reflects both on the richness of biblical texts and on the energies with which scholars will engage these texts in working through matters of gender, sex, and violence.

Donna Haraway notes that "Gender is always a relationship, not a preformed category of beings or a possession that one can have. Gender does not pertain more to women than to men. Gender is the relation between variously constituted categories of men and women (and variously arrayed tropes), differentiated by nation, generation, class, lineage, color, and much else" (Haraway: 28). In general parlance and the language of documents for the United Nations for over two decades, gender pertains to the socially constructed or fabricated differences between women and men and the related, ensuing unequal power relationships. Understanding gender suggests that the differences between men and women are not unavoidable, inescapable, or basic products of biological sex differences (Women's Caucus for Gender Justice). Gender, then, focuses on the behavioral, cultural, or psychological traits typically associated with one sex. In biblical texts, an individual's gender has strong ties to the process, necessity, and context of marriage, genealogy, inheritance, kingship, sociocultural location, land, right relations, and finding favor with God. Gender issues always concern one's notion of sex.

Sex and sexualities often get constructed around whether one appears to be male, female, man, woman, boy, or girl. Males are those who produce sperm. Females are those who produce eggs. Thus, in one narrow sense, sex pertains to the total structural, functional, and behavioral characteristics of living things that are involved in reproduction by two interacting parents and that distinguish males and females. Such a definition fails to allow for the reality of sex and sexuality that includes, but is not reduced to, activity among human beings for the sake of procreation, where there is a distinct need for female eggs and male sperm together to combine their genetic material to reproduce. Most species have two sexes, female and male. Some organisms and fungi involve more than two sexes but produce in pairs. Species such as geckos and earthworms can produce either sexually or asexually. In casual conversation the term *sex*, as shorthand, is used to mean sexual intercourse. In many species, including birds and mammals, sex chromosomes determine one's sex. Females usually have two X chromosomes (XX) and males have one of each (XY). While some people use the terms *gender* and *sex* interchangeably, in contemporary parlance *sex* usually refers to biological markers and *gender* to markers of social and cultural construction. For some, *gender* refers to differences between male and female, and *sex* refers to the erotic (http://www.wikipedia.com/wiki/Sex). These definitions are part of but not the whole picture, for pertinent to the conversation are matters regarding lesbian/gay/transgendered/bisexual persons: those who may appear male or female but who remind us that there are more than male and female sexualities; there is more than a heterosexual experience. The articles in this volume have not addressed homosexuality, bisexuality, or transgendered realities in a primary way, though some reference emerges in a few articles, notwithstanding the biblical text as primary focus. Sex and sexualities in many cultures are rife with taboos and much misinformation. Biblically speaking, one's embodiment of sexuality has ties to feasts and famines, betrayal and bloodshed, seduction and sensuality, power and politics, virtue and violence—from Tamar, Judah and her twins, Esther, Vashti, and Xerxes, to Herodias, Salome and John the Baptist, and the hemorrhaging woman and Jesus. Much work still needs to be done regarding biblical texts, biblical interpretation, sex, and sexualities, given how frequently misreadings of particular texts have been used to demonize persons because of their orientation or because of the use of their bodies. The parameters of this volume, however, has not been to explore the specifics of sex or that of gender but the intersection of the two with violence.

The prevalence of the intersection of gender, sex and violence begs for a volume that explores some of the dynamics of power, place, and personality. How intriguing that a so-called "good book," one used as the basis of denominational authority and for slogans to get people through the day is so filled with violence—a violence orchestrated by divine and human hands. Violence is that which violates, destroys, manipulates, corrupts, defiles, and robs us of dignity and of true personhood. Violence is the use of thought and deed within a continuum of the physical, the philosophical, and the psychological that oppresses and robs an individual or community of their gift of freedom and the sacredness of their person. Violence is a practice of idolatry: that which defames God's created order. Divine and human violence have intimate ties to covenant obedience. That alleged texts of freedom, liberation, and elevation, from Exodus and the Deuteronomistic texts through Psalms and the Gospels, use violence as a means to a good end of covenant relations, salvation, and resurrection ought to cause us some pause, though many of these concepts can only be mentioned here and not fully addressed in this particular work.

This volume presents essays that explore the dynamics, intersection, and relatedness of gender, human sexuality, and violence in the Bible. All contributors to this volume carefully worked through the related definitions of the categories of gender, sex, and violence in their essay, particularly analyzing how these categories function in their selected pericopes. The volume intentionally engages new ideas and diverse voices and exegetical styles to unpack the prevalence of violence in sacred texts. Further, the volume allows for how when questions of sex and gender intermingle with violence, a teleological ethic comes into play. The violence is justified if the right players and the right god wins. Each author ultimately names the pregnant passion in the particular text and reflects on how such rhetoric resonates with a twenty-first-century reader.

The volume is divided into three parts: Part 1: Passion, Power, and Relational Conflict; Part 2: Legal and Regulatory Matters; and Part 3: Types, Stereotypes, and Archetypes. "Love, Honor, and Violence: Socioconceptual Matrix in Genesis 34," by Mignon R. Jacobs, Fuller Theological Seminary, examines the concepts of love, honor, and violence as exemplified in the behaviors of Dinah, Shechem, Jacob, and his sons. Genesis 34 is a text ripe for exploring the correlations between the occurrences of love and violence amid personal relationships and the institution of marriage. "Slingshots, Ships, and Personal Psychosis: Murder, Sexual Intrigue, and Power in the Lives of David and Othello," by Cheryl A. Kirk-Duggan, Graduate Theological Union, engages in a comparative analysis between Othello and David, two ambitious leaders, in their relationships to family, power, and oppression. These two tragic stories afford a fascinating laboratory from which to view emotional and political issues central to private and public life in the brokerage of power and control. "Who Wants to Marry a Persian King? Gender Games and Wars and the Book of Esther," by Nicole Duran, United Theological Seminary, pits a modern, popular television show (*Who Wants to Marry a Multimillionaire?*) in dialogue with the book of Esther to explore the issue of proximity to power in Esther, including the risks for Esther and the dynamics of court life. In view of the beauty-pageant phenomenon that occurs on all levels, including globally, this essay encourages us to explore them toward understanding the underlying relationships, the place of competition, and how student scholarship, prize money, and making a name come to be connected; such games ought not be totally ignored.

Part 2 begins with Hyun Chul Paul Kim and M. Fulgence Nyengele, Methodist Theological School in Ohio, unveiling more intrigue in "Murder S/He Wrote? A Cultural and Psychological Reading of 2 Samuel 11–12." Their essay does a cultural analysis of the issues of gender, sex, and violence, pregnant in the literary subtlety and ambiguity in 2 Sam 11–12, in dialogue with Korean customs and folklore. Where Kirk-Duggan focuses on a comparative analysis of the two male protagonists, including David, Kim and Nyengele focus on matters of dependency, submission, and cultural expectations with regard to gender in the relational dynamics between Bathsheba, David, and Uriah. In "Cry Witch! The Embers Still Burn," Madeline McClenney-Sadler, Duke University, explores the immanent dangers and consequences of archaic, androcentric, misogynist, and oppressive readings of two biblical texts, Deut 22:5 and 1 Tim 2:9, with extrabiblical texts such as Tertullian's treatise on women's apparel, which have been used to mystify and demonize women's bodies. Bringing into the conversation these texts with an early eighteenth-century Virginia woman who was accused of witchcraft and making a pact with the devil, she explores the gross maltreatment, ostracization, and intimidation in the twenty-first century where any human who fails to meet a "standard" of dress is ostracized. Mixing jurisprudence with theological-ethical discourse, Barbara A. Holmes, Memphis Theological Seminary, and the Honorable Susan R. Holmes Winfield, Federal Judge, Washington, D.C., explore the nuances of law and religion in John 7 and 8 to unearth the complex nuances of gender, power, and violence in "Sex, Stones, and Power Games: A Woman Caught at the Intersection of Law and Religion (John 7:53–8:11)." Addressing matters of violence sensationalized in twenty-first-century media, which convey the miscarriage of justice and the desire to falsely manipulate the law, these two sisters show how issues of gender and violence are layered over issues of institutional power and religious authority.

Valerie C. Cooper, Wake Forest University, begins Part 3 with "Some Place to Cry: Jephthah's Daughter and the Double Dilemma of Black Women in America." Based on the story of Jephthah's daughter in Judg 11, which has served as an archetype, tragic myth, or cautionary tale of man, woman, and society, she examines selected historical and modern hermeneutics of the story, toward a womanist understanding given the reality of contemporary life for black women. Mary Donovan Turner, Pacific School of Religion, Graduate Theological Union, in "Daughter Zion: Giving Birth to Redemption," provides a historical overview of the use of the terms *virgin, daughter,* and *virgin daughter* that identifies the female metaphor used to personify Jerusalem (Zion) in the prophetic material and the book of Lamentations in the Old Testament. She notes how through lament in Second Isaiah and in Lamentations, the redemptive process is given birth. Susan E. Hylen, Emory University, uses rhetorical and sociological criticism to offer a reading of Rev 18, in which the metaphor is multivalent, in "The Power and Problem of Revelation 18: The Rhetorical Function of Gender." She compares this limitation of the metaphor and its meaning to a familiar dynamic in which some feminists focus on concerns of sexism to the exclusion of racism.

I am especially indebted to the three respondents who offer insightful dialogue following the particular sections: part 1, Randy Bailey, Interdenominational Theological Center; part 2, Gina Hens-Piazza, Jesuit School of Theology, Graduate Theological Union; and part 3, Barbara Green, Dominican School of Theology, Graduate Theological Union. Their response is rich and expansive and offers fertile reflections for the ongoing dialogue that must happen if we are to learn how not only to read but also to listen. As exegetes with a conscience, one must be able to read the danger in these texts and see the implications wherein a person can take biblical texts to justify unjust, oppressive, illegal acts. This is particularly the case as homileticians, theologians, biblical exegetes, other teachers, and politicians use these texts as authority, as gospel, as law, without giving credence to what can happen when one takes everything in the Bible literally. Just as some truly believe that the red-letter edition of the King James Version is the one and true and only Bible, others pick and choose about what is literal, metaphorical, or mistaken history. We need only think of Jeffrey Dahmer and his heinous acts. The only difference between Dahmer and the man in Judg 19, for example, is that Dahmer had more victims and cannibalized them. The man in Judg 19 merely butchered his victim and then sent off her twelve body parts to the twelve tribes of Israel. Such an indictment indicates that we must be careful and cautious in dealing with dangerous texts, for regardless of our own intent, what others hear and how they live them out can result in horrific violence, via gender and sex, and other categories of oppression. Is this the legacy we want? This volumes offers a resounding "No!"

A thousand, thousand thanks and much gratitude to all of the contributors for this volume. We have transversed new vistas and provided rich conversation for all who care about living out an ethical, moral life, for those interested in social justice, and for those committed to dignity for all people.

"And She Remembered: In the Beginning, God"

And in that moment
All that was real
Seemed unreal
As the unthinkable
The unconscionable had happened.

She felt the pain, and saw the blood
Violence was no more a theory
But a reality for her
And the culprit
Had the audacity
To cite scripture
As the authority
As the sanction
For his barbaric act.

And then she remembered:
That a female friend
Had used biblical authority
To beat up on her kids
And was pleased and proud to do so.

And then she remembered:
All the acts of violence
She had come across
In the sacred pages
She had come to revere.

And then she remembered September 11th
The trail of tears, the holocaust, slave trade,
200 million dead because of war in the 20th century
And folks dying by state ordered execution, who may have been innocent.......

And then she had to stop and ask?
What's going on?
Are we that unconscious?
How often on a daily basis do we violate?
Do we punish, kill, maim, hurt
Abuse, lie, beat, defame?

And in that moment,
Too overwhelmed,
Too disenchanted
She started all over again, reading:
In the beginning, God.......

Cheryl Kirk-Duggan, September 2002

PART 1:

PASSION, POWER, AND RELATIONAL CONFLICT

LOVE, HONOR, AND VIOLENCE: SOCIOCONCEPTUAL MATRIX IN GENESIS 34

Mignon R. Jacobs
Fuller Theological Seminary

INTRODUCTION

The story of Dinah and Shechem presents itself within the larger framework of the Jacob narrative. As part of this framework, it exemplifies relationship dynamics that are analogous to others found in its primary intertextual context of the Pentateuch—for example, concerns about the relationship of Israel to its neighbors; Israel's identity defined from intra- and intergroup perspectives; appropriate sexual behaviors; and the place of violence.

The focus of this discussion is the socioconceptual matrix of Gen 34 in light of its intertextual framework (von Wolde: 1–28).[1] Such a matrix affirms that the extant text is generated by a conceptuality that itself is in a dynamic relationship with its social matrix (see Washington: 324–63).[2] Here the term *matrix* is used in the following sense, namely, "something that constitutes the place or point from which something else originates" (*Random House Dictionary*). Love, honor, and violence in Gen 34 are manifestations of a socioconceptual matrix within which they are sometimes inextricably intertwined and linked. Genesis 34 may modify the perspective of its larger conceptual framework, where violence as an act of vengeance is not prohibited and sexual violation may be an anomaly in that it deviates from the social

---

[1] Intertextuality is used here in reference to the synchronic aspects of a text perceived by the reader. This perception is regulated by the textual signals and the conceptual limits imposed on the reader by the text.

[2] This perspective is comparable to the New Historicist perspective. Washington states that "a literary text is no longer regarded as the reflection of an historical setting, but rather as a part of a larger discursive complex, where text and culture are understood to be in a mutually productive relation to one another" (327).

norm, but it is regulated by prescribed consequences for both male and female.[3]

1. Summary: Genesis 34

A summary of the content paired with observations appears at the onset of the discussion in order to document the basis for the discussions in sections 2 and 3. The summary has at least two presuppositions. First, it presupposes that the narrative framework is deliberate and that it sets the conceptual parameters for its interpretation. Second, it presupposes that the narrator generates the multivalency within the text and facilitates discernible conceptual tensions. Accordingly, one needs to appreciate the tensions in the narrative as a microcosm of the complexity of their socio-conceptual matrix.

Genesis 34:1 indicates the action of Dinah, that she went out with a particular purpose "to see the women of the region." There is no indication that Shechem went out (Gen 34:2). Rather, his seeing Dinah does not necessarily exclude the possibility that he was lying in wait for someone. If this were the case, it would at least suggest that the fact that Dinah was the person he seized had more to do with his intent than the ensuing feelings toward her. These feelings are as incidental as the fact that it was this person and not some other person. Whether or not she was presumptuous or unwise in her actions, her violation is not caused by those actions but by the actions and motive of Shechem.

Yet the narrative builds on the incidentality of the encounter and demonstrates the deliberate course of actions that ensues (Gen 34:3–4). The account depicts the independent actions of the two family representations: first the independence of Dinah and then that of Shechem. Subsequent to the encounter between Dinah and Shechem, the families are further depicted as acting independently to ensure their own agenda: Hamor acting on behalf of Shechem, his son, and Dinah's brothers avenging the loss of their family's honor.

The report of what happened to Dinah reached Jacob before Shechem and his father reached Jacob with an offer (Gen 34:5). How did this happen? While the text does not make any attempt to indicate how the information was uncovered and transmitted, it seems that the text is just as concerned to indicate that what happened was known. If this fact of the news is taken in light of Deut 22:23–29, it may suggest a

---

3 Cf. Deut 22:23–29. Verses 28–29 represent a provision for an offender to marry the female with the consent of the one sanctioned to grant that consent, namely, her father. See below for further reference to this text.

few scenarios, including: the one represented in Deut 22:28–29 that they were "caught in the act"; or the incident was reported to others and Dinah was given the benefit of a doubt regarding her culpability in the violation (cf. Deut 22:25–27). She remains an object of actions and does not emerge as a participant in any action other than her initial "going out" (Gen 34:1).

However the report was transmitted, the brothers responded to the news with an evaluation of Shechem's behavior: it was vile (נבלה; Gen 34:7). This was regarded as a violation of a particular standard and a foolish act. The evaluation further indicates a societal ethos in which there were parameters placed on appropriate and inappropriate behaviors (see references to sexual violations: Deut 22:23–29; Judg 19:23–24; 20:6; 2 Sam 13:12; Jer 29:22–23). In the cases of Gen 34; Judg 19:30; and 2 Sam 13:12, the parameter is indicated by the pairing of the label and the declaration "that such a thing is not done" or some variation of the expression. The expression signals the deviation rather than the non-occurrence of the event.

The evaluation of Shechem's behavior toward Dinah as vile is further depicted in Gen 34:8–12. The negotiation of Hamor with Jacob indicated the admission of wrong or a breach of the group norms. The "wrong" was the violation/rape of Dinah. In this case, the nature of the wrong was not simply the fact that Shechem and Dinah engaged in sexual relations but rather that the appropriate group norms (of Jacob's family) were not followed. Furthermore, appropriateness as defined by those norms was not necessarily constituted by the age of Shechem and Dinah but by their genders and the possession of the rights to sexual relationship. As a male Shechem had the right to consent to his sexual behavior, but he did not have the right to consent to Dinah's behavior. He was not her father or male relative/protector. Additionally, if he was her relative he would have had the right to consent to her sexual behavior but with the restriction that he did not engage in sexual relations with her (cf. Lev 18:6–18). To do so would have been a violation of the group norms.

The violation created a setting wherein all ensuing behaviors were conditioned. Without the violation of Dinah the specific type of negotiations would not have happened. Also, this negotiation would have been normative in as much as the law allowed for a violator to pay a bride price for the woman he had violated to become his wife (Deut 22:28–29). The deviation from the norm in this instance (Gen 34) would become both the focal point of the negotiations as well as the catalyst for deceit (מרמה). As related to the negotiation, the concession not only included the prospective groom and his entire people but also stimulated some questions: Why did the prospective groom agree to the price? Was he attempting to compensate for his wrong? Seen within the larger conceptual framework of the laws in Deut 22:23–29, Shechem was compensating for his wrong. The text indicates that he longed for Dinah (Gen 34:18), and it also allows for the possibility that the magnitude of the concession was regulated by the awareness of wrongdoing.

In Gen 34:13 the response of the brothers is labeled "deceit" (מרמה), a term usually used in reference to duplicity, as in the case of Gen 27:35 (Esau and Jacob). מרמה (deceit) refers to a particular intent to misrepresent the desired outcome. Consequently, one outcome is represented (union of the families) while another is the focus of the behaviors (revenge). This is not an instance in which the plan to kill Shechem and his people came after the communication to allow the marriage of Shechem and Dinah. Rather, the decision to exact revenge preceded the communication, such that the communication was duplicitous—concealing an ulterior motive.

The brothers' deceit involved maintaining a sense of normalcy in merging the two groups: Jacob's family and the Hivites. However, there are indications from the brothers' perspective that Shechem deserved to be punished rather than welcomed into the family—regardless of the wealth that he might have brought to the family. Even so, Gen 34:26 at least implies that Dinah was already married to Shechem. So what was to be accomplished by removing her? She was returned to her father's house, and the rape-marriage was terminated. A synchronic reading of Gen 34 with Deut 22:28–29 provides the socioconceptual framework for understanding the possibility and acceptability of the marriage. Giving her in marriage would have been consistent with the law.

Even with the marriage in place, the brothers persisted with their plan by engaging the rules of war in their acts of vengeance (Deut 20:14–18; 21:10–14; cf. Num 31), namely, plundering the city and taking the wives of the Hivites. As with other acts where sexual violation was used as a catalyst for war (e.g., Judg 19), in Gen 34 the acts of vengeance extended the scope of the offense they aimed to avenge.

Jacob's awareness of the possibility of retaliation by the Hivites, their allies, and other nations prompted his concern for his safety among these foreigners (Gen 34:30). On the other hand, Dinah's brothers had little concern about their number but much about the violation of their sister. Yet the tension within the story is that the brothers' actions ensured the marginalization of Dinah—or at least that she might most likely remain in her father's house without the prospect of becoming a wife. She was widowed at the hands of her brothers and moved from girl, to violated person, to wife, then to widow. She was the object of displaced passions that redefined her social possibilities (the rape) and sealed her fate by placing her in particular sociocultural constraints (cf.

Pitt-Rivers: 126–71; 182–86).[4] These social constraints were generated by their social matrix, which in turn is manifested and discernible in the conceptuality of Gen 34.

2. CONCEPTUALITY OF GENESIS 34—SOCIAL MATRIX

What is the primary conceptuality of Gen 34? Some have argued that, while the story of Dinah factors into the primary conceptuality of Gen 34, the narrative's primary concern may not be Dinah as much the honor of her father's household. The validity of this argument necessitates an understanding of how the depicted relationships are constitutive of that conceptuality, namely, Dinah and Shechem/Jacob's family/Hivites.

The story is best understood as a presentation of an intergroup tension brought to the foreground by the proximity of the groups and their interaction. The conceptuality of the story also betrays multivalence about the constituents of the relationship dynamics. Pitt-Rivers discusses the story as part of the evolving attitudes about exogamy and more specifically within the matrix of "sister-wife" stories (156–61). Streete also endorses this perspective and observes that in these stories "women's honor is related to their sexual function and is always situational" (Streete: 31). The intergroup tension in this case manifests itself as the reluctance of the Israelite to intermarry with the Hivites, compounded by the fact that Shechem raped Dinah.

2.1. Relationship Dynamics—Dinah and Shechem

Within the social matrix, the dynamics of this relationship exist as that of a dominant figure and a relatively subservient if not marginalized figure. The narrator presents these contrasting dynamics in the introduction of each character and gives the relational and behavioral descriptors. "Leah's daughter" is the primary descriptor used to introduce Dinah (Streete: 31).[5] The preceding narratives already established Leah as Jacob's wife but as the less favored wife—the wife accepted through a process of deceit and retained out of custom and duty. The second descriptor gives the information that Dinah was borne to Jacob. Even in

---

4 Pitt-Rivers claims that his summary is representative of the story "as it is told in Genesis 34." While it does well in this venture, his summary, like all others, includes interpretive presuppositions, e.g., the relationship of Gen 34 to its immediate literary context.

5 It has been noted that the typical introduction is the identification of the father. Here her mother is noted first. Whether this is intended by the narrator to indicate the diminished position of Dinah in the family is at least a possibility.

this descriptor, the relationship to Jacob is introduced as a subordinate clause. Both descriptors serve as appositives of a named individual, Dinah. Yet the relationship to Jacob is presented as a secondary designation vis-à-vis the primary relationship to Leah.

As important as it is to the relational dynamics of Dinah and Shechem, gender takes a lesser role in the relationship of Dinah and Jacob. The fact that she is her mother's daughter may be a distant secondary matter to Jacob's concern about survival (Gen 34:30) and may betray her place on his list of priorities.

The behavioral depiction follows the appositive. She, Dinah, went out with a distinctive purpose, namely, to visit the women of the region. She went out beyond the relational boundaries. Her independence had intergroup ramifications, in that an Israelite woman was deliberately fostering relationship with foreigners. Nonetheless, no indication is given as to whether or not she was accompanied. Even so, some scholars suggest that her excursion—her being alone—was a factor in the ensuing incidents. Because of the apparent discrepancy of honor in relation to her behavior, Pitt-Rivers casts doubt on the importance of her honor (e.g., Pitt-Rivers: 156). Certainly one can find this meaning at some level in the socioconceptual framework of the text, but perhaps the fact of her being alone or accompanied does not factor in for the narrator as a significant part of the behavioral sequence. The text already indicates her familial connections, thus indicating that she exists in relational context. She may have been physically alone but noticeably a part of a group. What may be significant is the representation of Dinah in the depiction of the behavioral sequence.

Immediately after introducing her and reporting her behavior, the text introduces Shechem. Like Dinah, Shechem is named, and the subsequent descriptors enumerate the elements of his identity. In both cases, it is clear that these persons are connected to a family and community. The discrepancy in the introduction is already noted. Dinah is introduced as the daughter of her mother, Leah, while Shechem is introduced as the son of his father, Hamor—his mother unnamed while her father is named as a second point of identification. In each case, however, the significance of the connections to the father is inescapable. The fathers on both sides are determinants in the community. By placing Jacob in the second position, does the narrator already signal social dynamics that are more significant to the outcome than the fact of Dinah being Jacob's daughter? Does the introduction of Jacob in the second position anticipate his apparent adaptation of a secondary position in his response to the Hivites, his sons taking the dominant role?

The behavioral sequence presents Shechem as the actor and Dinah as the recipient of his actions. In the short sequence of four actions, Dinah is

not identified by name or as subject but through pronouns as the gram-
matical object.[6] Shechem, the named subject, engages in four acts: sees her
(ראה), seizes her (לקח), lies with her (שכב), and afflicts her (ענה) (Gen
34:2). Bechtel notes that when used of sexual relations, ענה "to afflict" a
woman typically means to humiliate her (Bechtel: 23–27).[7] The social
matrix defines humiliation and the parameters for appropriate sexual
relationships. Accordingly, sexual relationships are considered illicit if
they occur apart from the appropriate consenting group/person and/or
challenge the marital norms set by the group.

The resumption of the named Dinah indicates a transition in the
sequence; however, in Gen 34:1–4 Dinah and Shechem are not named
together. When the text identifies Dinah by name, it does not identity
Shechem; he is not named (34:3), and when he is identified by name she is
not (34:2, 4). Within the sequence in which Dinah is unnamed, she is the
recipient of the actions, and the text indicates no response from Dinah—
unlike the reported responses of Tamar (2 Sam 13). This is not to suggest
that she is a willing participant in the sexual encounter with Shechem. I
will argue further in the third part of this essay that the issue of consent is
paramount to the socioconceptual framework of this story. Here, suffice it
to say, the lack of reported response is not necessarily indicative of her
culpability in the behavioral dynamics any more than she is culpable in
the brothers' behavior, where her response is also notably absent.

The transition indicates that Shechem was drawn to Dinah—the
daughter of Jacob (Gen 34:3). The subsequent sequence speaks of Dinah
by the use of common nouns and pronoun forms: the girl (הנער and
הילדה), her (pronominal suffix ה), wife (אשה). He loved (ויאהב) the girl
(הנער) and requested that the girl (הילדה) be given to him as his wife
(אשה). Does calling her girl refer to her age or her innocence? Does the
designation indicate that Dinah is not authorized to consent? The fact that
Shechem forces her already indicates that he has overlooked the process
of consent. This is also signaled in the attempt to rectify the situation after
the fact.

His premeditation of the act is as significant as the fact that he forced
her. Was he lying in wait for her? It so happened that Shechem was
drawn to Dinah after the fact; however, he could have very well been
repulsed by her. Amnon was repulsed by Tamar after lying with her

---

6 The sign of the direct object plus pronominal suffix (אתה) follows the first three verbs
(ויקח, וירא, and וישכב). The object of the fourth verb in the sequence is indicated by the
pronominal suffix (ויענה).

7 She considers the difference between Deut 22:25–27 (does not use ענה and the rape is
not humiliating) and 2 Sam 13:11–14 (use of ענה and the rape is humiliating.

(2 Sam 13). Whether or not he was repulsed by Dinah, and in spite of the fact that the narrator describes him as "the most honored of his family" (Gen 34:19), Shechem is hardly the figure of a noble suitor. Being drawn to Dinah is not indicative of commendable behavior; the violation had already taken place. The moment of encounter between Shechem and Dinah was a pregnant moment—a moment of possibilities for many outcomes. Within that moment was the unfulfilled passion of Shechem that he sought to fulfill. The fulfillment resulted in other pregnant moments, but the possibilities of these moments were irrevocably altered by Shechem's choice of expressed passion—unsanctioned sexual relationship. Furthermore, restitution does not erase the past; it is an acknowledgement that there is a need for restitution. Shechem seized a girl and by chance was drawn to her. While the narrator presents this sequence of his affection for Dinah, it presents the affections as incidental to the previous actions.

Who would question the character of Shechem, the prince? Who would dare to entertain the notion much less to suggest that Shechem had access to women and as prince would not have been in want for female company? So, who would dare to further entertain and postulate that the seizure of Dinah by Shechem points to more than a man's attraction to a beautiful woman?[8] Like David and Amnon—men of privilege and status—Shechem had access to countless women. Why Dinah? Dinah was in the wrong place at the wrong time. She is the backdrop of a larger issue, namely, Shechem's behavior. Even in the backdrop she is the central part of the event—the catalyst that is forgotten is no less the catalyst. Nonetheless, she is incidental even to Shechem. The prince lying in wait for...? Perhaps the apparent affections for Dinah are to be recast into the drama as reflex response born out of an inherent tendency if not pattern of behavior. Shechem as predator is not a farfetched notion for this narrative. Dinah just happened perchance to be the recipient of his "after-the-fact affection." But it could be that she may have been just another object of his princely pursuits—the object of untamed passion.

The narrative appears to show sympathy to Shechem for his "after-the-fact-affection" and effort to secure Dinah. Yet even in this characterization of Shechem, there are conceptual tensions, not the least of which is his reversion to the appropriate channels of behavior. The characterization shows Shechem, prince and independent actor, as capable of taking action to ensure the acquisition of what he desires. He is drawn to Dinah and decides to have her as wife. The implicit presentation depicts another

---

8 The narrator says nothing of her beauty, thus leaving that aspect open or even unimportant. This discussion postulates that her beauty is a nonissue for the behavioral sequence.

facet of his desire that may not need the societal assent to secure its object. For all his status, Shechem is subordinate to Hamor, his father; but he is dominant in relationship to Dinah. This dominance ensues from gender specific roles and status. Within the social matrix, Dinah's gender dictates that if she is to be the sexual initiator, there is no other way than being a prostitute (see Gen 38, Judah and Tamar). Even so, as a female, here sexual expression is regulated by her culturally specified role, namely, to continue the family by bearing children.

Bach interprets the Dinah story as indicative of a potential ancestress story. Dinah's value is that she is a potential ancestress whose potential is endangered by foreigners. Her inherent power of carrying on the lineage of the man to whom she bears a son is not her own, but her power is dictated by the societal laws and customs (Bach: 30). Her behaviors are thus regulated to ensure the appropriate execution of the societal expectations. If she abides by the rules and produces an heir, she is viewed as an asset to the family. Conversely, if she does not abide by the rules, she is a liability to the family. Within the social matrix, her gender restricts her to the scope of her sanctioned behavior both with respect to the behaviors and their consequences. The story of Dinah is analogous to the David-Bathsheba story, in which a royal uses his power to gain sexual access to a woman he desires (see 2 Sam 11; Bach: 30). In both stories the man finds a way to transform a socially inappropriate sexual union into a socially sanctioned one. In both instances, death ensues from the effort to legitimize the previously illicit union.

Bledstein suggests that Dinah's representation in this story at best minimizes her status as compared to the social elevation of Tamar, accentuated by the lineage and depiction of her garment (2 Sam 13). Tamar is in a favored position in much the same way that Joseph is in such a position marked by the tunic he wore (Bledstein: 78–83).[9] The highlight of the comparison of Dinah and Tamar illustrates the relative social location of the women. The comparison further indicates that the social matrix was such that the status of the woman did not serve as a hedge of protection against sexual exploitation. The princess and the pauper are both victims of the princely power.

2.2. Relationship Dynamics—Jacob and the Hivites

The relationship of Dinah and Shechem is one factor of the intergroup dynamics. Their relationship is an example of the fact that all of

---

9 Bledstein presents a case of both Tamar and Joseph wearing a tunic that is indicative of exalted status, a status analogous to the priesthood.

these characters are part of a social reality that defines their roles, that is, how they are perceived in the group and fundamentally the parameters of appropriate behavior. The relationship dynamics are also constitutive of a network of intragroup elements. In addition to generating a network, these elements are decisive to the nature of the network with respect to the points of convergence and divergence within the intergroup dynamics.

The intragroup network consists of at least the following elements: Jacob as father in relation to his children as group or as individuals or subsets; Jacob's children in relationship to each other, also with various subsets defined by gender, age, or mothers. The point is that the relationships within Jacob's family constitute a matrix that exists in connection with the Hivites such that the Jacob family matrix will define itself in relationship to the "others" according to how the family views itself. Consequently, conflicts of love, honor, and violence did not begin with the encounter between the Israelites and the Hivites. Rather, all of the previous conflicts in Gen 27–33—such as Jacob versus Esau, Jacob versus Laban, Rachel versus Leah—attest to the intragroup dynamics. These conflicts are simply redefined by the distinctive nuances that ensue from the intersection of the two groups, that is, the intergroup dynamics. In Gen 34, the intra-Israelite group is thus depicted as fractured. At no point in the story does Jacob interact with his daughter. His closest contact appears to be his negotiations about her. Additionally, Simeon and Levi are in tension with Jacob because of their revenge on the Hivites. The semblance of unity portrayed in Jacob's family is discerned in the intergroup dynamics: the family consenting to the terms of the intermarriage between Dinah and Shechem and subsequently between the Israelites and the Hivites. Even in the act of revenge there are apparent fractions: Simeon and Levi (one subset) joined by others of Jacob's household (another subset).

Camp notices this intragroup fraction and comments that Dinah's brothers, with particular focus on Simeon and Levi, attacked and killed the incapacitated Hivites, only to be condemned by Jacob for endangering the family. She questions who was right in their choice of response to the sexual violation (Camp: 277).

The question of who was in the right recognizes one of the many socioconceptual tensions in the narrative and further demonstrates the ambiguity if not the multivalence of the texts on the matter. The multivalence comes out of the perspectival nature of the narrative constituted in part by its intertextual framework. From the brothers' perspective their action is the right one because of the deed done against their sister. This is not to say that they did not have other alternatives for addressing the perceived dishonor; however, their behavior mirrors that of Absalom in avenging Tamar's honor (2 Sam 13). Seen in the context of Gen 35, where God places terror on the cities, the brothers' behavior is apparently protected by God, if not favored. Likewise, Gen 35 seems to address Jacob's concern for safety amidst foreigners and allows for the possibility that Jacob's choice and actions are not commended. The issue may be that Jacob is responsible and thus behaves on behalf of the whole rather than the individual (Sternberg: 463).[10] Even in this light, the text suggests that Jacob is condemned while his sons are commended. If the latter were the case, it would mean that violence is condoned or perhaps simply tolerated as a vehicle of vengeance.

Another socioconceptual tension is intersection of identity and morality. Does identity define the parameters of morality? Camp examines the dynamics of identity and morality. She labels the intergroup dynamics between Israel and the foreigners as identity, the intragroup dynamics as morality (Camp: 280–81). In agreement with Camp, the intergroup dynamics are both identity and morality to the extent that the moralities of the groups come into contact with each other as an inextricable component of identity. Furthermore, the intragroup elements are part of the focal point of the narrative. The intergroup conflict is an extension of the intragroup reality or self-perception whether or not that perception is that the group/family is endangered. The intragroup identity also coheres around circumcision, which is used as the mode of the revenge.

Noting that the Hivites' intragroup presents itself as united, we may summarize the intergroup dynamics. Hamor supports Shechem even though Shechem committed a social infraction. The people likewise conform to the wishes of their leader by becoming circumcised. On the contrary, the Israelite intragroup is fragmented in its approach to the social infraction committed by Shechem. Jacob's initial inactivity (Gen 34:5) may best be seen in his objection to Simeon and Levi (Gen 34:30). He is more concerned about the family, but to suggest that the brothers' behavior shows no concern about the family is to misunderstand the narrative. The difference between father and sons is their views about handling the situation. Jacob resolved to intermarry presumably with the concern for safety. The brothers resolved to avenge the honor of Dinah and the family since her violation demonstrates an affront to the family. The violation also demonstrates that the consent of one who owned Dinah's sexuality was bypassed in the use of that sexuality. This act of bypassing the channel of consent and gaining access to her sexuality

---

10 Sternberg discounts the idea that the narrative is rebuking Jacob. Cf. Fewell and Gunn 1991: 208–11.

constituted the shame of Dinah and her family within the socioconceptual matrix of the text.

3. Socioconceptual Matrix

The present assessment of the text necessitates further understanding
of the customs of the time and generates several questions, including: Is
there a normitivity of violence and love in relation to honor? Does the
Gen 34 narrative depict an incident of sexual violence? How does the narrative define love and violence? This concept-critical study examines the
concepts of love, honor, and violence as exemplified in the behaviors of
Dinah, Shechem, Jacob, and his sons. Central to this examination is an
assessment of the relationship or possible correlation between love and
violence—for example, love and Shechem's behavior toward Dinah; love
and the acts of vengeance against the Hivites.

3.1. Love As the Definitive Element

The socioconceptual dynamics of love and violence is depicted in the
relationship of Dinah and Shechem. Love "after the fact" does not erase
or alter the fact of the sexual violation. Dominant love may be a type of
love if one considers the popular saying that love has as many manifestations as persons who love. One must not mistakenly identify Shechem's
love with that of other presupposed loves within the text—e.g. Jacob-
Rachel (Gen 29); Dinah and her brothers (Gen 34).

3.1.1. Love and Violence. Shechem possessing Dinah as sexual property
generated his love for her. If on no other basis other than conceptual
grounds, one must at least consider this fact: his offer of marriage that
could give a respectable status would hardly have been necessary apart
from the sexual violation. Any dispersion on her character and action is
nothing short of blaming the victim and thus acknowledging the inability
of the perpetrator to control himself. If there is a correlation of love and
violence in Gen 34, it must include a sequential aspect. This is a type of
sequential aspect that prevails upon Jacob to offer and commit himself to
seven years of labor for Rachel (Gen 29). Shechem loves after he commits
the act of violence against Dinah.

Shechem's act demonstrates one thing among others: this is a man
out of control and/or a person used to his own way. The fact of the offer
of marriage is at once an acknowledgment of guilt or of unsanctioned
social behavior. Sheres advocates a perspective in which she looks sym-
pathetically on Shechem's behavior. She argues that Shechem is in love
with Dinah and has the most favorable pathos toward her—more so than

the brothers. In Sheres's perspective Dinah is responsible for the rape in that she (Dinah) ventures out alone. Accordingly, rape is Dinah's punishment for her presumptuous behavior (Sheres: 8, 17; cf. Scholz: 191–92).[11] The misfortune of Sheres's perspective is that it makes the villain into a hero by minimizing the violence he committed. Her perspective ignores the narrator's view of the socially deviant behavior, albeit that that perspective is seen in the brothers' evaluation of Shechem's act as "vile" (Gen 34:7). Furthermore, Sheres's perspective represents a trajectory shared by Bechtel, who vilifies the brothers. She does not consider Shechem's action toward Dinah as rape or even shameful (Bechtel: 19–36; cf. Scholz: 194). On the contrary, Sternberg protests against a favorable view of Shechem. In response to Fewell and Gunn (1991: 207–10), Sternberg argues that the narrative is not favorably disposed toward Shechem (Sternberg: 473).

While the narrator emphasizes Shechem's love and willingness to pay the bride price, one can hardly ignore the possibility that forces other than love generate the determination and attention of the negotiations. Perhaps Shechem's guilt generates his willingness to offer compensation. This willingness to please or comply with Israelite tradition is noticeably absent from the initial behavior toward Dinah. Rather, Shechem's aggression toward Dinah exhibits an attempt at self-gratification. Perhaps the appearance of love and willingness to comply are clearer in Hamor's words of encouragement to his people, words that indicate his awareness of the socioeconomic advantages to an alliance with this people (Gen 34:21). The text seems to allow for the possibility that Hamor also conceived of an opportunity to assimilate the Israelites. The violation of Dinah by his son is simply the occasion for the merging of the two groups.

At best the love of Shechem is born out of premature attachment or forced intimacy. Love in this instance appears to be a bond formed by sexual contact. The narrator makes it clear that Shechem loves Dinah and will do whatever it takes to secure her. His initial unsanctioned possession of her culminated in a desire for a long-term possession. Yet one cannot ignore the comparison between Shechem's love for Dinah and her brothers' love for her, since both disregard Dinah in their passion to achieve a goal. First, Shechem's seizing her and violating her jeopardizes her social status as a marriageable woman. His fulfillment of a desire overshadowed the repercussion. Second, the brothers also contributed to the marginalization of Dinah. Who would marry such a woman? According to Dinah's brothers, Shechem treated her like a prostitute, the woman who stands for herself socially and consents to sexual behaviors with a

---

11 Scholz does not endorse Sheres's view.

variety of men. However honorable their intention, the brothers' passion for revenge secure her a social status alongside this group—who would marry such a woman? But would her existence with Shechem have any less social status than a prostitute? At least one should consider more than a sociocritical argument for exonerating Shechem, but one must equally consider the effect of the brothers' behavior as being no less violent than Shechem's toward Dinah.

Historically speaking, the measure of the nobility or honorable nature of an act is often not so much the motivation as the effects. Honorable motives do not lessen the adverse effects of violence. The anomaly is that death ensuing from violence is just as final whether or not the motive is good or evil. Even so, the historical measure of violence and its governing framework is ideologically conditioned and as such relative.

3.1.2. Love and honor. Love and honor are not unequivocally synonymous. In Gen 34, the relationship of love and honor has more to do with intent than with reality. Shechem's claim of love leads to an attempt to make Dinah his wife. Even so, marrying her moves her away from the margins but does not necessarily restore honor. The rape, according to the text, leads to love that in turn leads to an offer of marriage. At the root of the practice there seems to be the presupposition that the woman is used and unfit for marriage, apart from marriage to her violator. The implicit concern of the practice is the honor of the family, and secondary, ostracizing of the woman. Even so, the focal point is not the quality of life for the woman who has already been violated. What real possibility is there that this woman will not be further violated in her marriage? Or does the marriage become a sanctioned way of violation. The rape/marriage becomes a form of pardoning the rapist and further subjugating the woman. The fact that a man enters a rape/marriage is hardly a consolation to the woman. Even the law that seems to be for the protection of the woman is a further insult to injury in that it is punishment to the man to remain with a woman he may want to divorce (Deut 22:28–29).

Culturally, rape results in the dishonor of the victim and not the violator.[12] Even the brothers' behavior reflects this perspective. Is not the dishonor that of the villain as one who violates another—or one who is out of control and a social deviant? Societies support the idea of the violator as untainted by punishing women or isolating them or killing them for being violated. Societies that allow rape/marriage as an exoneration

---

[12] For an understanding of some of the ideology behind the correlation of sexual violation and dishonor, see Wenham.

for the violator embrace the acknowledged wrong and further violate the woman by marrying her to her offender and thus again denying her of her option if not her right to terminate connection with her offender (Scholz: 196).[13] Marriage connects the event of the rape to the larger historical context in other ways not already included and/or ensuing from the rape. There is little or no probability for closure in a rape/marriage. The conceptual framework of the text is that the rape/marriage is a sanctioned union made of socially deviant behavior. In the first place, the woman is violated in that she is subjected to a sexual relationship without proper avenues of consent. Second, she is again violated because, with consent, she is given to her violator by her family—her protector (cf. Exod 22:16–18; Deut 22:28–29). Hence her violator and protector become one in the same. Dinah's story exemplifies the path toward the latter scenario. Her honor in the socioconceptual matrix would be restored with the marriage.

3.2. Honor As the Definitive Element

3.2.1. Honor and violence. The socioconceptual dynamics of honor and violence exhibits gender differentiations. The woman's honor is the delicate flower to be protected, defended, or avenged at all cost. Perhaps a contemporary example may allow insight into the conceptual dynamics of the Dinah story. The contemporary "honor killing" is an example of the marriage of violence and honor in which violence is used to restore honor. In such cases, the violence is directed against the one who is deemed to have brought dishonor on the family. Ironically, it is the woman who has already suffered by being sexually violated who is the recipient of the violence. She was raped, but she is killed because of the dishonor that the rape brought to the family. Her purity is the essence of her family's purity; thus, her defilement is the defilement of the family. Consequently, the one who avenges the family is commended for restoring the family's honor, and the violence of the victim's death is seen as the necessary means of the restoration. The woman might be involved in a romantic relationship with an unsuitable suitor; if so, she has violated the family honor. Thus a brother who kills a sister in an effort to restore family honor is a hero. But the death of the sister is no more than a necessary social event. Honor before life—violence for honor (Makiya).

As tragic as the events are that use violence to restore honor, these events show the influence of "silent power." Such power is unrecognized

---

13 Scholz reviews a few of the well-known cases, including: "Justice in Peru: Victim Gets Rapist for a Husband," *New York Times* (12 March 1997): A1, A12.

as power but exemplifies the characteristics of power, that is, female culturally induced power wherein sexual purity and sanctioned behaviors
are the basis for honor. In so far as a woman's dishonor constitutes the
dishonor of the family, the centrality of the marginalized is demonstrated. This means that the margin is the decisive determinant in the
behaviors and in the course that the center dictates. Nonetheless, this
silent power is an unfortunate possession, since others regulate its
socially sanctioned execution, and the socially unsanctioned execution is
the only unregulated execution of that power, namely, prostitution.

Fewell and Gunn's argument that Dinah could have made her own
choice is a misunderstanding of the ethos (Fewell and Gunn 1991: 193–
211). Whether or not Dinah is a helpless girl or a young woman is less the
point than the right of consent. Dinah, girl or young woman, did not have
the right to consent—primary consent. Any consent to socially sanctioned
sexual behavior and marriage is the right of her male protector. With
respect to the parameters of consent, the Dinah story differs from the
laws in the United States, where the right to consent is determined by age
(Lagassé: 576). One must therefore consider that whether or not Dinah
"gave in to" Shechem, the very fact that she did not have the right to consent constitutes a sexual violation—regardless of her age. Consequently,
the stipulations of Deut 22:28–29 are an appropriate framework for
understanding the proposal and marriage.

Scholz discusses the marriage proposal as an exonerating factor,
noting that some see it as such (Scholz: 190). I agree that the rape takes at
least a secondary if not a tertiary position to the ensuing actions. But in as
much as the rape is the catalyst of the behavioral sequence, it is a problem
for Gen 34. The narrator is hardly illustrating the conflict of Israelite
behavior toward women vis-à-vis non-Israelite behavior. If that is the case,
the narrator's perspective stands in tension with Exod 22:16–17; Deut
22:23–27, and most certainly 2 Sam 13 (Amnon and Tamar). So while the
narrator may be concerned about the encounter between an Israelite and a
non-Israelite and that delineation or the possibility of respect for Israelites
and their practices, the story demonstrates that the propensity for violence
is not monopolized by any group or exclusive to a particular realm or type
of behavior. Both the Hivites and the Israelites involve themselves in violence, and a sanctioned religious act—circumcision—is used as the vehicle
for deceit and violence (cf. Scholz: 192).[14]

Camp notes the "insolent disregard of circumcision" in relation to the
"sojourner" (גר). She notes that while Exod 12:48–49 makes circumcision

---

[14] Note Scholz for discussion of insider/outsider as the basis for violence. The violence
itself is a manifestation of a larger group ideology.

the condition for participation in Passover, Gen 34:15 makes circumcision the condition for intermarriage (Camp: 316–18). Yet even the identity makers do not clearly demark the boundaries of identity. Violence is both against the Hivites and the Israelites. For Brenner the dominant force in the sequence of events is not so much to avenge Dinah's honor as much as it is to preserve clan identity (Brenner: 116). The particular aspect that this signals is the tendency in cases of sexual violation for the act of violation to become subsumed under a larger agenda. Often the larger agenda is articulated as justice for the abused, but in many instances the abused is a lost entity in the conundrum of noble intentions buffeted by a lack of understanding of the true nature of the abuse.

The violence in Gen 34 begs the question of the acceptability of violence, but acceptability is relative even within the story. Shechem's violence against Dinah is regarded as an offense—unacceptable. On the other hand, for Dinah's brothers their violence against the Hivites is acceptable in that it was a response to dishonor. They are in the company of others who either by their silence or their participation sanction violence as an acceptable option for dealing with violence. Certainly Gen 35 suggests that God was not displeased with their violence; however, it does not indicate how God regarded the deception.

3.2.2. Honor and deception. Are honor and deception mutually exclusive? Is deception a violation of morality, or is the end toward which deception is employed constitutive of its morality? According to Garcia, "deception is deceiving [that] ... consists in inducing (or confirming) in her apprehension, expression, or belief that is not true or veridical" (Garcia: 515). In agreement with Garcia it is argued that deception is not contingent upon the articulation of misinformation. Whether or not one has the intention to deceive is also inconsequential to the effects of the deceit (518–19). The nature of the outcome of any act is measured by the effect, not the intent of the catalyst. As such, misinformation in some cases may not have adverse effects, while accurate information may be used to violate others. In Gen 34 deception is achieved by the intention and the effect of planned behaviors. Dinah's brothers intended to avenge the family's honor and chose to do so using otherwise sanctioned practices—circumcision.

Honor is the value assigned to particular practices, beliefs, or persons by a group and is measured by particular actions and relationships within that group.

> Honor is simultaneously internal and external to the individual, a matter of both one's own feelings and the judgment of society. The two aspects are often closely linked because an individual frequently judges himself,

as well as others in terms that reflect the values of the group with which
he identifies. (McCord: 106)

In Gen 34 the narrative signals the value assigned to Shechem's
behavior. His behavior is measured by Dinah's brothers and deemed to
be outside of the parameters of honorable behavior. The Hivites by their
standard deemed Shechem to be honorable, thus illustrating that relativity of honor in the intergroup dynamics of the story. The merging of
the personal and the public aspects of honor manifests itself in the various activities used to demonstrate honor. One such act of honor is the
duel. The offended and the offending parties both have their reputations at stake. Often regardless of the office of those involved, their
participation in the act, such as a duel, can overshadow the catalyst
such that the act of defending becomes the focal point if not the whole
point of the defense.

The Gen 34 narrative does not delineate the aspects of the brothers'
deceit. The deceit is the tool used to ensure an opportunity to defend the
honor. The defense of honor is analogous to honor killing seen in various
cultures. In these cultures it is common for the one identified as the one
bringing the dishonor to be killed. The rationale is that the removal of the
object of dishonor removes the dishonor. The practice illuminates the
social matrix in which persons are in symbiotic relationships. The woman
is an integral part of the social matrix for several reasons, including her
ability to continue the lineage of the male whose offspring she bears—
legitimately or illegitimately. Likewise, the woman is a subservient figure
within the surface social operations but is the hub of the wheel in the
existence of the social matrix. To the extent that her honor defines the
honor of her family, she carries the social destiny of the family. The irony
of the property being the center of power is inescapable. One need not
focus on the passing mention of Dinah and her disappearance from the
narrative to be struck by the salience of her location in the social matrix.
Even so, one must focus on the patterns of the negotiations to uncover the
conceptual tensions exemplified in the social matrix. These are the
nuances that give the story its captivating complexity achieved through
its very simplicity of presentation.

The interrelationship of honor and deception also highlights essential
aspects of deception. Seemingly, the ease of deceit and its effectiveness in
achieving one's goal is contingent on trust. Dinah's brothers planned and
effectively executed their deceit because of a generated and fostered trust
between them and the Hivites. For the Dinah story, the deceit is not the
end of the plan but the means to an end. The question at this point is
whether the goal for which deceit is employed influences the nature of
the deceit. Are these honorable acts of deceit?

Notice that the deceit utilizes the socioreligious norms to establish trust. The normitivity of the planned activity (circumcision) enabled the parties in the plan (Hivites) to trust the instigators of the plan (Israelites). This is part of the trust that was essential to the plan. Circumcision was the norm for the Israelite. Why would Shechem and his people question the custom or the desirability of their participation in the custom given their agreement to an alliance? Are honor and deceit compatible? Does the use of deceit to defend honor invalidate honor as honor?

In agreement with Prouser, lying (and the present author would add deception) is not a moral issue in the Hebrew Bible. If anything, deception is a sanctioned way that the weaker party exercises power over more powerful people (Prouser: 15).[15] As in the story of Isaac blessing Jacob (Gen 27–28), there was a context of trust established that facilitated the deception. The trust came out of the relationship between Isaac and his family. The narrative describes him as old and vision-impaired. While this fact in and of itself was not enough for the deception, the family relationship context was. Isaac questioned whether he (Isaac) was talking to Esau but was assured that he was. There were clues that led Isaac to a conclusion, but Isaac deviated from that conclusion because he trusted Jacob. The other essential element for Isaac and Jacob was the vulnerability of the deceived: Isaac was old, vision-impaired, and dependent on his family to carry out his wishes. There are also some of these elements of the deception pattern in the Jacob-Laban story (Gen 29–31). Jacob agreed to work for seven years in order to get Rachel as wife. At the end of the seven years, Laban gave him Leah and requested an additional seven years of service for Rachel. Jacob accused Laban of deceiving him (Gen 29:25–26) and was told that the practice of giving the younger before the older daughter into marriage was not done. Did Laban discover in that moment that the custom existed and would challenge the previous arrangement that he made with Jacob? Was Laban somehow unconscious of the custom? Apparently, Laban was cognizant of the custom but neither communicated it to Jacob nor signaled that the arrangement would contradict the custom. Laban deceived Jacob at the inception of the plan. Consequently, Jacob did not question Laban but carried out his part of the plan.

In both cases, the narratives in Genesis depict situations involving deception without showing a distinctive pattern of the deceiver. They are not in agreement with Prouser, who advocates that deception is the tool used by the "underdog." The Jacob-Isaac interchange suggests a

---

15 Prouser cites the following texts to demonstrate the use of deception by the relatively weak: Exod 1:15–21; 1 Sam 16:1–2; 1 Kgs 22.

dual aspect of the underdog. If by *underdog* we mean the weaker person or the one with the lesser opportunities, then Jacob in both instances is the underdog—but he is both deceiver and the deceived. One may also argue that Isaac was the underdog as the vulnerable person in the Jacob-Isaac interchange.

Turning now to Gen 34 several observations are noteworthy. Here is another situation pregnant with possibilities and as pregnant with passions for different outcomes. First, Simeon and Levi deceived Shechem at the onset of their negotiations. They facilitated trust and then capitalized on that trust much as Laban did to Jacob (Gen 29). Second, their violation of the trust placed in them was a violation of their religious norm as well as the norm for possessing a woman's sexuality. Dinah was Shechem's by virtue of his fulfilling the requirement for the union. To murder him and his family would be a way of stealing from him what he first seized unlawfully and then gained legitimately.

In presenting this aspect of deception and honor, it is hard to escape the impression that one is in favor of Shechem. Let it be said here that the intent is not to favor or disfavor Shechem but to reflect the multidimension of the socioconceptual matrix wherein Shechem's behavior patterns are examined in light of the intertextual framework of the matrix. Furthermore, it may also be said that the vulnerability of both Dinah (and her family) allowed for their exploitation by the Hivites, but the vulnerability of the Hivites was used as a necessary precondition for their demise at the hands of Simeon and Levi.

Does honor necessitate honor as a means of defense? The text seems to suggest that honor does not necessitate honor to achieve its desired goal (see Gen 35). Jacob's response to his sons signals that the means of their efforts to defend the honor was unacceptable. Even so, the unacceptability of their behavior is not a commentary on the universal acceptability of the means. Note that Jacob's response is particular to the context (see above). Following these observations, the final part of the conceptual matrix evident in Gen 34 is violence.

3.3. Violence As the Definitive Element

Violence is represented in at least two spheres, namely, interpersonal (Dinah and Shechem) and intergroup (Jacob's son and the Hivites). In the preceding discussion, much attention has already been given to the interpersonal dimension of violence. Even so, there is another aspect of this dimension that is inextricably linked to the intergroup aspect. Simply stated, violence is any aggressive act or expression resulting in the harm of person(s) or a living entity. While violence is often seen as the intention of an act or speech, here violence is not defined solely by the intention from which it ensues. Violence may be the effect of well-intended behavior whose unregulated and/or unanticipated course results in harm. Such harm may be physical, psychological, and/or social. In reference to social harm, it may include a rift in relationships as well as a disruption of the customs and laws of a particular community.

Particularly as it relates to war and masculinity, violence appears to have gender distinctions. Washington recognizes this, stating that "warfare is emblematically male and discourse of violence is closely imbricated with that of masculine sexuality." (Washington: 330). Notably, gender distinctions and violence are further seen in the characterization of the defeated male as female (cf. Nah 3:13; Jer 51:30). In agreement with Washington, note that sexual violence is "elemental to normative masculinity," as seen, for example, in Judg 19 and 2 Sam 13; 16.

The narrative in Gen 34 highlights the social dimensions of harm/violence. The social harm to Dinah is that she was defiled and thus marginalized or restricted in her marriageability (cf. Deut 21:10–14; 22:29). This assertion finds support both in the intratextual focus as well as its intertextual framework. Intratextually, Dinah is referred to as defiled (Gen 34:5,13), and the way she has been treated is equated with a prostitute (זנה).[16] Additionally, the text at least opens the possibility that after she is married to Shechem, her brothers kill Shechem, making her a widow.

Intertextually, Gen 34 exists in the conceptual framework of other texts that are concerned about the sexual violation of females (e.g., Exod 22:16–17; Deut 22:22–29). In this conceptual framework where such sexual violence was both attested and regulated, the presence of Gen 34 facilitates questions about the intent of the brothers to avenge their sister's honor. The law required "reparative marriage for an injured woman" (Pressler: 103) and was aimed at ensuring that a woman dishonored by sexual violence did not lose out on being a wife. The law therefore created a type of security for those who would be otherwise marginalized and with negligible probability for marriage. The brothers presumed the punishment of Shechem as indicated in Deut 22:28–29 and in this way would reverse the opportunity for Dinah to be a wife. Consequently, the provision of the

---

16 The two terms here are seen as descriptors of the harm/violence that resulted form Shechem's act toward Dinah. First, the result of his action toward her is that she is defiled (טמא). Second, the behavior is that associated with the behavior done toward a prostitute (זנה). Typically to act like a prostitute is to do unsanctioned sexual behavior. This presumes a social standard that was violated by the woman since men are not labeled as prostitute (זנה), and their behavior is measured by different standards. The term is used of the nation to designate its unsanctioned behavior toward deities other than yhwh/God of Israel (e.g., Deut 31:16; Judg 2:17; Hos 9:1).

law was overlooked in favor of revenge, and the probability of Dinah's marginalization became a reality.

Perhaps the reaction was more to the identity of the offender than the offense itself. Thus, for example, Thistlethwaite notes that the male protector (e.g., father, husband) is compensated for the loss of property value (Thistlewaite: 64; cf. Pressler: 91). Additionally, the intertextual framework contributes the conceptual view of a rape/marriage. Since the text does not prescribe punishment for Dinah in the way that Deut 22:23–24 does, it may be suggested that the narrative of Gen 34 does not assign blame to Dinah for what happened. Yet assigning blame to Dinah is well documented by some, including Graetz, who delineates the argument as follows: "[s]ince girls of marriageable age did not normally 'go out' to visit friends in the city, it is possible that the text itself criticizes Dinah's behavior by" implying promiscuity (Graetz: 312; cf. Nicol 1997: 43–54).[17]

As extensive as the harm is to Dinah, she is not the only one harmed. One aspect of social harm/violence to Jacob and his sons is the challenge to their sense of honor. As Dinah's male protectors, they are portrayed as ineffective. In their absence, their "protectee" (daughter/sister) ventures out and is violated. On the one hand, one may argue that their absence is the reason for the success of the violation. On the other hand, it may also be argued that the violation attests to the fact that their influence in the region was not highly regarded or even respected. Apparently, they were present in the land of the Hivites but were not perceived as a force to be reckoned with. This is seen in Jacob's response to his sons—he appears to be fearful of the repercussions to him and his family (Gen 34:30), which further suggests that he was afraid for the fact and quality of his existence. Hamor's negotiations with Jacob for Dinah are not indicative of the Hivites' fear of Jacob and his family nor necessarily of their respect for them. Rather, the negotiations appear to be a combination of factors, including the compensation for and thus acknowledgement of the wrong done to Dinah and the perceived social and economic advantages of a merger between the two groups.

Another aspect of the offense to their honor is related to the issue of property and consent. Pressler's discussion highlights the framework in which this dishonor would have been perceived, namely, the "male possession of female sexuality" (Pressler: 91).[18] Notably, issues of consent to

---

17 Nicol's argument is an example of inferring the culpability of the woman in the sexual violation. Nicol asserts that Bathsheba cleverly plotted and secured the object of her desire, i.e., David.

18 Pressler discusses this in reference to Deut 22:13–29, noting that "the sexual offense laws, therefore, must be understood in the first place as protecting the rights of husband" (91) of the betrothed and the rights of the father of the unbetrothed.

sexual relations would not apply in war conditions (cf. Deut 20; 21:10–14). First, in the intergroup dynamics the women captives of war are non-Israelite. While their sexuality may also have been the property of the male, the context of war allowed for reformulation of the lines of consent. The death of their male protector left the women vulnerable. According to the rules of war, Israelite men were allowed to seize these women and make them their wives. Consequently, while the behavior of the Israelite men is the same as that of Shechem, the context of war may imbue their behavior with a different significance. War allowed for such seizing of women, but outside of the war context that behavior is reprehensible. The questions that the narrative seems to leave open to discussion are: What constitutes war? Is Simeon and Levi's act of revenge a declaration of war? If it is, then their seizing the Hivite women, as destructive as it may be in their social matrix, is normative.

Second, the intergroup manifestation of violence also represents itself along social and political lines. Brenner argues that in rejecting Hamor's proposal, Jacob and his household rejected political alliance. "It seems, therefore, that the pretext of a sister's honor—although it is one of the reasons for attacking the city—is less significant [than] the reluctance to lose the clan's unique identity through intermarriage" (Brenner: 116).

The intergroup manifestation of violence highlights a tendency that is prevalent in the social dimension of family's response to sexual violence. In Gen 34, as in some modern settings, the rape itself somehow becomes incidental to the ensuing actions taken in response to or even in an attempt to avenge the rape. The phenomenon may be referred to as the invisibility of the subject of the rape. In her discussion Keefe examines the intertexuality of Gen 34; Judg 19; and 2 Sam 13 to explore the "relationship between sexual and marital violence in these texts, demonstrating how the violated body of a woman functions as a metonym for the social body as it is disrupted in war" (Keefe: 79). She examines rape in ancient Israel literature while recognizing that the representations in the literature do not have a one-to-one correspondence to the social reality. She is on target in noting the relationship between rape and war in these texts (ibid.). While rape is the catalyst for the retaliation of war, the violence of war is on a different scale than the rape itself. This is not to suggest that the essence of violence in its propensity to produce adverse effects is less in rape. Rather, the immediacy of the effect may be more extensive in war than in the rape that was the catalyst. The dangers of this observation are the minimization of the effects of rape and the magnification of the effects of war. Likewise, the danger is to misconstrue the immediacy of the effects of violence for the extent of its effects. The immediacy of the effects of rape is most often focused on the object of the rape, but the extent of the long-term effects may encompass an entire community over a long period of time. The effects of violence are not regulated by the motivation for the forms of violence—love or honor.

CONCLUSION

Genesis 34 allows for extensive discussion of the interrelationship of love, honor, and violence. The story suggests that: (1) love is defined by the one who claims to love, not by the social ethos of the time; and (2) Shechem's love for Dinah was true in its manifestation of effort to win her. Love, however, may lead to behaviors that further involve violence. Such would be the case in the brothers' act of vengeance against the Hivites. This act of violence transcended the boundaries of the infraction that it aimed to avenge in that it substituted death for sexual violation (cf. Deut 22:23–27). Furthermore, Jacob's family took its mark of identity and exploited it in the service of vengeance. In addition, Dinah's brothers engaged the rules of war, plundering the cities and taking the Hivite women as captives.

One way of seeing the story is that the apparent ambivalence is intended by the narrator to demonstrate the complexities of the intra- and intergroup dynamics. First, the story demonstrates the nondeterministic aspect of violence. Violence sometimes begets violence, but sometimes there is a change in course that leads to nonviolent negotiations. Second, the characters are consistent in their behaviors. Shechem is focused and deliberate about getting what he wants: he is passionate in his pursuits. This is seen in his assaulting Dinah as well as his negotiations to get her as his wife. Simeon and Levi faithfully carry out their revenge, even to the point of violating their religious norms. The fathers (Jacob and Hamor) act in response to their children. Hamor conforms to the wishes of his son, while Jacob does not.

Finally, one can discern in the socioconceptual matrix of Gen 34 at least three models of responding to oppression. All of these models reflect a type of passion and the choice in moments pregnant with possibilities. The first model is that of Shechem, who oppresses and then takes measures to cover the negative repercussions of his behavior. His passion is self-centered, untamed, and aimed at self-gratification. The second model is Simeon and Levi, who show solidarity with the violated and thus seek to right a wrong. In this model, violence is not only an option—it is necessary. While their passion appears to be altruistic, their actions result in violence against Dinah. Like Shechem's passion, theirs is untamed. The third model is represented by Jacob, who is easily appeased because of his fear for his safety. This model shows a high tolerance for violence and recognizes violence for what it is but chooses to focus on nonthreatening alternatives. Jacob's passion is highly regulated to the extent of inertia in some matters, but the passion for preservation is vital. Finally, Hamor also represents a model. His is that of joining in on the side of the violator because of a prior relationship and defending the violator in spite of the nature of the violation committed. His passion is for solidarity with family and community. Like Jacob, he is passionate about preservation, and hence the operative criterion for standing with the violator is the prior relationship.

On the basis of Gen 34 one may suggest that some violence appears to be sanctioned in light of a larger goal of honor. Similarly, it may be argued that honor and deception are not mutually exclusive. Every action is a manifestation of a choice among possibilities, and the choice itself is the exhibition of personal passions. Difficult as this may be to accept, Shechem is that part of all of us that will do just about anything to achieve self-gratification. He is the part of every person and the persons who continue to have familial support even after they have committed heinous crimes. Jacob is the voice in every person who plays it safe even in the face of blatant wrongs. Genesis 34 is a story of love, honor, and violence—the story about the human propensity to exercise one's passions in choosing possibilities.

SLINGSHOTS, SHIPS, AND PERSONAL PSYCHOSIS: MURDER, SEXUAL INTRIGUE, AND POWER IN THE LIVES OF DAVID AND OTHELLO

Cheryl A. Kirk-Duggan
Graduate Theological Union

The Shakespearean saga of Othello and the Deuteronomistic saga of David both display obsessive desire, jealousy, sexual intrigue, premeditated murder, mental instability, and war. Othello, a Moorish noble in the service of the Venetian kingdom, alienates Iago his ensign, who feels slighted for not being promoted to lieutenant. This Black general marries a Venetian woman, Desdemona, without getting paternal consent from Brabantio, her father, a Venetian senator. For some critics, matters of Black and White confront each other as one of the bases for turmoil and the downward spiral from nobility to the wreckage of human bodies and spirits.

David, the youngest son of Jesse of Bethlehem (the grandson of Ruth and Boaz) and the anointed[1] king by Samuel (a prophet of the Lord), seduces and impregnates Bathsheba (daughter of Eliam, wife of Uriah). David then orders an assassination hit on Uriah the Hittite, Bathsheba's husband—one of David's outstanding warriors (2 Sam 23:39)[2]—because Uriah will not sleep with Bathsheba; as a warrior, he is pledged to be with his men. He is probably unaware that she is already pregnant by David. King David alienates his son and heir, Absalom, who then tries to dethrone the king. David's lust for Bathsheba and his obsession with absolute rule creates a dysfunctional home and destroys his kingdom.

---

[1] While priests were anointed, from the time of kingship, kings are the one's deemed anointed of the Lord. Anointing indicates that the Lord has separated the person out for a particular task and has divinely equipped the individual for the particular task.

[2] Uriah, formerly a sojourner or foreigner living in Israel, enjoyed some protection but not full civil rights. He converted to Yahwism and reached a rank of high office under David's regime. See Bruce C. Birch, "The First and Second Books of Samuel," *NIB* 2:1044, 1098.

Othello's insecurities and poor judgment are catalysts for his murder of Desdemona and his own suicide. Both King David and General Othello are men of distinction who have difficulty maintaining themselves in the interconnected public/governmental and private/domestic spheres. My essay engages a comparative analysis between Othello and David, two ambitious leaders, in their relationships to family, power, and violence. Both narratives are endemic with envy, guilt, pain, and death. After summarizing a *Womanist* biblical methodology, I then dialogically juxtapose the characterizations of David and Othello; investigate the familial and political relationships and the role of scapegoating, sex, and violence; and explore the roles of faith and infidelity, and irony and discernment as prompters or detractors of power: all markers of pregnant passion.

THE LENS OF SCRUTINY: WOMANIST BIBLICAL HERMENEUTICS

Many seek to give the Bible secular and religious authority, both as a spiritual guidebook and as a political manual. In the process, they often confuse the actual texts of biblical narratives with oral mythology about what is in the Bible and disregard the literal words of the sacred text, inserting an admixture of the ideologies scholars ascribe to the text from contemporary biblical studies. Biblical scholarship often searches for a privileged metadiscourse toward some "Truth" about biblical history and ancient Israel. Biblical stories contain multiple and often conflictual truths. Thus, this brand of scholarship tends to assign certainty and reality to stories that are inconsistent, ironic, and ambiguous. Popular insights and misunderstandings attributed to biblical texts spring from a psychological need to assert unequivocal and infallible authority to church authority and tradition.

Biblical stories parallel Lyotard's (xxiv) sense of postmodernist incredulity regarding any kind of metanarratives with their great multiplicity, whereas modernist biblical studies retain a variety of nineteenth-century quests for metanarratives vested with authority. Other biblical scholarship attempts to reconstruct the sociopolitical and religious history of ancient Israel and the Near East. The histories within the Bible relate to the narratives that are often reconstructed into particular contemporary ideologies, which are then used to justify the oppression of others.

Regina Schwartz notes that biblical narratives are redacted amorphous stories rife with multiple thematic tensions, contradictions, and repetitions, where characterizations and identities are devised, shaped, broken, and remade as a reality known as Israel evolves. Many messages seem contradictory, such as the succession narrative and the house/palace/temple scenario, wherein at once David is secure in his power by God, yet God does not want David to build God a house. God is the benefactor, not David. In this development of Israel's story, in the biblical text, conflict and struggle are at the forefront (Schwartz 1992: 36, 40–51).

Many of the same dynamics occur in Othello's tragedy. Conflict and struggle occur in the play from the outset. For my essay, the received text of King David's life and reign, rife with conflicts and struggles, is the dialogical entity that I connect to the tensions, perceptions, and leadership of Othello. Grounding this comparative analysis is my understanding of *Womanist* biblical hermeneutics.

Womanist theory invites, actually insists, that one live in the present, while simultaneously being a student of history, engaging in radical listening and discerning to see, know, challenge, analyze, and make a difference. *Womanist* theory is a field of study and a way of thinking that takes seriously the exposure, analysis, and transformation of societal and personal injustices and oppressions that affect those who usually matter least in society, as symbolized by poor Black women. *Womanist* theory is interdisciplinary and examines experience present in living, written, oral, visual, aural, sensual, and artistic texts to create its epistemology, hermeneutics, and philosophy. *Womanist* thought, as theory and praxis, appreciates ongoing intellectual, spiritual dialogue to prepare individuals to experience their own reality to the fullest in a holistic, healthy manner. *Womanist*, derived by Alice Walker (xi) from the term "womanish," refers to women of African descent who are audacious, outrageous, in charge, and responsible. A *Womanist* emancipatory theory embraces a message of hope and transformation toward engendering mutuality and community amid the responsibility and stewardship of freedom and honors the *imago Dei* in all persons, regardless. *Womanist* theory builds on the essential goodness of humanity and focuses on liberation amid personal and societal fragmentation for all people in general and the healing and transformation of peoples of African descent in particular. In so doing, Womanists take seriously people's lived experiences and their realized, creative imagination, canonized in cultural production of stories, poems, sermons, novels, art, music, video, gardens, dance, and the like. Embracing matters of town and gown, of society and the academy, *Womanist* theory always relates to praxis and is challenging, multifaceted, complex work.

The body of knowledge and research of *Womanist* thought includes, but is not limited to, issues pertaining to theology (divinity, dialogue, identity; sacrality; spirituality, and power); Bible and narratives (texts, authority, characters, rituals, language, and history); ethics (value, behavior, emotions, visibility, integrity, and praxis); and context (autobiography, culture, aesthetics, power dynamics, ecology, and community). *Womanist* theory is a tool to name, expose, question, and help transform the oppression of women, particularly those affected daily by race and

class domination. Womanists champion the struggle for freedom, ultimately the freedom for all people. Freedom is a gift and a right, both
bequeathed by God. God is personal, not an abstract, philosophical construct. Since God spoke the world into being, many Womanists take the
use of language seriously between the divine and the human and within
human community, as they are the *imago Dei* incarnated. The politics of
language, where words and expressions can inspire or subjugate, are vital
to analysis, particularly that of biblical texts. A move toward a *Womanist*
reading of biblical texts requires a hermeneutics of tempered cynicism,
creativity, courage, commitment, candor, curiosity, and the comedic.

Tempered cynicism or suspicion invites one to question with a sensitivity that knows the joy of the impossible, the hope of the embedded
faith, together with the scholarship that helps one appreciate the complexities of such work. Creativity affords a context where customary
interpretations and traditions do not hinder exploring oral or canonical
texts in new ways. Courage provides the cushion for moments when the
analysis leads to more of the same or to mystery, with the audacity to ask
questions and engage comparative analysis of unique and seemingly
antithetical texts and themes. Commitment to the hearing and just,
appropriate living of these texts undergirds the process of discovery that
can and needs to be relevant to the lives of people from a *Womanist* perspective. Candor provides the impetus to reveal the oppression within
the texts and the communities that have incorporated such tenets to produce an oppressive, though mainline faith. Curiosity presses one to keep
searching the realm of the sacred to push the envelope toward an atmos-
phere of inclusivity, mercy, justice, and love. The comedic reminds us not
to take ourselves so seriously that we fail to grow and to respect other
ways of seeing, though we may disagree.

Womanist biblical scholarship signifies the fire and passion of *Womanist* scholars as they study, teach, write, interpret, preach, and minister.
Located in a cosmological setting where Black women intimately know
the multivocal oppressive experience of race/sex/class/age/ableness,
Womanist biblicists commit to the gift of education as transformative
power. *Womanist* biblical scholars wrestle with the Hebrew Bible, New
Testament, and apocryphal scriptures as they deal with the madness and
absurdity of oppression—calling for a cease fire, new kinds of hermeneutics, of accountability, and change. Womanists scholars want us to name
systemic and personal evil in our society and then move to transform that
evil, whether apathy, abuse, or affliction. *Womanist* theology (Hayes:
102–19) is the study or discipline of God-talk that emerges out of the rich
yet oppressive experience of women of African descent. Such theology
analyzes human individual and social behavior in concert with the Divine
toward seeing the ramifications of injustice. Based upon a "least of these

theology" (K. B. Douglas: 76–77), *Womanist* theology embodies a God/ Spirit who cares and who looks with disgust on anyone who dismisses, disregards, or denigrates a person made in the divine image. A "least of these theology" is a mode of God-talk in which every person is important and relational. Injustice, the antithesis to liberatory theory and praxis, produces a malaise due to all oppression, other phobias, and the abuse of power. *Womanist* theology sees, studies, and then wishes to exorcise oppressive evil, moving toward change, balance, promise, and healing.

Womanist biblical theology merges the study of theology and exegesis to examine and learn from biblical texts toward the survival, wholeness, and health of all people.

As a Christian *Womanist,* I am a *Womanist* scholar, storyteller, preacher, poet, and performer. My belief in the Christian story as I appreciate God's revelation through many faiths supports an interfaith, interdisciplinary, theological bent and ethical sensibility toward creating new methods and ways of reading and new avenues of possibility for nurturing communal solidarity. Consequently, my use of *Womanist* theology embodies redaction, reconstruction, and reformation: bringing new questions and new ways of listening while juxtaposing multiple texts for enjoyable, provocative scrutiny. Such reformation shapes a reading of biblical texts that yearns for social justice toward engaging and stimulating conversation and life transformation in the communities of faith and the academy. Some biblical texts make such a quest next to impossible. Nevertheless, I search for a way to champion the freedom, dignity, and justice of *all* people—a prelude to dance a praxis of morality, to the rhythm of sacred words, of poetics. Using a *Womanist* biblical exegetical paradigm allows the working definition of "pregnant passion" as a metaphor for intense, powerful engagement that crosses boundaries, causes harm, and squelches creativity by taking those energies and relegating them to the realm of disregard, deviance, and destruction. *Womanist* biblical hermeneutics provides the lens through which I explore the mystique, camouflage, perceptions, and illusions surrounding two men called to lead: David and Othello.

David and Othello: Harbingers of Facades

We first meet David as he enters the court of King Saul, a musician with presence, valor, and eloquent speech (1 Sam 16:14–17:58). David's music helps refresh and soothe Saul, one fraught with mental illness, probably an obsessive-compulsive, paranoid schizophrenic, or bipolar disorder (1 Sam 16:14–38). David, the youngest son of Jesse, was told to carry provisions during the skirmishes with the Philistines, but he approaches the scene of battle. Intriguingly, his older brother Eliab

reproaches David for leaving the sheep and says, "I know your presump-
tion and the evil of your heart" (1 Sam 17:28). Is this a foreshadowing of
what is to come? Saul lets David meet the Philistine and yokes the God of
Israel with David's deliverance and triumph. David successfully kills
Goliath with a slingshot in 1 Sam 17:50, although 2 Sam 21:19 states that
Elhanan actually killed Goliath of Gath later.[3] Early on, we see David's
pride, arrogance, and capacity to do violence, for David not only fells
Goliath with the stone but kills Goliath and then decapitates him (1 Sam
17:50–51): the beginning of David's taste of blood and victory, which one
can imply, escalates David's reputation.

Three varied stories in 1 Samuel narrate how David comes to fame
and distinction in Saul's court. These sagas involve Samuel's disappoint-
ment with Saul, Saul's insanity running amuck as his courtiers search for
a good therapist, and the epic around Goliath, wherein Saul appears not
to have had prior knowledge of David. These three different, unrelated
stories depict Samuel's harsh critique, his unanticipated hatred of Saul,
and the need to find a therapist—outweighing any military or sacred
anointing, given Saul's heightening insanity—as critical to David's rise to
esteem in Saul's court. David's attractive personal appearance, his
demeanor, and his ability to play music to soothe Saul's mental and emotional illness make him a match for the role (North: 524, 543–44). David's
excellence at court parallels his eminence at war.

With each battle, David is more successful. For example, the ransom
for Michal's hand, procuring the foreskins, necessarily disposing of the
Philistines, conjures up sadomasochism, brutality, and premeditated
murder: barbarically maiming sexual organs and committing homicide, a
cornucopia of violence and an act of pregnant passion (1 Sam 18:20–30).
When David joins legions with Achish and the Philistines, he becomes a
terrorist, a renegade. He slaughters women and men, plunders, and steals
animals and garments. He is ruthless, this guerilla fighter, warrior, and
robber baron. Achish finds no fault with David but must comply with the
wishes of the other Philistines and sends David from Aphek. David
returns to Philistines as the Philistines go to Jezreel. When David returns
to Ziklag and finds their wives and children kidnapped, David's followers
want to stone him. David recoups, calls on the Lord, and is triumphant:
he recovers all persons and commodities and shares the spoils with all of
the men (1 Sam 27:8–12; 1 Sam 29). Is David a complex character or a
shallow chameleon, that is, one who tells people what they want to hear?
How is it that David gets away with what he does?

---

[3] For the purposes of this analysis, we assent that David killed Goliath.

In studying David's characterization, one can categorize the narrative of his life experience from the perspectives of plot, characterization, and theology. Within the plot, there is much ambiguity, issues of divine election, and divine rejection. David appears to be the winner, favored by God. Yet many would have selected Saul over David, given the human drama that unfolds within the books of Samuel, where Yahweh serves as one of the supporting characters. David enters the stage after Saul's previous introduction as "the prototype, the antitype" (Noll: 51) and seems to be typecast for the role of king: David is young and wants to find favor with God. The narrator sets David up as the desired one but never conveys what so attracts the deity. David, an opportunist, aggressively inquires about warrior status (1 Sam 17), about being part of the royal family[4]—first modestly, then later contentiously with military mastery. David's ambition combined with his faith, in the name of Yahweh, seems to gain him God's favor. Kurt Noll finds David "moving from a kind of hero cliché to a fully rounded character in I Samuel 18 to II Samuel 9" (Noll: 54). I find such an assessment problematic. How can Noll find the character "fully rounded" when he himself expresses disgust at David's negative attributes—his rape of Bathsheba and most egregious slaughter of Uriah—unless "fully rounded" implies no reference to David's dysfunctional character. Thus, David may have developed his expertise and acumen as a king, but his character is a quagmire. Noll himself notes that David is manipulative, shrewd and mercilessly deceptive, indifferent, apathetic, opportunistic, self-serving: he postures publicly, though he is often incompetent when dealing with Joab, his hooligan accomplice (Noll: 43–45)—public élan and emotional debacle.

David is a rather competent administrator, as governor, as soldier, with a deep respect of the Yahwistic traditions. Yet moments of ugliness tarnish his rule, especially the lustful descent of his son Amnon, who

---

4 David has an extended family, including eight named wives. Ahinoam of Jezreel bore Amnon, David's first born. Abigail, the former wife of Nabal, bore Chileab; Maacah, daughter of Talmai king of Geshur, bore Absalom and Tamar; Haggith bore Adonijah; Abitai bore Shephatiah, Eglah bore Ithream (2 Sam 3:2–5). David also told Abner to bring him back his bride Michal, Saul's daughter, now married to Paltiel, son of Laish. Paltiel did not want to let her go, but Abner convinced him to return home (2 Sam 3:13–15) and to let her go. David also married Michal, who had no children. Bathsheba, widow of Uriah, bore Solomon and three others sons. According to 1 Chron 3:6–8, David had nine additional sons. After David became king of all Israel, he obtained more concubines and wives from Jerusalem; more sons and daughters were born, which was the custom then; it was a matter of prestige for which David was not criticized, though Solomon was (1 Kgs 5:1–12). Though Solomon is included in 2 Sam 3, he is not born until later.

rapes his half-sister Tamar. Cousin Jonadab,[5] son of Shimeah, David's brother, goads Amnon. Amnon rapes Tamar after she pleads for him to ask their father for her hand in marriage. After the rape, Amnon shames her, puts her out, raping Tamar a second time, psychologically. Jonadab is to Amnon as Joab is to David and Iago to Othello. Like Othello regarding his sensual, passionate side, David has a propensity for demonstrating exorbitant affection for particular people: Jonathan, Bathsheba, Absalom, and perhaps Amnon. He shows extravagant emotional outbursts when dancing before the ark, his repentance before Nathan, his total reconciliation with Absalom after Amnon's death, and his numerous acts of generosity to Saul's family. His emotional surges often result in impetuous actions that hasten the demise of the nation (Maly: 93–97, 104), a nation previously under the kingship of Yahweh.

David's elevation to kingship locates a political development framed by a theological interpretation, at the will of Yahweh.[6] Such apologies are documents that defended or justified a particular king attaining a throne by force. The received, apologetic text indicates David's guilt-free, legal accession to the throne, despite charges of escalating Saul's and Abner's demise to charges of David being a deserter, outlaw, and Philistine mercenary (Carter: 494–96, 498–502). Walter Brueggemann offers such an apologetic treatment of this boy who becomes king.

Embracing the methods of sociological and literary analysis, Brueggemann explores how Israel remembers and imagines David. We receive their view of David's truth in the canon as a drama in three acts: "The Trustful Truth of the Tribe" (1 Sam 16:1–2 Sam 5:5); "The Painful Truth of the Man" (2 Sam 9–20; 1 Kgs 1–2); "The Sure Truth of the State" (2 Sam 5:6–8:18). Act 4, the related theological derivative construction as "The Hopeful Truth of Assembly," will not be considered here (Brueggemann 1985: 8, 9, 19, 41, 67, 87). These polyvalent truths are not the essential, historical David but the recorded memory and presence of David that moves in many directions, from many different contexts, included for different reasons. The trustful tribe concerns David's ascent, his key relationships, the legitimation of David and the values of the tribal community (who accepts its story uncritically), and how David's story is both told and heard (Brueggemann 1985: 19–39, 72). The painful truth, or pathos, offers a critical or at least suspicious knowing of David, a faithful yet self-serving man of power, with all of his foibles amid the text of the Succession Narrative and

---

5 Jonadab is the one who later tells David that only Amnon is dead and that it is the result of Absalom's revenge.

6 This course of action echoes the royal apology tradition of the Hittite kingdom.

the intersections of "personal temptation and self-deception" amid public responsibility and power; amidst adjudicatory matters of divine indictment and human repentance because of evil called good (43–45, 47, 53, 62–67). The third saga of state's truth relates an unambiguous story of royal theology and public certainty, while God disassociates from this king and standard royal theology. This story is ultimately couched in the language of the promise of dynasty, incongruity, and the leveraging of all old power, images, legitimacy, and metaphor with the state, truly "under God and indivisible," which allows for subjugation and conquest under David's reign (67–84). Bruggemann's reading allows how David moves from shepherd boy to chieftain to king with divine sanction: point well taken. A return to the man prior to the throne makes my case for the complexity of pregnant passion and David's full participation in its implicit violence.

Under fire, David is the consummate actor, schemer, and manipulator. When trapped in Achish of Gath's territory, after fleeing Saul, David pretends to be mad, which allows for his escape. In another instance David uses the Gibeonites' complaint as carte blanche to give over two sons and five grandsons of Saul to be hung in front of the mountain before the Lord (1 Sam 21:7–9), as an expiation of the heritage of the Lord (1 Sam 21:3). Though David prayed Ps 22, confessing that God saves him *from* violence (22:3b), David *perpetrates* much violence, *in the name of the Lord* (e.g., the attack against the Philistines to save Keilah [1 Sam 23:5]). While David schemes against others and Saul continues to plot evil against David, David spares Saul's life when David gets the upper hand at Engedi (1 Sam 23:9–24:7). Saul and David seem to reconcile; Saul lauds David as more righteous than he and asks David to swear not to harm his descendants, while noting that David would be king (for many scholars, late source material; 1 Sam 24:8–22). Again, David spares Saul's life as Saul sleeps (1 Sam 26); once more, David asks Saul why the king pursues him: because of David's activities? Is he guilty? Does God anoint Saul's act of revenge? Yet again, Saul confesses his wrong, and they part in blessing. Unconvinced, David, his wives, and his warriors flee to the Philistines and affiliate with Achish (1 Sam 27:1–7). Interestingly, God often empowers David to commit violence, particularly against the Philistines when they search for David, giving him the strategies to defeat them successfully (2 Sam 5:17–25). Some of the violence is incited by God's anger against Israel (2 Sam 24:1). Although compelling, crucial, and needed, a critique of divine action that condones violence cannot be explored here. Even though seemingly directed by God, when David realizes that his act is a sinful one, he does confess (2 Sam 24:1). Is David an ancient version of a twenty-first-century "bad boy," a sociopath of the arrogant, self-centered, sly persuasion?

Many criticize David for not being present during the actual battle, when he remains home and seduces Bathsheba. Mindful of historiography, rhetorical and literary attitudes of the text, however, kings during that time may or may not have participated in a particular battle. David's presence would lift morale, yet also make him a sitting target; thus, one would weigh the risks regarding the magnitude of the battle and the expectations of its outcome. In 1 and 2 Samuel, a king's success is a function of the king's behavior, not of his accomplishment or any inherent value. H. P. Smith argues that, given the existing peace treaties between other kings and David and Ammon's great isolation, David's choice of staying in Jerusalem does not indicate a dereliction of royal responsibilities. Tinged with a little irony, only later does the reader learn of David's victory, after he admits the wrongs he has done and receives partial forgiveness. This account is not "irony enjoyed by the narrator for its own sake" but intensification of the moral criticism of David's sins (Garsiel: 253). What of Bathsheba and Uriah? Bathsheba is not involved in collusion nor an opportunist but a tragic figure: a woman in a monarchial patriarchy who has to deal with adultery and murder, not of her own making, forced to marry the king to avoid persecution for adultery. The narrator keeps us in the dark about Bathsheba's perceptions and feelings of these monstrous events. Uriah is a dutiful warrior, a member of the "Thirty," a select order in the service of the king. We see the story's actions, but the characters' feelings and sensibilities regarding their experiences remain untold (Garsiel: 249–61).

Thus, part of the Davidic saga is the triangle of David, Bathsheba, and Uriah/Joab. Ironically, David's story involves actual adultery with Bathsheba, but Othello's story involves the lack of adultery by Desdemona. Othello's cataclysmic triangle involves Othello, Desdemona, and Iago. Othello's phenomenal domestic and emotional tragedy involves deception, bigotry, envy, treachery, struggle, passion, and crime. Shakespeare quickly dispenses with the war, where Othello achieves a heroic victory as general, to move on to emotional matters, with a major theme of appearance and perception. The unfolding of this complex play of many characters finds that Othello, the Moorish general, marries Desdemona, daughter of Brabantio, a Venetian senator. Earlier, Brabantio had rejected Roderigo, a Venetian citizen, as Desdemona's suitor. Roderigo, who still loves Desdemona, is Iago's pawn. Iago, Othello's ensign, is jealous of Cassio, Othello's lieutenant and friend. Iago, married to Emilia, Desdemona's lady in waiting and confidante, is an ensign to Othello and the main instigator for this drama. Moreover, Iago is livid with Othello for becoming general and not appointing Iago as second-in-command. Bianca is Cassio's mistress. This tragedy presents themes of loyalty and respect of office, duty, jealousy and envy, marriage, naïveté, projection, betrayal, the politics of identity and place for women, and racism. Some scholars argue that the question is not the antagonism between Black and White ethnicities but between good and evil (Lamb: 24). The story of public versus private ends with four deaths: three murders and a suicide. The once noble Moorish general and his beloved wife die. Iago, the one who cuckolded and manipulated everyone, shuffles off in chains. How can one begin to come to grips with such a tense, multifaceted narrative?

The gaze through which the audience sees connotes power and skews how and what we see. As the play opens, we see and hear through the sensibilities of Iago, the exasperated employee. Othello is painted in a negative light, as the story of an intricate matrix of relationships unfolds. Iago manipulates anyone who can help him in his drive to defeat Othello, beginning with Roderigo—who, blinded by his unrequited love for Desdemona, is a willing pawn. Because Iago confesses his deception to the audience, the onlooker remains privy to the key threads that unravel throughout. Iago's second pawn is Brabantio, Desdemona's father. Iago taunts and demeans Brabantio, who does not know that Desdemona has eloped with the Moor, by ridiculing Othello. Iago manipulates every character to control someone else. Iago tells Brabantio that his new son-in-law is animalistic, boorish, and bestial, setting up oppositional polarities between light and dark, white and black—playing the race card, long before O. J. Simpson, Mark Furman, Nicole Simpson, and the sensationalized murders of 1994. That Othello is an outsider, a military man, and a Black Moor removes him from the category of desirable husband material for Desdemona, from the view of her society and her father, who finally views Desdemona as property. (Interestingly, when Shakespeare wrote *Othello,* Venice had banned both Jews[7] and Moors from residency.) Othello enters the stage at the end of scene 1 and at the beginning of act 1, scene 2, which occurs on the same evening. Iago continues to spin his web of deceit as he intimates to Othello that either Brabantio or Roderigo have been vilifying Othello. As Iago works to endear himself to the general, he convinces Othello that he, Iago, is loyal, honest, and devoted (Lamb: 34–37).

This provocative, passion-laden Shakespearean tragedy unveils intense, unbridled, natural desires and anonymous, unnamed fears that most persons mask on a daily basis, set in the story of a well seasoned,

---

7 See also Shakespeare's *The Merchant of Venice* and the interactions between Shylock, the Jew, characterized as a hard-hearted, vengeful usurer; Antonio, the Christian and Venetian merchant who takes no interest for lending money; Antonio's friend Bassanio, a noble Venetian; and the ingenuity of Bassanio's wife Portia.

victorious general with a solid reputation who is systematically destroyed via envy, greed, and betrayal, resulting in a murder-suicide. His alleged friend, Iago, dupes, manipulates, and betrays the general. Ironically, Othello continually labels Iago innocent.[8] Innocent he is not; far from it: orchestrating Othello's demise, preying on his superstitions, and using his intellect and cunning to exploit all of the characters as pawns, for he believes he is undervalued. As Iago schemes and weaves a matrix of deceit, he makes seemingly positive statements that have evil intent and ends, in true Machiavellian fashion (Shakespeare: x), with Othello killing his innocent wife Desdemona and taking his own life: a time and place all too similar and familiar, and different from our own times of the twenty-first century.

Shakespeare wrote *Othello* (1603–4) during a time when Ptolemaic thought was central; that is, official Church dogma stated as truth that a stationary earth was the center of the universe, encircled with nine concentric rings, then surrounded by six planets, the sun, and moon. Thinkers only began accepting Copernican thought around 1610. In accord with a hierarchical view of the planet system was a hierarchical view of creation, of men over women, humans over animals, animals over vegetation, and so on. The four Greek elements thought to make up everything in the universe—*fire, water, air,* and *earth*—were also contained in the body as humours: *phlegm, blood, black bile,* and *yellow bile.* The dominant humour determined one's persona: heightened phlegm caused one to be kind and dull; yellow bile or choler made one irritable; black bile signaled sadness and melancholy; blood signified lightheartedness. Physicians assumed that illness resulted from an imbalance in one's humours. In *Othello,* Shakespeare assumes the knowledge of this system with his audience.[9] Society relegated women to the domestic or emotional realm or the convent, with little to no autonomy, no ability to inherit, no benefits of education, and no rights after marriage. Thus in *Othello,* Desdemona has problems because she asserts her own power and brings the appearance of impropriety to her family, thus signing her own death warrant. Any inference of embarrassment or dishonor to her family, particularly of being unchaste prior to marriage, de facto signaled an affront

---

8 Dramatically, Othello's continued blind eye to Iago's duplicity creates a tension, where the audience either has incredible empathy for him or incredible disgust because of his naiveté and either incapacity or refusal to see.

9 In the England of Shakespeare's day most of the female characters have phlegm as dominant; most of the men have a choleric disposition, amid tremendous religious discord. The class hierarchy included the haves (the nobility or aristocrats with power, wealth, and ancestry) and the have-nots (everyone else).

to Elizabethan social order. Critics note that during this era England banned Blacks and Jews, particularly, and all foreigners in general, given that English society saw them as menaces to cultural homogeneity. Ergo, such connoisseurs argue that Othello, as an outsider, is a protagonist regardless of his race, perhaps signaling that we are all outsiders (Lamb: 8–13, 20). The race question remains for the reader in the twenty-first century a question of social mores, role, and character.

Shakespeare's plays involve a wide spectrum of deviant and criminal characters. Crimes inherently declared wrong universally, the *mala in se*, include rape, theft, robbery, and murder; those acts made crime by law/ statue, *mala prohibita*, receive different weight in different societies. One views the crimes based upon levels of seriousness and type of punishment. That is, felonies connote grave, serious offenses; misdemeanors pertain to lesser infringements and petty crimes. Categorically crimes vary: from those against a person, to crimes of habitation or property. *Othello* includes premeditated murder, attempted murder, and criminal solicitation. Under the rubric of murder, the "unlawful killing of a human being by another with malice aforethought, express or implied," there are three categories. These include (1) justifiable homicide, an act of self-defense or in the line of duty; (2) excusable or accidental homicide, when one is unaware of what she or he has done (e.g., insanity); and (3) criminal homicide, negligent, reckless homicides committed purposefully or knowingly. Othello kills Desdemona as a premeditated, deliberate act. This first-degree murder occurs out of Othello's own gullibility, as Iago was able to set Othello against Desdemona because of her alleged adultery with Roderigo. Othello moves from loving to loathing her in a cruel, emotionally tormented fashion (Time: 25–27, 29, 32). This rendering does not fully tell us, however, who Othello is as leader, general, and military mastermind or strategist. Like studying David, it is difficult to separate the public from the private persona, since they are so integrally intermingled. In public sojourns with Iago, we often learn more about Othello the military strategist and the man.

There is a relationship between Othello and Iago, for example, before the drama begins. Othello is Iago's superior, and when Othello becomes a general, Iago remains under his command but without a promotion. Iago convinces Othello that he is loyal, honest, and devoted. Iago continues to build his case as a faithful lieutenant who is genuinely concerned about the general's reputation. Since Othello has moved up in rank, this indicates his leadership acumen, that those with higher authority saw those traits for keen military strategist in Othello. Moreover, he has been victorious on the battle field and is seemingly respected by Venetian society, if not his person, that he held the rank. Reading from twenty-first-century eyes and ears, one cannot help but wonder if Othello was regarded as a novelty in Venetian society, not unlike Paul Robeson or Sarah Baartmann, the Hottentot Venus in Parisian "polite" society.[10] In the first act we meet a general who moves with some ease, though his bantering makes one suspect. Is he comfortable? Has he paid too great a price to move in the Venetian court, or has he acclimated to his new environment and is merely enthusiastic? When he meets Desdemona's father, for example, Othello is not worried about Brabantio's possible actions because he views himself as vital to Venetian society: he holds himself in their esteem. The general proclaims his profound love for Desdemona, and the audience must begin to wonder about the statements Iago made earlier. Cassio, Othello's lieutenant, comes to relate the shift in politics and the need for Othello regarding the Cyprian wars. Given the three search parties that had been sent to search for Othello, since he is not present for the battle skirmishes, one wonders how Othello could have been so unconscious to the mounting political tensions. Is this disregard of the political situation an indication of Othello being completely besotted by his wife? Is he seeking to shift his foci from so public a venue to a more private one? Is he an irresponsible leader? Given that King David took advantage of Bathsheba while his men were also at war, is Othello's obtuseness and David's philandering the result of the privilege of leadership? Finally, with his rank and apparent social acceptance, why did Othello and Desdemona have to run off?

Using a market motif, Iago tells Cassio that Othello has married. That Desdemona is wealthy probably so irritates Iago that he uses her socioeconomic status as an excuse to project his venom again on Othello and Cassio, because ultimately he wants Desdemona for himself. On some level an accomplished politician, Othello tries to assuage Brabantio and successfully presents himself as a sophisticated gentleman, that is, worthy of Desdemona. Yet Brabantio believes Othello used magic to seduce Desdemona, setting up a contrast between paganism and Christianity, pandering to an exotic, mysterious, stereotypical view of this man with an ebony hue. Brabantio creates an explanation that can save the family's reputation from the shame his society would attach to his daughter marrying without parental consent, the shame to a father who cannot control his daughter. Both Brabantio and Othello are absent when the council meets, which calls attention to Brabantio's lesser importance to Venice and Othello's focus on his personal disquiet and not upon his

---

10 Sarah Baartmann, a native of the Khoi San tribe of South Africa, was a twenty-year-old slave in Cape Town in 1810. Taken to London and exhibited as a freak across Britain, she was usually locked inside of a cage and treated like a dancing bear.

state obligations. Ironically, Iago remains apprised of both the emotional and political realities and continues in Othello's esteem (Lamb: 41–43).

Act 2, set in Cyprus, presents Othello as a great man and leader, through the eyes of Montano. We learn that the war is over, due to inclement weather. That Othello is now a general gives us pause. How did he get to this position? How did this Black Moor move up the ranks from private to lieutenant major to general? Clearly Othello must have demonstrated military acumen, intellect, commitment, and physical stamina. In the process of his rapid ascension, Othello must have showed a talent for victory in conflict, for excellence, for being able to achieve goals, a conquering mentality, and an allegiance to a higher authority. This is the one to whom Cassio has great allegiance, as his commanding officer. As Cassio adoringly affirms the marriage of Othello, Iago and his entourage, which includes Desdemona, approach Cyprus by sea. Cassio's honorable nature and his devotion to Othello as general cast a foil for the devious nature of Iago and will make Cassio's afterward apparent betrayal of Othello even more devastating. The plot moves back and forth from matters of leadership to matters of relationship.

Iago mercilessly castigates his wife, Emilia, to Cassio, despite Desdemona's efforts to intervene. This dialogue highlights several themes, in addition to Iago's persona and mindset: Iago views women as unfaithful and manipulative. The theme of irony unfolds as the most untrustworthy man controls the downfall of honest Cassio and unsophisticated Othello due to their misplaced confidence in Iago. Desdemona disputes Iago about his misogynic views concerning women and then turns to Cassio for his opinion. Iago will use this exchange between Cassio and Desdemona as additional artillery against his enemies, Cassio and Othello. Early on, Desdemona is a leader in her own right and does not play the subservient role demanded of a Venetian upper-class woman. When Othello arrives, he and Desdemona embrace with deep affection, joy, comfort, and tenderness. Othello cannot perceive Iago's true nature, although the audience knows the Iago who manipulates Roderigo and works to convince Othello that Desdemona is having an affair with Cassio. Othello's instincts and skills, which allow his rapid and unprecedented elevation from private to general, are not on display in his relationship with Iago, a subordinate staff member, which is mystifying. But then again, many who are brilliant often lack street smarts, the everyday perspicacity that helps ordinary people to avoid indiscretions and stupidity. Convinced of this lie, Roderigo agrees to kill Cassio. Iago's ensuing monologue reveals his own love for Desdemona; he admits the nobility of Othello yet schemes to make Othello go insane (Lamb: 74–79). Othello's categorization is a paradox, strong in many areas, weak in others. His military strategy does not help him clearly discern Iago's treachery. An analysis of the psychological underpinnings helps illumine the complexity of Othello, of how his unquestioned ability to lead and direct others in the military sphere is not transferable to his personal/social relationships.

Iago blindsides Othello, an introverted, repressed persona who dreadfully responds to Iago's stimuli. Othello's reality of Desdemona spirals down recklessly to regarding her as a common whore. In Othello's subconscious, Desdemona must have been a whore to marry a Black Moor. In Jungian terms, Iago, the extraverted thinker, creates incredible confusion between Othello, an introverted, sensation type, and Desdemona, an extraverted, intuitive type. Othello is more oriented to his inner reality; Iago and Desdemona are more oriented toward their outer reality (Coursen: 101–3).

With Othello's persona, he embodies an integral connectedness and identity with the self and ego, a reduction of the former and inflation of the latter causing a tremendous power complex that results in a profound break with reality causing delusional behavior. Objects take on horrid and magical qualities. All change becomes problematic, causing mistrust and fear. Othello's utopia would be to live on a lonely island where he has total command. His obsession with his career is the space of an introverted sensationalist who focuses on the subjective insight stimulated by the objective catalyst. For example, Othello's fixation on the handkerchief fuses "the blending of an existential event with archetypal timelessness, confusing Christian and pagan values.... The handkerchief, first gift of a Christian marriage, absorbs the negative shifting of Othello's perspective as it is shadowed by the past he thought he had left behind, but had merely repressed" (Coursen: 103–4). Othello usually appears to be unbelievably calm, but his pathology causes him to be unable to tell the difference between the actual object and his subjective perception. The objects embody powerful, fear-inspiring qualities, qualities he is not consciously aware of, but through his imagination, he sees through his unconscious cognition. Othello, as an introverted sensationalist, becomes the victim of someone else's aggressiveness quite easily. An easy prey for abuse, Othello exacts revenge at inappropriate times with heightened obtuseness and obduracy. His ultimate target is Desdemona, whom he can love only as a reflection of his own ego. Othello's obsessive infatuation, like that of Amnon for Tamar (2 Sam 13), leads quickly to animosity. Manipulated masterfully by Iago, the vulnerable Othello ultimately betrays himself. In the chaos throughout, Othello confuses truth with falsehood. He is convinced that he is executing a witch when he strangles Desdemona. His murder and suicide erases all that had contrived his perfection from within (Coursen: 107, 109–13, 115, 117–18). Iago and Othello tell us other discrete qualities of Othello's personality.

Iago notes that Othello is a Black Moor who is open, has a free spirit, and believes that people are who they present themselves to be; Othello is naïve. Othello also has a noble, loving, and constant nature. Othello acknowledges that he is not of the aristocracy, for he claims rude and unpolished speech and notes that prior to coming to Venice nine months earlier he lived among his simple people, who live a hard life. He has aged prematurely, in large part due to his military career. Iago describes Othello's relationship with Desdemona as "an old black ram/Is tupping your white ewe" (act 1, scene 1, lines 90–91). In sum, Othello and Desdemona grew up in very different worlds. One might think he would probably have a difficult time, at his stage in life, of adjusting to Venetian society and to his marriage (Somerville: 69–70). At the same time, Othello has risen through the ranks and publicly expresses his love for Desdemona to Iago: "But that I love gentle Desdemona" (act 1, scene 2, line 25). Both parties need to make serious adjustments; however, in the right set of conditions, people can triumph over cosmic differences. Othello's trusts of his betrayer, Iago, demonstrates both Othello's gullibility and his insistence on seeing only the best in people (à la *Candide*) as well as Iago's sociopathology and manipulative mindset. In addition to the general personality profile, it is essential for mapping out the "pregnant passions" to note how David and Othello relate to women and family, the politics of marriage amidst the politics of state.

Politics of Marriage

In studying the men of the Bible, David's maleness stands over that of many. He kills his ten thousands to Saul's thousands, but he does not come across stereotypically macho, as his pledge of undying love is not made to Bathsheba or the other women in his life but to a male, Jonathan. Jonathan equally loves David, to the point of foregoing an opportunity to become king. Given that neither the Hebrew Bible nor the New Testament speaks of people loving other people in a casual manner and that David did not love just Jonathan but Jonathan's soul, several scholars have argued for a homosexual relationship between the two; a definite possibility, when adding to David's seduction of Bathsheba, might portray a bisexual human. Clearly David's lament for the deaths of Saul and Jonathan are overwhelmingly passionate. Whatever David's feelings regarding Jonathan, David often fails miserably as husband and father, even while decisive in political matters of state. David is the man who finds favor with God, loves those who hate him, and hates the people who love him (2 Sam 19:6). David appears keen on moving ahead and advancing his career, but the text does not make us privy to his motives. David lives and rules in a patriarchal world where women exist in and against culture, sometimes with options to transform culture. David is not one who follows the discernment of the Song of Songs, which celebrates the sexuality and the profundity of a male and female in love, sated with joy, enthusiasm, happiness, wonder, fulfillment, anticipation, acceptance, and delight (Goldingay: 178–79, 181, 183). On the contrary, David the consummate diplomat strategically marries some of his wives for their political capital. His marriage to Ahinoam is strategic to David ruling Israel, and his relationship to Abigail is more peripheral. David is expert, early on, at playing various peripheries against the center, and he makes connections that avail for him opportunities (Levenson and Halpern: 518) of passion and power under his reign.

Sex, politics, and militaristic pursuit go hand in hand in David's dynasty: rape, adultery, and incest results between various militaristic escapades and claims of victory. Sexual violence and wars help define Israel. The integration of politics and sexuality involves David's public responsibilities, his private desires, and his ability to galvanize more power, a power that grants David the ownership of women's sexuality, which invests more power in this patriarchal system, defining power relationships with other men amidst sexual and military conquests. In the case of Bathsheba, David orchestrates homicide and adultery. He entraps a loyal soldier, Uriah, and has a "contract" put out on Uriah by having Uriah intentionally placed on the front line to die, after he refuses to sleep with his wife, Bathsheba, impregnated by David. David violates Uriah's property right. David's adultery is a disruption of societal rules and identity strategies. David uses his office to have his way in adultery with Bathsheba.

Tamar's words to her rapist, Amnon, indict David, by saying: "this [rape] is not a thing men do in Israel, ... but David is Israel" (Schwartz 1992: 49). Taken in a larger context, Israel continuously lusts after other gods, committing spiritual adultery. Sexual infidelity is used to symbolize idolatry. David's adultery juxtaposed against Uriah's faithfulness puts askance David's allegiance to God alone, the creator of the nation, to bring about an expanded nation: a gross violation of many commandments. David's life parallels the complex, multifaceted, inconsistent, fractured life of Israel (45).

In David's story, especially, 2 Sam 9–20, part of the Succession Narrative, one finds mimetic and objective desire, rivalry, collective violence, and *scapegoating*. From the Greek tragedies, biblical texts, opera, and modern-day cinema, tragedies and ritual sacrifices have usually been resolved through the process of *scapegoating* someone, that is, by identifying and killing a victim. The victim's death provides a catharsis and produces a sense of social camaraderie to a heightened extent that the crowd or perpetrators began to understand the experience religiously.

With the scapegoat we see the intersection of religion, violence, and culture. René Girard, literary critic and cultural anthropologist, theorizes
about these notions based upon mimetic desire, the imitative way human
beings learn and often respond in culture. For Girard, the scapegoat is part
of a larger matrix he names mimesis, particularly mimetic rivalry. Mimesis, to imitate, is central for our epistemology, the way we know and
learn. Mimetic desire is that experience where two or more people desire
the same thing, person, place, or status. Mimesis, a destructive or creative
force, is present within human discourse and dialogue. When persons
imitate each other, imitation can lead to rivalry. When such rivalry escalates between two persons, this can spill over to others, moving one
person from a single enemy to the status of public enemy. For Girard,
mimetic desire and its ensuing ritualized conflict is the process of resolv-
ing and containing the resulting violence. The scapegoat becomes the
culprit, which allows the satiation of lust and thirst for calm, moving the
given group of persons from a violent catastrophe into peaceful unifica-
tion. This shift allows for the invoking of a sacred structure, rooted in a
sacrificial altar, the locus of creating and re-creating communal, social solidarity. When one person, named other, is targeted as scapegoat, this
common enemy becomes the sacrificial victim. That this person is the
scapegoat remains hidden from the public, for the success of the scapegoating process often hinges on the invisibility of the victim. While we
know more about the experience of victims and the process of scapegoating that usually releases the pressure valve of discontent and internal
violence, the violence and need for scapegoating only seems to intensify
(Jensen: 39–40; Kirk-Duggan 2001a: 33–34). In David's case, his family
ends up being scapegoated for David's indiscretions, his sexual dalliances
and disregard of familial violence of murder and incest—pregnant passion simultaneously run amuck and imploding within.

    In King David's story, issues around sex and violence are plentiful, as
David's saga with Bathsheba sets up a pattern later replicated in David's
own family. Girard analyzes the mimesis by identifying the subject of
desire, the object of desire, and the obstacle or disciple of desire: David,
Bathsheba, and Uriah, respectively. One finds a similar pattern with
Amnon, Tamar, and Absalom. Both scenarios feature a sexualized, objectified female body as the object of desire. In the saga of Absalom's
rebellion, kingship and power, not sex, is the object of desire. Between
David and Absalom, one finds the double bind—where subject and
obstacle of desire covet the same thing and are not sure what they want
from each other until the triangle of desire collapses into a monstrous
double. Absalom no longer desires what David has but wants to subvert
David and then become David. In Absalom's death, one finds collective
violence, collective lynching, as Joab stabs him first, but Absalom dies

finally at the hands of nameless young men. Uriah's death is also collective violence, as no one person actually causes his murder, though David puts out the contract on him. The location of his home and his membership in a royal-military circle indicates that Uriah was probably known to David's courtiers and perhaps to David himself, causing one to wonder just what was in the mind of David and Bathsheba (Jensen: 43–54, 58).

The David-Bathsheba story is not a harlequin romance or a torrid affair. David did not want Bathsheba as a concubine or paramour, for he tried to get Uriah to claim paternity. Examining the verbs, we note an interesting interaction. David *sent, took,* and *lay*—terms of acquisition and control. Bathsheba *came* and *returned,* framed by a backdrop of war, violence, and aggression as all of the men except David are away fighting. Because David sends for Bathsheba, does she have a sense of freedom to refuse? The force implied here echoes not only Amnon's rape of Tamar but Absalom's later rape of David's ten concubines or secondary wives; thus, David's punishment for his force against Bathsheba is the rape of his wives. The text does not make us privy to Bathsheba's thoughts. The absence of her subjectivity violates her "by means of the story" as much as David's assault and "leaves her open to the charge of seduction" (Exum 1996: 50). This text, like many contemporary interpretations of culture, narratives, and law enforcement, often wants to blame the victim for the vile acts of the perpetrator. In addition, the narrator helps to make the reader complicit by invading Bathsheba's privacy as we assume she is either partially dressed or nude, which makes us undress or dress her mentally as she bathes and David watches. The text implies another voyeur is also watching Bathsheba (2 Sam 11:3) and makes Bathsheba guilty for being seen, making her taking a bath sexually suggestive because Bathsheba the woman is bathing and David as male desire is affected. When Michal sees David dancing seminude before God, she gets angry, not desirous. When men appear naked, this is glorified activity, active sexuality, public, with him in control.[11] When women appear naked, this activity is private, passive, and shame-based, linking sexuality to female nakedness (Exum 1996: 48–53, 68).

One reading of Bathsheba is that she is passive, as she is hardly ever called by her name but referred to as "Uriah's wife," "she," or "her." The narrator silences her grief by describing only David's pain at the loss of their first child.[12] David may have married Michal, Abigail, Ahinoam, the other concubines and wives (2 Sam 5:13), and Bathsheba because having

---

11 As in the Greek Olympics of this era.

12 Is it possible that this first child was not lost, that it did not die but was actually Solomon, and the redactors decided to do a "whitewash"?

a large number of wives and concubines symbolized a king's authority and political connections. One wonders about the political implications of the rape of Tamar. In addition to the vicious rape by her half-brother, Tamar's story is one of revenge, when Absalom her brother[13] places a contract on Tamar's rapist, half-brother Amnon, and Absalom begins to plot his revolt against his dad, King David, and to devise his own rule. Tamar's story is ripe with abuse of power, manipulation, vengeance, scapegoating, and loss grounded in suggestive, relational words, some with erotic overtones, such as the "heart-shaped[14] dumplings" that Amnon asks Tamar to make for him. Tamar's pleadings for her half-rother not to rape her go unheard. When Tamar further suggests that Amnon could go to David and get his permission, it is not clear whether brothers and sisters could marry (Hackett: 92–94),[15] as could the Egyptian pharaohs.

While the story clearly articulates David's sexual conquest of Bathsheba daughter of Eliam, his ordering the murder of Uriah, Nathan's critique, and Solomon's birth, some scholars question Bathsheba's motives and demeanor. Was she being seductive or provocative in bathing in view of the king's residence? Was she a pawn in David's chess game? Or was she a manipulative woman who took advantage of the circumstances in 2 Samuel? Was she too willing to become another of David's numerous wives? Does the narrator's ambiguous silence around Bathsheba's feelings regarding the alleged death of the infant and the prospering of an apparent legitimate heir, Solomon, denote the more important issue of her marrying David, placing little value on the infant's life? Or is this an affirmative view of pregnant passion? Perhaps the reality is that Bathsheba was considered Uriah's then David's property, so her experience is of little consequence: pregnant passion reinscribed as the violation of Bathsheba as objectified, sexual partner. The consummations leading to both births are poignant: earlier David *"took her."* With Solomon's birth, David *"went in to her,"* as she *"came to him."* Did she really have a choice? In 1 Kings, as David is deteriorating, we see a strong, resourceful Bathsheba who convinces David that the just and proper action was for her alleged second son, Solomon, to ascend as king. Taking all of her appearances together, Nicol argues that Bathsheba is always resourceful. As opposed to a victim, she is a clever woman who brings every prospect to fruition (Nicol 1987: 360–63).

---

13 Absalom's experience can be that of indignation at the heinous, barbaric nature of Amnon's betrayal of their sister, Tamar. Absalom could also be jealous of Amnon sleeping with Tamar.

14 Perhaps implying the vagina.

15 This scenario brings to mind the story of Lot and his daughters and of the mystery wives of Cain in Genesis.

Randall Bailey, citing Richard Bowman, contends that the verb *šlḥ* in 2 Sam 11 indicates use of authority; thus, as Bathsheba is sent for, it indicates an authority, indicating influence and power, a politically prime mover. In proving his argument, Bailey does a comparative analysis of other women whose narratives include this verb: Rahab, Deborah, and Delilah. While I do see the parallels and would concur that David's interest is more about political associations and networking than her marital status, the problem is that, in the case of these three women, their power does not concern a summoning about their bodies, thus sexual politics. The moves are political but more related to communal war, not the battle for one's body. How would such a woman think she had more power than the king or that she could say no to any requests made by him, Bathsheba's influential family status notwithstanding, since her grandfather Ahithophel was one of David's key advisors (Bailey 1990: 86)? Here pregnant passion is ultimately giving umbrage to or the consummate denial of sexuality and individuality, with greater regard to the communal state, which avoids all investigation to the essential Bathsheba.

Conversely, George Nicol's study of Bathsheba concludes that she is resourceful and clever, particularly given the ambiguities—the piquancy, the spice of biblical stories—within the Bathsheba-David episode. Nicol contends that ambiguity abounds. Does Bathsheba hope to be seen or not be seen by David as she bathes? Does David use coercion to get Bathsheba brought before him? Is a passerby watching? Does her bathing indicate that this was Bathsheba's postmenstrual time of purification? Does David bring Bathsheba to the attention of a third party? Did Bathsheba tell David that she was probably fertile at that time? But how would she know? At that time, they did not know that fertility occurred in the middle of the cycle. What if she was irregular with her menstruation cycle? Nicol also argues that David is not a warrior, for he is often not present during battle or war, though one wonders if this is credible, given David's triumph over Goliath. Nicol responds to the critique by J. Cheryl Exum in her work, *Fragmented Women: Feminist (Sub)versions of Biblical Texts.* Nicol argues that David's absence from war leads to the adultery, and he takes exception to Exum's interpretation, that one can only conclude that David does exploit Bathsheba, given her title, "Raped by the Pen," and conversation there around David's exploitation of Bathsheba. Nicol argues that the narrator's reluctance to portray Bathsheba's experience with David with details does not put the reader in the space of a voyeur but actually works to protect and not violate Bathsheba's privacy and vulnerability. Further, Nicol finds that the mention of purification appears after we learn of the intercourse and that there is no clear sense of force in this activity (2 Sam 11:4). Nicol finds no persuasive evidence that Bathsheba did not consent to having sex, even though the two may not have been participating with equality as they engaged in adultery.[16] Nicol also takes exception to Exum's statement that the narrator rapes Bathsheba in the treatment of her in the text (Nicol 1997: 43).

Exum takes seriously the violation that occurs within the text through the voice of the narrator and sees the potential for encouraging the objectification of women, particularly via sexual aggression. She argues that the rape of Bathsheba occurs, not at the hand of David, but with the pen of the narrator, that is, the means of the narrative, an androcentric, constructed representation: not depicting a historical Bathsheba but portraying societal values. Such representations teach and encode particular modes of sexual aggression, gender roles, cultural expectations, and sexual limits. Exum contextualizes her argument within the connection between war and rape, though David is not at war and does not take Bathsheba as hostage per se. She does note the many ways sex can be coerced and extorted. Exum does not question Bathsheba's motives or the possibility of resistance but about how little access the reader has to Bathsheba's reality, and she critiques the narrative for not exploring the idea of force versus consent and for annihilating Bathsheba's subjectivity. Exum further indicts the narrator for forcing the voyeurism of the reader, David, and a third party, and she criticizes H. W. Hertzberg for blaming the victim for her "rape" because she bathed in view of the king.[17] Exum views David's "rape" of Bathsheba in parallel with Amnon's rape of Tamar and Absalom's rape of David's ten wives. Interestingly, for having Uriah killed, for taking Uriah's wife, and for his adultery, David does not experience direct punishment. Bathsheba as Uriah's property has no recourse. David's wives are raped; this is David's punishment; these wives have no recourse. While the text seems too ambiguous to cry rape of Bathsheba, Exum certainly is on solid ground when she reminds us of the critical role of gender in the matter of analysis, cultural expectations, and punishment. When men bathe communally, heterosexual people usually do not view such a scene as provocative. When David dances naked at another time, his wife Michal's anger, not her desire, is triggered. How curious that Michal is punished, in ancient terms, for she does not conceive. Spotting Bathsheba, however, whetted David's desire. The text seems to imply that Bathsheba asked to be "sent for" and "taken." In the process of blaming the victim, men get to control and set behavioral norms through engendering fear (Exum

---

16 This episode echoes contemporary issues of equality with sexual-misconduct activities between priest/pastor and parishioners and professors and students.

17 A similar treatment occurs in the film version of David and Bathsheba, which blames Bathsheba for arousing David.

1993: 170–76, 184–85). Neither Exum nor Nicol wrestle with the complex dynamics of kingship nor with how much implicit and explicit power comes with the territory of kingly authority.[18] Is this a seduction scene? Does she submit out of respect for the office? Who really has the power in this scenario, and what kind of power? What is the status of Shakespearean women? What is the nature of the relationship between Othello and Desdemona?

In addition to Desdemona, the play has two other female characters: Emilia and Bianca, each representing a particular class and social status for Elizabethan times, each scrutinized regarding her sexual behavior. Desdemona, a woman with privilege and high status, is subjected to doom because people perceive her as acting with indecency or bad taste: she asserts power and is perceived as being unchaste—placing herself, her family, and ultimately society in a bad light. A complex character led by her passions as opposed to conventions Desdemona is innocent, though not subservient and dutiful to Othello, though she ran away from her father and secretly married Othello. Desdemona is a paragon of virtue compared with Iago, an embodiment of hatred and envy. Emilia, Iago's wife, depicting middle-class status, though devoted to Desdemona, does retrieve Desdemona's handkerchief at Iago's bequest, showing mixed loyalties and a naïveté about her husband's motives and the implications toward Desdemona's demise. Her actions follow the Elizabethan patriarchal sensibilities, so that she ends up being complicit. Bianca, Cassio's mistress, representing lower-class women, and Cassio have a conversation about Desdemona's handkerchief. When Bianca inquires about the origins of the handkerchief,[19] after which he wants her to replicate the handiwork, Cassio says he found it in his bedroom. The interchange shows Bianca as astute with a great deal of savoir-faire. The conversation is curious because, since Cassio had served as a go-between for Othello and Desdemona, it is highly unlikely that he did not know the owner of the handkerchief. Bianca's presence completes the cast of women in the play: Bianca, the mistress; Emilia, the middle-class woman; and Desdemona, the upper-class woman (Lamb: 13, 22, 136). The "pregnant passion" of the violated word or deception and lying, crossing class and gender lines, plays constantly through *Othello*, including in this scene. What does the relationship between Othello and Desdemona denote?

---

18 Consider the medieval tradition where the lord or the king had the right or duty to take the hymen of the brides in his fiefdom.

19 One could imagine that the handkerchief comes to symbolize her virginity, her trustworthiness, and her love.

In act 1, scene 3, when Othello states his love for Desdemona before the council, he uses his military demeanor to account for any shortcomings in his persona and for not first going to Brabantio to ask for Desdemona's hand in marriage. This scene occurs primarily before the Venetian council. Elements and themes developed here undergird what unfolds later domestically: matters of trust, strategies, and perceptions, that is, whom one ought to trust, the contrast between overt and covert activity, and appearances versus reality. Thematic parallels abound, as the impending military struggle between Venice and Turkey echoes the struggle for power between Iago in his quest over his alleged enemy (control, triumph) and that of Brabantio (Desdemona's objectification, accusations of sorcery, quest for justice) over against Othello. Interestingly, the duke backs off from supporting Brabantio in his quest for justice, which raises questions about the former's judgment (paralleling Othello's poor judgment regarding Iago). For his entire prowess in military affairs, however, Othello is blind to the pursuits of Iago. We do learn that Othello identifies himself as being a warrior who has fought for most of his life (Lamb: 55–57).

Before the Venetian council, Othello invites them to have Desdemona come and give her account of her romance with him. Notably, Othello is the only one to suggest that she speak, signaling a break with societal sexism and the silencing of women, as he places his reputation in her hands. Othello's account shows a strong woman with desires—or perhaps a man domineered by a woman. As Desdemona and Othello proclaim their love for each other, the question remains as to the nature and dimensions of that love. Clearly Desdemona is a feminist of her times, as she is not demure and retiring or passive but strong and articulate: one who does not follow the norm of an arranged marriage for political purposes, one with whom the audience can readily empathize. Brabantio, a father who refuses reconciliation, suffers his humiliation because of how society views the elopement and seethes with hatred for Othello. Though Othello's marriage is only hours old, the duke calls him to be patriotic toward matters of state, placing public affairs over private matters. Accordingly, Desdemona will go with Othello. Then three key things happen. The duke approaches Brabantio again to help him get some perspective, using the race card established earlier, but the duke remains unconvinced. Second, Othello entrusts Desdemona into the care of Iago and his wife Emilia. Third, Iago taunts and plays on Roderigo's desire for Desdemona, insinuating that Othello, being Black, is base and animalistic. Iago both shows his contempt for women and has Roderigo under complete control. For Othello, love is honorable; for Iago, love shows weakness. Iago is a self-serving, villainous coward. He intends to ruin Cassio, Roderigo, and Othello. Othello calls Iago honest, and his true persona is despicable and evil. Like a chameleon, Iago changes every moment only to his benefit (Lamb: 57–61). Iago's sociopathic sensibilities and the complex cauldron of romantic sensibilities and desires for power afford a complex scapegoating mechanism: multiples of triangular mimetic desire.

Subject of Desire	Object of Desire	Obstacle to or Disciple of Desire
Iago	Desdemona	Othello
Roderigo	Desdemona	Brabantio
Cassio	Desdemona	Othello
Brabantio	revenge	the duke
Iago	revenge	Othello
Iago	power, privilege	Othello
Iago	jealousy, position	Cassio

In this drama, Iago is most often the subject of desire; the object of his desire is either Desdemona, emotional acts of revenge, a quest for power, or a combination of all three desires; and Othello is the most frequent obstacle of Iago's desire. This rampant mimetic desire of Iago's is apparent in both political and emotional affairs, often collapsing into monstrous doubles fueled by rivalry, ending in destruction.

Othello focuses on his emotional affairs in act 2, scene 2, to the exclusion of Venice's need for his talents as a military tactician, seeing his marriage to Desdemona in market metaphors, as a profit that will bear fruit, probably a child. Everything has a tone of merriment and a celebration of peace, love, and prosperity. Most scholars think that Othello and Desdemona have not yet consummated their marriage, which was just as critical during Shakespearean times as it remains today. An official wedding involved three phases: proclamation of the engagement (reading of the banns), the ceremony proper, and the consummation, often witnessed in noble marriages of political considerations, in order to forestall future opportunistic declarations of sacramental nullity. The consummation becomes an issue when Desdemona calls for her wedding sheets in act 4.[20] The newlyweds leave the scene; Iago returns. Iago continues to bait Cassio, getting him drunk. Paradoxically, Iago uses people and destroys their lives while giving the appearance of a loyal and trustworthy friend to those whom he deceives and to those whom he destroys. Iago keeps the diabolical side of himself hidden within a

---

20 Perhaps the handkerchief becomes Shakespeare's symbol for consummation.

mask of duplicity, adapting at will and revealing only what he desires any particular person to believe. Iago convinces Montano, governor of Cyprus, that Cassio is unfit to serve and that Othello used poor judgment in selecting him. In a skirmish between Roderigo and Cassio, Montano receives a wound. Upset by what he sees, Othello asks "honest" Iago what happened. Iago feigns ignorance. Othello personally inquires as to what happened, and Montano says little. The audience is aware that the action moves via the antagonist, Iago, and is pressed in on the protagonist, Othello. When he still cannot find out what happened, Othello lets his emotions get out of control and loses his temper. That lack of control is what Iago has sought. Iago's account makes Cassio righteous and Roderigo a villain. Under Iago's persuasive rhetoric, Othello demotes Cassio, again reflecting snap judgment with little evidence, punishing a former trusted officer and advisor. Iago's next encounter with Cassio signals a recurring theme, that of reputation: from Cassio, who feels crushed by Othello's demotion as well as Desdemona's rejection of him, who must always be above board; to Othello, who is driven insane by believing himself to be cuckolded by Cassio. Iago succeeds in his goals of creating deceptive reputations, disorientation, and peril for others. Iago continues to amuse himself with Cassio, making Cassio believe he can get back into Othello's good graces through Desdemona's intercession, when actually this is the best possible strategy for Iago to employ: Desdemona certainly will help. Othello most certainly feels betrayed, not only because of Desdemona's actions, but because Iago plants the seeds of jealousy within Othello to assure a terrible end. That is, Iago signifies to Othello that the virgin Desdemona is being unfaithful with Cassio. When Roderigo returns, he seems to realize that Iago is playing him, but shortly thereafter Iago has Roderigo back under his thumb. Iago then proceeds to launch the complete downfall of both Desdemona and Othello. Iago convinces Emilia to participate in his nefarious machinations. She speaks to Cassio and ensures that Desdemona will help him and that Othello now regrets he fired Cassio. Othello and Desdemona are awash in naïveté (Lamb: 80, 92, 98, 105, 106).

Strong Desdemona is yet so youthful and naïve that she tends to disbelieve what she sees and manages to misapprehend her own status and position in this situation, so much so that she seems to be a fatalist. Like her husband, Desdemona is a unknowing pawn in the hands of Iago: Iago perverts her persona in the eyes of Othello by accusing her of racist prejudice. Incredulously, Othello places the onus of perfection on Desdemona, with Iago as interloper. Where Desdemona could have facilitated Othello's psychic integration, the mimetic desire framing their relationship results in their downfall. Iago succeeds in sabotaging both her total commitment to Othello and his total faith in her (Coursen: 106, 110, 117). "Her commitment is the central irony of this tragedy" (110).

In act 3, scene 3, Desdemona and Cassio confer, and she agrees to support his reinstatement by Othello. Conversation that ensues indicates with deepest irony how something that, on its surface, appears sound and complimentary is in reality deceptive and negative—as a foil for the villainous actions of "honest" Iago. Cassio remains fearful and doubts that he and Othello will be reconciled. Consequently, the time Desdemona and Cassio spend together foreshadows the pain and trickery to come, noticeably indicating the questions around Othello's ability to lead and make decisions on the emotional front. When Desdemona mentions Cassio's situation, Othello is hesitant to believe Iago's insinuations but remains affectionate with her. Desdemona urges Othello to reconsider Cassio's demotion, and Othello agrees to see Cassio—Desdemona begins to get under Othello's skin. After the women leave, Iago begins to interrogate Othello, socratically, taunting and torturing Othello with skillful rhetoric. Othello thinks Iago is hiding something, so the questioning of Iago by Othello continues. Iago leads Othello further and deeper into his deceptive web of innuendo and half-truths. Iago feigns jealousy and warns Othello that he might not want Iago's opinion. As Othello's curiosity heightens, Iago's deception intensifies. Othello does not heed the one truth that Iago has told him, *not to trust him!* Conversely, Othello believes everything Iago says, even as Iago, using reverse psychology, tells Othello to avoid believing that there is any impropriety going on between Cassio and Desdemona. Iago continues his intrigue as he reminds Othello that Desdemona deceived her father when she ran away and married Othello, thus implying that she would also deceive Othello. Iago warns Othello to watch for signs of Desdemona championing Cassio, as an act of her unfaithfulness. Desdemona drops her handkerchief for Emilia to retrieve. Iago, delighted to have the handkerchief, hides it where Cassio can find it, so that when Othello finds out about the handkerchief, a gift of significance[21] from him to Desdemona, Othello will experience betrayal. Othello now falls into utter despair over Desdemona's apparent infidelity. Othello is swayed easily and fails to question Desdemona, instead asking Iago for more proof of her unfaithfulness. Iago states that he had seen Cassio wiping his beard with the handkerchief. Betrayed, livid, enraged, and fully Iago's pawn, Othello calls for revenge, ordering Iago to kill Cassio. Iago, on a roll, suggests that Desdemona, too, must die (Lamb: 122–27).

---

21 Note the earlier mention of the symbolism of the handkerchief.

Othello, thoroughly convinced that Cassio and Desdemona are having an affair, plunges deeper into rage and paranoia, which seems to elude Desdemona. Desdemona asks Othello if he will see Cassio. Othello says he is not well and then asks her about the handkerchief. When Desdemona says she lost it, Othello becomes quite hostile. She escalates the situation by shifting the conversation back to Cassio. Enraged, Othello leaves, and Emilia tries to calm Desdemona. Iago and Cassio enter, and the latter speaks with Desdemona about his hoped-for reinstatement. Desdemona says she will continue to press Othello when she thinks the time is right, though both she and Emilia later worry (Lamb: 135–37).

When Othello questions Emilia, she declares Desdemona quintessentially faithful and not engaged in impropriety. Othello assumes that Desdemona has simply tricked Emilia, and he settles for Iago's lies instead.

Othello's perceptions of Desdemona and Iago are creations of Othello's internal imagination, tempered by stoked suspicions and an unwarranted trust based on stereotype. Like any outsider, Othello is ripe for deception and exploitation by an insider, Iago. As a long-time soldier and a newly married man, Othello stereotypically must choose whether he believes his comrade in arms, Iago, or his wife (Hirsh: 136–38).

In the last scene of act 4, there is a deeper development of the ethical and moral differences between women and men. The either/or paradigm has women as either disloyal, lascivious, and lusty or grand, highly praised, and objectified as divine and superhuman—the aesthetic skewing of pregnant passion as sexism and classism. Women are established as subservient, we learn, from an internal perspective, how Desdemona and Emilia relate to and perceive their Venetian world. Desdemona quickly extols her love for Othello, for she is a "lady" who knows the requirements necessary for fulfilling her obligations. Such dedication indicates Desdemona's purity to an Elizabethan audience. In conversation with Desdemona, Emilia confesses that she would be unfaithful if the price were right and that women are capable of the same things that men can do. With all that has happened, Desdemona continues to love and proclaim her love for Othello—in her innocence, she is blind to what is unfolding (Lamb: 169–71).

The final scene opens in the bedchamber of Othello and Desdemona. The tensions of public versus private, political versus emotional culminate here. As Desdemona sleeps, Othello has failed to see the ambiguity and the trickery that has unfolded under his very nose and is quite rigid in his thinking, as he connects her beauty with her alleged infidelity. His notion of Desdemona shifts from that of an alabaster monument to a rose to a foil for justice. Her only sin is that of loving and caring for Othello. Desdemona knows that she is no longer dealing with a rational person.

Civility and manners are no longer in place. Othello strangles her. As she lies dying, Desdemona speaks of her innocence and notes that she is the one who is responsible for her own death—a sense of duty and obligation in her last moments of life. That is, she made various choices in her life that resulted in her end. Her sense of loyalty and love for him finally helps Othello emerge from his depths of madness. Emilia castigates Othello, using his race as a weapon—pregnant passion from the underside, denigrating Blackness and implicating male gender. Emilia engages her husband, Iago, who shows no remorse or guilt. Othello continues to seek Iago's support in justifying his acts. When Lodovico questions him, Othello responds that everything he did, he did for the sake of honor. Then he and Cassio reconcile, and Othello asks Iago: Why? Othello learns how much he was used and calls himself the fool. Relieved of duty and aware of the truth, Othello takes his own life (Lamb: 195–200). As the curtain falls on the stories of Othello and David, Emilia also lies dead at the hand of Iago, and Othello commits suicide. David dies an old man, but a part of him dies sequentially over time, as he murders and suffers the loss of his children and wives. Who, then, are David and Othello, and what can we learn from them regarding the role of power as a factor in the experience of pregnant passion?

PREGNANT PASSION INTERROGATED: ARENAS AND MANIPULATIVE USES OF POWER

The worlds of David and Othello have many parallels and many more disconnects. Both have high office, know the esteem of others, and in various ways exemplify many human foibles. Their popularity and their use and misuse of power makes them superb candidates for this kind of analysis, for exploring "pregnant passion" as a metaphor for profound, powerful engagement that ruptures boundaries, causes harm, and squelches creativity toward disregard, deviance, and destruction. Power denotes an influence, a permission, and an ability to choose, make decisions, responsibly or irresponsibly to effect change. In the spousal/partner category, David's characterization provides more fertile ground for analysis, regarding the specific relationships with his children, over a long life span.

David reflects both sensitivity and savagery, sometimes connected with others being punished as the result of his own shortcomings.

David's interaction with Michal around him dancing before God is rife with questions and innuendo. When the ark's residence is a blessing for Obed-edom, David decides he wants to have the ark of God in Jerusalem. To have the national religious symbol and being the seat of politics and military can add much prestige to David's city. When he does retrieve the ark, David dances before God wearing only an ephod, an apronlike garment that only covers the front and back. When Michal sees David dancing, she despises him. The text is ambiguous as to the root of Michal's ire. Michal possibly gets upset: (1) because she was kidnapped from her husband Paltiel; (2) because she was only one of many wives; (3) because of the former relationship of her father, Saul, and David; (4) because of the change in her family's fortunes, now that her brother, heir apparent, is dead; or (5) because Michel actually found David's dancing ludicrous and unbecoming of a king. Michal receives punishment: she is made barren. In ancient Israel and in many cultures today, to be childless, to be barren is viewed as a curse, as misfortune. Thus, a barren woman is not really a woman (2 Sam 6). Similarly, in David and Bathsheba's case as in Othello's and Desdemona's, a background of military sagas frames all of the ensuing emotional and political troubles. Uriah is honorable and dies for that stance. David commits adultery and impregnates Bathsheba before Uriah is killed in battle at David's order. David takes Bathsheba as a wife. This entire scenario displeases Yahweh (2 Sam 11), who sends Nathan to rebuke and critique David. God gave David the anointed kingship of Israel, delivered him from Saul, gave him all that belonged to Saul, and put him over Judah and Israel. Intriguingly, the Lord punishes David by raising up evil against David, his house, and his family. Absalom has sex with his father's wives publicly Their son, Solomon, also known as Jedidiah, is born—a son "the Lord loves" (2 Sam 12). Perhaps it is the hand of Absalom (2 Sam 15–20) that assures the punishment of David in a profound sense.

Absalom revolts against David and induces the people of Israel to side with him by convincing them that David has neither time nor concern for them. Absalom is like Joab, greedy for power, and like Amnon, one who cannot or does not want to wait. When Absalom and his entourage come to Jerusalem, they sleep with the wives David left behind in the palace, so that all Israel will know that Absalom has betrayed and disrespected his father (2 Sam 16). Ahithophel, Bathsheba's grandfather, even offers to go out and kill David.

David and Othello share the military connection and often share their understandings of domesticity, though Othello at least initially fares better than David. In comparison, David has many wives[22] and children. Many of his marriages involve using marital status to make political connections, as a way to expand his rule and authority. Othello

---

[22] That David actually procures the two hundred foreskins as a dowry for Michal, at the cost of two hundred homicides, is gruesome, barbaric, and breaks the commandment, "do not kill"—the work of a psychopath?

marries Desdemona, which brings Othello political advantages in the Venetian court.

Othello is smitten and in love with Desdemona. Perhaps what he names as love is a cornucopia of feelings fleshed out across diverse needs in a "multicultural" situation, at a time in his life when his habits were set. Clearly there is need, adoration, passion, perhaps even novelty: Desdemona and Othello on one level are so attracted to each other because they are so different from each other. Perhaps each one mesmerizes the other because the societal norms of the day deem their relationship, especially without the consent of Brabantio, as immoral, debasing, and disgracing the family. Perhaps the novelty of the other spikes an irresistible impulse from both persons. Perhaps both have a need to defy convention. Both Othello and Desdemona are clear about the sexual attraction. Though Othello spirals down in madness, he confirms his love for Desdemona Blinded, he demands his murder-suicide. Was this the more honorable course than that of David as it comes to love?

David *never* pronounces his love for God, Bathsheba, Abigail, Merab, or Michal, nor for any of his other wives or for his children. God loves David (Isa 55:3); David praises God (1 Sam 25:32), sings of God's unfailing love (Ps 52:1), and accepts God's love for him as beloved (2 Sam 23:1). Israel and Judah love David, and Michal loves David. David *only* pronounces love for Jonathan (1 Sam 18; 20:17). Perhaps the tragic underpinning of David's characterization is that David loves only David, and Jonathan. The pregnant passion operative at the point of love, in both the David and Shakespearean drama *Othello*, is unhealthy, for these loves lead to contempt, deception, deep pain, and loss of life.

In the realms of this contempt, of deception, of using others, and of being used are themes of seduction and betrayal. David seduces and betrays women; Othello is loved unconditionally by Desdemona. Othello's insecurities and, in today's parlance, mental illness cause him to judge poorly, to be manipulated, to become a pawn, as his own dignity and self-worth dwindle in the process. In both the David and Othello settings, there is dysfunctionality. Interestingly, the role of anger pushes Othello and is submerged in the David. David appears angry at Amnon's rape of Tamar but does nothing. Othello becomes enraged at Desdemona's alleged infidelity and becomes a homicidal maniac. In both stories, the reality of the male protagonists is explored in depth. The female characters experience their reality, but in the Davidic story they do not respond to that reality; for example, we never hear from Bathsheba or Tamar. Desdemona and Emily speak for themselves, so, despite a patriarchal environment, via Shakespeare, the voices of some women do get heard, though unfortunately, not believed. In both sagas, class and race are prevalent matters.

Recognizing that "race" is more a later sociological constru
category acts more like a matter of lineage as opposed to cultura.
ical difference in Shakespearean literature. In the time of Da
national community and persons connected by geography and faith belief
systems seem to be most prevalent. In twenty-first-century listeners, by
virtue of domestic and global context, the race card and class distinction
are always present. Racism negates that which is pregnant and ripe and
makes beautiful, innocent passion into a farce—into stereotypical language and vulgarity. Similarly, class forces the boundaries, demeans and
objectifies those deemed other. Thus, Othello is the Black stud and Desdemona the White virgin whom the dirty Black man seduced. Bathsheba
was a Hittite by marriage, of a conquering people in Asia, a foreigner. The
class differences, particularly for the women, are made painfully clear in
how they are treated by each other and then how others, how "outsiders"
treat them. In this instance, Othello and Bathsheba would have been outsiders, race-wise; Bathsheba and Desdemona outsiders, gender-wise; and
Othello and Bathsheba, from the perspective of class, outsiders or at best
objects for display and performance. In sum, what does the analysis bear
witness to, regarding a *Womanist* biblical reading of David and Othello,
regarding pregnant passion?

Tempered cynicism or suspicion pressed the question of violence to
both major figures, amid ambiguous information and historic texts that
argue that neither David nor Othello are totally sinners nor saints: both are
somewhere in between. That they were human gives us a dual lens from
which we can learn regarding our own weaknesses, boundaries, and
foibles. Creativity affords the opportunity to see these characters and their
texts in new ways, where ultimately we see the *pregnant passion* as a context, choice, and potentially liberatory arena. Freedom, however, only
comes with one willing to take on the responsibility. Courage provided
the avenue for making bold statements and for challenging the readings
of these two characters, noting where particular characters do or do not
exert courage. Commitment to hearing and justice allowed for much discovery within these two texts that can support twenty-first-century
interpretations and provide a cautionary voice for not making these two
characters into demigods. Candor paved the way for naming the countless moments of oppression and the confusion around love in both texts.
Curiosity skirts about these texts and raises questions of culture, timing,
and intent. Irony, as a form of the comedic, surfaces within both texts.
Thus, both the Davidic texts and *Othello* are inundated with questions of
morality, passion, justice, and power, public and domestic. David dies
an old, worn man. Othello dies ravaged of heart and soul. Iago walks
away in chains as Othello, Desdemona, and Emilia lie on their
deathbeds. Israel and Judah continue to pay for David's mistakes. The

Venetian court continues to pay for Othello's mistakes. Is this the end of the stories? These stories teach the importance of relationships of integrity, commitment, and competence—in family and the public. One ought not take these relationships for granted. Othello was being deceived by Iago, and David focused on possessions. Imbalance is precarious and can be deadly: and that is a conclusion pregnant with a passion of life, health, existence, moral and just authority, and the brokerage of power.

The curtain falls now,
Midst greatness, fragility
How does your text read?

WHO WANTS TO MARRY A PERSIAN KING?
GENDER GAMES AND WARS AND THE BOOK OF ESTHER

Nicole Duran
Rosemont College

> Not only has Queen Vashti done wrong to the king, but also to all the officials and all the people who are in all the provinces of King Aha-suerus. For this deed of the queen will be made known to all women, causing them to look with contempt on their husbands, since they will say, "King Ahasuerus commanded Queen Vashti to be brought before him, and she did not come." This very day the noble ladies of Persia and Media who have heard of the queen's behavior will rebel against the king's officials, and there will be no end of contempt and wrath! If it pleases the king, let a royal order go out from him, and let it be written among the laws of the Persians and the Medes, so that it may not be altered, that Vashti is never again to come before King Ahasuerus; and then let the king give her royal position to another who is better than she. So when the decree made by the king is proclaimed throughout his entire kingdom, vast as it is, all women will give honor to their husbands, high and low alike.
>
> Esther 1:16b–20 (NRSV)

Considering the acknowledged reign of brutal patriarchy in Esther, the similarities between its opening chapters and the recent television debacle *Who Wants to Marry a Millionaire?* are disheartening in the extreme. The kind of gender setup that many of us would like to think well-contained with the boundaries of the biblical narrative's ancient world leapt into the present tense via the American television screen last year. In both cases, young women from far and wide come to compete for the hand of a rich and powerful man. In both cases, the powerful man seems to rule the proceedings, which are set up for his benefit and amuse-ment. But the differences between the biblical story and the television show are perhaps even more disheartening than the similarities. Namely, the short-lived but courageous character of Vashti in the biblical story has been completely erased from the story surrounding the television show, and the mitigating circumstances that make Esther's character sympathetic even to feminists are missing from the television show.

Beginning from these points of comparison in this essay, I explore the issue of proximity to power in Esther. Through the characters of Vashti, Esther, and Mordecai, I trace the issue of access to power in this book, and the different ways in which this issue connects to gender and ethnicity.

THE COMPETITION AND THE PRIZE, BIBLICAL AND TELEVISED

The period of beautification described in Esther, during which contestants are provided with expert help to set themselves off to their own best advantage, was largely hidden in the airing of the reality game show. But in the publicity beforehand, it became clear to any who doubted that such a process was happening. Informing the press about the swimwear portion of the show, Darnell said, "We explain that our millionaire is an outdoorsman," and added, "They chose whatever they wanted to wear. Most of them went with two-piece swimsuits, but with taste. Whatever they were comfortable wearing" (Carman). The scene conjured up by this remark lacks only the relative modesty of Esther's story world, in which presumably the women's adornment would display less of their bodies than would the average bikini.

Let me rush to point out that, in the case of the television show, women volunteered for the competition, apparently eager for the fame and fortune it promised. We could debate the extent to which the contestants on *Who Wants to Marry a Millionaire?* were fully in charge of their decisions to be contestants, but the fact remains that contemporary American women scrambled headlong toward what should have been (and proved to be) a rather scary prospect, namely, that of entering into a binding legal contract with a total stranger.

Not only did the general public and the prospective contestants know nothing of Rockwell before the show aired, but even on the television show itself Rockwell was hidden from view until the last minute. "He's in a sort of pod," executive producer Mike Darnell told the *San Francisco Chronicle* before the show aired, "You can't see him except his shadow" (Carman). Rockwell's identity was unimportant, except insofar as he could claim to be a millionaire. The show actually emphasized this fact, thus calling attention to the contestants' apparent eagerness to marry the wealthy shadow. In the biblical story we can at least give Esther the benefit of the doubt that, like the other virgins of the land, she was "gathered" by the king's representatives—taken, if not against her will, at least regardless of it. Esther's contest seems in general more dangerous than Darva Conger's. The king sleeps with each of the gathered virgins in turn, as part of his decision-making process. The fact that sex is part of the competition and the virgins, win or lose, are no longer virgins once they have been in the competition lends Esther's story a scarier tone than Conger's. These women—more likely girls—are forced to compete, and, in a society where virginity is a girl's only ticket to respectable adulthood, the losing contestants stand to lose a great deal.

By contrast, winning the prize on *Who Wants to Marry a Millionaire?* proved to be a good deal more frightening than losing it. Darva Conger, not unlike Esther, found herself married to a stranger who had abused his previous partner emotionally and physically. But the land of television is far more magical than that of biblical legend; in the former, all fortunes can be reversed, and no answer is every really final. Conger's marriage was annulled at her initiative, leaving her a great deal richer and, one would hope, a tiny bit wiser. In Esther's case, as we will see, what has been decreed cannot be undecreed, even by the king himself. On this one point, Conger may better be compared with Vashti than with Esther, since, while the latter wins the right to enter the powerful man's circle, the former refuses to enter it when summoned. But the virtues of Vashti, like those of Esther, are substantially missing from the contemporary story. Conger displayed herself voluntarily while Vashti refused to do so even on the king's command, and while both in the end turned the king down, Vashti did so at great cost to herself, while Conger went home a great deal richer.

Vashti's Story: What's So Funny?

Besides the fact that her brief story begins this book, Vashti's banishment is a helpful entry into the larger story because of its dramatic presentation of gender issues that elsewhere in Esther must be read between the lines. The abortive story of Esther's predecessor has been summed up by scholarship as "a harem story satirically showing how the willfulness of one pretty woman compelled the king and the highest officials of the realm to marshal all the instruments of government to assure male supremacy in the home" (Humphreys: 280; cf. White 1992). We are to read this summation with a knowing chuckle, although what we are knowing is difficult to say—perhaps that men are naturally supreme and need not use force to assure their supremacy; more likely that the struggle between the genders is a game enjoyed by both, not a war where some lose their lives.

Granted, the banquet that Vashti refuses to attend takes on legendary proportions. So many important people are invited that one wonders how the kingdom could have functioned while the banquet was going on, particularly since it goes on for 180 days (1:4). Some of this legendary quality perhaps extends to the described effects of Vashti's rebellion. But if the immediacy with which Vashti's example will lead all the women in the kingdom to rebellion is the stuff of legend, the point remains that, legendary or not, Vashti's example is a threat.

The dismissal of this book's explicit foray into gender politics interests me for two reasons. First of all, it effectively silences a certain discussion of the text; if this is satire of a frivolous variety, then suggestions of the text's actual political implications become an absurd mistake in analysis. Second, it seems to me to say a great deal about the cultural rootedness of interpretation that any portrayal of men as actively asserting their supremacy is read as humorous. Vashti is a woman with everything to lose by her rebellion, who refuses to submit to the man who is both her husband and her king; she risks and loses a great deal by rejecting the authority he claims over her body and her person. What— to ask a stereotypically feminist question—is so damned funny? Surely it is a threat to husbands everywhere when the queen refuses her husband's command. Judging from the reaction to the single motherhood of sitcom character Murphy Brown that Dan Quayle led a few years back, any prominent woman showing evidence of being able to function without a man is still considered threatening to the entire family and social structure. Conversely, the deep grip that the myth of women's dependence maintains on all of us emerges plainly from the wild popularity of *Who Wants to Marry a Millionaire?* and the fact that the show's title did not have to make the gender of the millionaire explicit: everyone knew that the millionaire would be a man and that the title question would be answered exclusively by women.

The effect of laughing off the court's turmoil over Vashti reverberates through the interpretation of the story of Esther. If Vashti's story is not about gender politics in any serious sense, then these issues are mute throughout the book of Esther. If, as I maintain, Vashti's is a social and political rebellion with the requisite effects of one, then the issues her story raises must color the story of her replacement. If Vashti is thrown out of court for her refusal to submit to male authority (which no one actually denies), then Esther is brought into court in the belief that she will so submit, and the reader must ask how this expectation is met in the story that follows. Sadly, this setup is missing from the contemporary story. Those women who declined to enter the contest are not perceived as particularly brave for having done so, because they are not perceived at all, having declined to enter the television's royal court.

ESTHER'S COMPLICATING JEWISHNESS

Feminists have found it easier to admire Vashti, however briefly she may appear in this story, than to muster sympathy for the woman who takes up Vashti's position and does for the king what Vashti refused to do, thus winning for herself the title of this biblical book. As Susan Niditch has pointed out, Esther is "a woman who offers a particular model for success, one with which the oppressor would be especially comfortable. Opposition is to be subtle, behind the scenes, and ultimately strengthening for the power structure" (1995: 33). Sidnie Ann White has suggested that the power Esther exerts through her femaleness is analogous to the kind of power that the diaspora Jew is urged to use within the foreign court. Direct confrontation would be fruitless and dangerous for either a woman—Vashti being a case in point—or a Jew. Esther's method of cajoling, flattering, charming, wining, and dining—that is, seducing—the powers that be therefore seems advisable. White sees the author as holding Esther up as a model for exilic survival; her story "is meant to teach Jews how to live a productive life in the Diaspora" (White 1989: 164).

Similar comments are made by more traditional readings that see Esther as subordinate to Mordecai in importance. W. L. Humphreys feels that "in essence, this tale affirms to the Jew of the Diaspora that it is possible to live a rich and creative life in the pagan environment and to participate fully in that world" (281). Humphreys's reading is a fascinating one on the issue of assimilation and difference. He notes the lack of Jewish religion in the text and appreciates the elision of the Jewish identity of both Mordecai and Esther. "The Jewishness of Mordecai and Esther did not prevent them from living full and effective lives in interaction with their environment," he concludes, a comment suspect on many levels (281). Humphreys seems to applaud the fact that Esther and Mordecai live like normal people, even though they are Jewish. I get the sense here that, conversely, those who maintain a different ethnic or religious identity from the societal majority are seen as disagreeable, antisocial, clannish.

Furthermore, both Esther and Mordecai are, at different times in the course of this story, a hair's breadth from execution on account of their Jewishness. It is not as if their being Jewish had no negative impact on their courtly success. Indeed, despite the fact that Esther hides her ethnicity and "passes" at Mordecai's insistence, he himself assures her that there will be no hiding her Jewishness when the decree to slaughter the Jews is enacted. The assimilation is tentative and partial, in other words; it is an effective temporary survival strategy, but it does not make the difference disappear, nor render it unproblematic.[1]

---

[1] Speaking of women's competitions for men's benefit, this element of the story evokes the controversy surrounding Vanessa Williams becoming the first African American Miss America. Since she was fairly light and quite assimilated, she was allowed the title until it

That Humphreys wants the difference to disappear is clear. He emphasizes the fact that "their success and the deliverance of their people are dependent, not on their keeping customs and practices distinctive to Judaism, but on their effective action," while failing to mention that it is only Esther's continued loyalty and identification with a "distinctive" people that saves their lives and hers. Beyond this, he even goes so far as to deny that it is the Jewishness of the Jews that makes them vulnerable, asserting that the central conflict of the story is "as much a result of the courtier's characteristic concern over rank and authority (3:1–5) as it is a result of the Jewishness of Mordecai" (280). Humphreys's reference here is to the personal grudge Haman bears toward Mordecai and to the undeniable fact that Haman is using anti-Jewish sentiment as a way of getting at Mordecai. But another way of putting this is to say that Mordecai's Jewishness makes him vulnerable to the attack of a resentful fellow-courtier. In fact, Mordecai's Jewishness means that when his fellow-courtier begins to hate Mordecai, the entire Jewish population is put at risk.

Here the perilous nature of the life of the successful diaspora Jew— the other who remains other, despite a lifetime of playing by the rules—emerges, for if Esther's proximity to the king in the end is the Jews' salvation, Mordecai's court presence is, in a sense, what endangers the Jews in the first place. To be at the court at all is to play with fire. To be near the center of power for the outsider promises on the one hand the acquisition of power for oneself and perhaps even for one's people. But being near the center of power also means proximity to the power of execution, a power that can be used as easily against you as against your enemies, as we see in the Mordecai-Haman exchange. The king, always a metonym for the society's power, is a malleable idiot—whether this is good news or bad changes by the minute.

The question of access to power is one central to Esther's story. Who is allowed entry to the king's court and whether they can ever come again; who is outside in the lobby; who is outside the gate—these are crucial to the movement of this plot.[2] Considering all of the maneuvering to gain audience to the king, it is remarkable in hindsight that Vashti's crime was that she did not want to go into the king's court. Strangely, her punishment is that she cannot go into the king's court.

---

became clear that she had previously done things to make money that did not mesh with the public's understanding of Miss America as a virgin innocent. Is the fact that she posed in the nude completely unrelated to her ethnicity, given the relative paucity of modeling jobs open to African American women as compared to European Americans?

2 Cf. Timothy K. Beal, who maintains conversely that the question prompted by the women's banquet in Esth 1 is "how to exclude without losing control" (93).

In her stead come a stream of virgins, gathered from the countryside like so many species of butterfly, among whom is Esther. White defends Esther against the charge that she is selling out by vying for the queen-ship in this way, saying that we must take the book on its own terms (1992: 126). She seems to mean by this that Esther cannot be expected to disdain the position of queen or to have a consciousness that competition among women of this kind was degrading. All of this is true but irrele-vant. There is no indication that Esther has the least choice in the matter of whether or not to enter the competition for queen. She is "gathered" (2:8) with the rest of the maidens—this is part of the king's privilege, to have his choice of the populace for his wives. This gathering is a kind of kidnapping, and, if Esther takes advantage of the situation to gain some privilege, it is for the same reasons that Joseph rises to be head slave and head prisoner—because a survivor is defined by his or her ability to suc-ceed in any circumstance.

Esther is in the court not because she wants to be but because the king is in search of an obedient wife. To this end he gathers the likely can-didates into the palace and admits them to the court one by one, where whether or not this will be their last visit is determined by how well they please the king. They are hustled from the first harem into the court and then out of the court into a second harem—presumably this is a method of keeping track of which women have been used and which are still being prepared for use. That the situation of the women is a frightening one is emphasized by the concern of Mordecai, who rather than celebrat-ing Esther's making it into the big leagues comes by the harem entrance every day to make sure she is alright (2:11).

As far as we know, the king's court is entirely the realm of men, the women being kept in a sort of cabinet to be taken out individually when desired. The boundary between the women's space and the men's is nav-igated only by the eunuchs, who being neither male nor female may have authority over the women within the women's place and also may move freely into the men's court, to bring in what women are requested.

Interestingly, it is a eunuch who prepares Esther for her night with the king and to whom in large part she owes her success there. For unlike the show *Who Wants to Marry a Millionaire?* this text shows no hesitancy in admitting that to please the king requires artistry.

Neither Esther's beauty nor her native charm wins the king's heart. First of all, it is not the king's heart that is won; there is a remarkable lack of romance in this entire story. This is not Cinderella, where Prince Charming searches out the woman he loves and she waits humbly, sweeping floors, for the happiness he promises. Here the king is not look-ing for love but for particular useful qualities, which include beauty, probably sexual talent, and certainly obedience. As for Esther, she has no feelings for the king one way or the other as far as we know but uses every effort to meet his criteria, in order both to survive and to gain some position and security for herself.

And the effort is large-scale. "The regular period of beautifying," which all the candidates go through, adds up to a full year (2:12). On top of this, Esther has the additional help of the eunuch Hegai, which includes several maids, a good diet, and the best living quarters in the harem. Beauty, and the art of making oneself memorable in the span of one night, is clearly something hardwon and utterly artificial; it is a skill, like playing the violin or running the four-minute mile, and it requires training and coaching as well as talent. According to this book, to be the king's wife, and by extension to be any man's wife, requires the rigorous shaping of one's womanhood into the particular desired configuration; the king does not love Esther herself, but, like an employer, he is pleased by her hardwon ability to be what he wants.

There is no doubt that Esther's skill in this area, like the eagerness of the television contestants, has a sour taste to the feminist reader. Vashti has asserted her own desires, refused to compromise, and made some kind of statement about who the king really is—a hedonistic fool—and she has suffered the consequence of being removed completely from the king's power. Now Esther comes in willingly to do what Vashti would not. Esther is, in effect, the scab undermining the impact of the striking worker's sacrifice. Indeed, where Vashti refused to appear before the king, Esther goes to the king uninvited, at the risk of her life. But here is the point, exactly. Vashti, whose ethnicity is a blank in this story (and as such must be assumed to match that of the majority, whose ethnicity generally goes unperceived), refuses to see the king, in a defense of her own dignity and integrity as a woman. But Esther's ethnicity is not blank. She is not distinguished simply by being a woman, but by being a Jewish woman. She may not want to see the king any more than did Vashti, but she must see him if the Jews, including herself and her cousin, are to live out the month. Ultimately, it is her identity as a Jew that makes her need what the king has and that makes her essentially sell her womanhood to get it.

MORDECAI AND ESTHER'S JEWISHNESS

If Vashti is Esther's counterpart in her identity as a woman, Mordecai is her counterpart in her identity as a Jew. Like Vashti, Mordecai is outside when Esther is inside; like Vashti, he protests while Esther finagles. It is Mordecai who insists that Esther conceal her identity as a Jew and her connection to himself. The instruction is vaguely reminiscent of Abram's to Sarai (Gen 12; 21) and Isaac to Rebekah (Gen 26)—in all cases the woman is asked to conceal her connection to the man in order to facilitate the relations of both the man and woman with the foreign king. By a combination of native cleverness and foreign avarice, the Jewish woman ends up in all these stories as the king's wife, serving the interests of the Hebrew minority from the king's court, where no one knows that she is herself a member of that minority until the story's final hour.

Strangely, Mordecai does not find it necessary to conceal his own Jewishness but advises Esther to conceal hers. Is it Esther's identity as a woman and all that that entails—her position in the king's harem—that makes it so much more dangerous for her to be openly Jewish than it is for him to be so? Perhaps it is not actually more dangerous for her, since Mordecai himself comes close to dying for the crime of being Jewish, in a couple of different ways. The fascinating part is that Mordecai must later turn back on his own advice and convince Esther that she is, after all, Jewish and shares in the plight of her people.

When Mordecai hears of Haman's edict against the Jews, he rends his clothes and mourns publicly. White sees this as an inappropriate and unhelpful response of panic, as contrasts with Esther's pragmatic and carefully strategized petitioning of the king (White 1989: 164). But the tearing of clothes, the putting on of sackcloth and ashes, and the act of positioning oneself in sackcloth and ashes in the king's gate—these are not the actions of a man paralyzed by panic. This kind of mourning is formulaic, conscious, and expressive—it carries a clear message to all who witness it, and that message is not panic but protest. The disturbing thing is that Esther does not get this message. Mordecai is outside the gate, mourning and protesting the king's edict, and Esther is inside the palace, ignorant of that edict. We must ask why Mordecai knows of the king's threat to the Jews before the queen knows. Is it the seclusion of the harem that has kept her in the dark? Or is it the privilege of her position that has distanced her from the concerns of her ethnic group? In either case, the selling of her womanhood in the interests of her Jewishness seems to be threatening her Jewishness itself.

Mordecai mourns just outside the king's gate because "no one might enter the king's gate clothed with sackcloth" (4:2). This is an odd law, and even if it exists only within the world of the story, I am inclined to speculate on the reasons for it. Namely, mourning within the court was an admission that the king's court was not a paradise. Mourning may have been prohibited because it was an act of protest, at least when done within the confines of the court. Again, the disturbing thing is that Esther's reaction to the news of Mordecai's mourning is to try and get him to stop (4:4). White reads this as solicitous, an example of how Esther has become Mordecai's protector, reversing the situation of her childhood

(1989: 169). But if the mourning is protest, then the effort to stop the mourning is not solicitous but silencing. Esther does not initially ask Mordecai why he is mourning; she does not appear to want to know. She does not want whatever is grieving him to end; she just wants this public expression of his grief to end. In this way, she is momentarily aligned with the interests of the court—that all within its purview should appear to be happy, so as to confirm the legitimacy of its rule and, for Esther, her precarious position of power within it.

This instance of Esther's ignorance and distance from the Jews is immediately answered by an instance of her knowledge, superior to that of Mordecai, of the workings of the court. In her first speech of the book, she gives Mordecai a swift lecture on what appears to be the court's organizing principle: who gets in and how.

> All the king's servants and the people of the king's provinces [except Mordecai, apparently] know that if any man or woman goes to the king inside the inner court without being called, there is but one law; all alike are to be put to death, except the one to whom the king holds out the golden scepter that he may live. (4:11)

What Esther has lost in contact with her own people's concerns, she has gained in an understanding of the court. Now, as Mordecai convinces her that the position for which she has exchanged her identity will not preserve her from the fate of the Jews, she must reconstitute an understanding of her ethnic identity in a Gentile world and join that understanding with her newly acquired knowledge of the court.

At this point, Esther becomes an actual character in this text, an agent whose actions drive the plot. Until this moment she has been a lump of clay, shaped now by Mordecai, now by the king's desires and the eunuch's advice. But at this juncture of her male-defined femaleness and her Jewishness, she suddenly becomes a human being, with a life of her own and resources on which to draw to accomplish her own will. We are notified of this change by the fact that she responds to Mordecai, whom until this time she has only ever obeyed, by telling him what to do. What he is to do is fast, a fast in which she and her maids and all the Jews whom Mordecai can assemble join. The fast is a preparation for her transgression of the law against going to the king uninvited, and, like the abstinence of a warrior before battle, it is an indication of how much this effort requires of her.

ESTHER AND THE LAW OF THE COURT

What is required of Esther in the end is that she risk her life on the hope that the king will allow her to transgress the boundaries of the court and the laws surrounding it. Transgression of the law is a central theme in this text, from Vashti's condemnation "according to the law" (1:15) to Mordecai's refusal to obey the royal edict concerning obeisance to Haman to Haman's decree against the Jews and onward. There is a continual question of who makes the laws and, more particularly, who writes the laws. Once written, the law must be obeyed and cannot be countermanded, even by the king himself (8:8). This law about the invulnerability of laws is ultimately the cause of the bloodbath that concludes this story. For the king's repenting of the decree written by Haman—or, more accurately, the king's understanding the decree written by Haman—has in itself no effect on the enforcement of that decree. A law cannot be unwritten; it can only be fought, and the energy required to defeat a written law is evident in the extensive, zealous description here of the victory the Jews finally win.

The slaughter of the Jews turns out to be a subjective, rather than an objective, genitive. The slaughter is, in fact, the reversal of this law that cannot be rescinded, just as Haman's plan for Mordecai's hanging is reversed on himself, rather than cancelled altogether. There is irony and a somewhat bitter humor in the statement that "many from the peoples of the country declared themselves Jews, for the fear of the Jews had fallen upon them" (8:17). The Jews' efforts to be Persian, evident in Esther's having to conceal her Jewishness, have now come full circle—who fears whom has reversed, and with it who becomes who.

What has not reversed is the relative positions of men and women. Esther gains in strength of character (in both the literary and ethical senses of the word), she orders Mordecai around to some extent, and she is established in the story as the heroine who has saved her people. But she accomplishes these things by using the gender role assigned to her, not by opposing it. When Haman physically throws himself at her mercy, the king interprets this as an attempted rape—an attempt, that is, to usurp the king's power by usurping his consort. Esther's acceptance of her role and its tools comes to disturbing fruition here, as she allows the false rape charge to stand because it serves her commissioned purpose (Esth 7:8). The king now believes that Haman is the king's own enemy, which it must be admitted is also not actually true.

The king's fulfillment of Esther's requests depends on her pleasing him; because she pleases him a great deal, she can request a great deal, and because she is ultimately a loyal Jew, what she requests is the salvation of her people. Her plea, "How can I bear to see the destruction of my kindred?" (8:6), is effective only because the king cares what she, the charming and pleasing wife he always wanted, can and cannot bear. She does everything in her power to make him want her alive and then says she cannot continue to live if the Jews are destroyed.

In fact, Mordecai's warning has emphasized that Esther cannot continue to live if the Jews are destroyed, because eventually she will be destroyed with them. But here with the king, the impossibility that her life may continue apart from theirs appears voluntary. No doubt this is part of her manipulation of the king, but it is also true that she has voluntarily thrown her lot in with that of the Jews. She has made a decision and said to her cousin, "If I perish, I perish" (4:16), and it is the courage in this statement that makes her admirable.

Yet her use of the gender role as a way of stepping into solidarity with her people acts to reinforce that role, so that at the end, although Esther has grown stronger, the gender trap seems to have grown stronger still. At the expense of Esther, Mordecai is suddenly, inexplicably, admired by all: "For Mordecai was great in the king's house, and his fame spread throughout all the provinces; for the man Mordecai grew more and more powerful" (9:4). In the tradition of interpretation, of course, Mordecai grows even more powerful, from the rabbinic writers to historical criticism, which has considered Mordecai to be both the more historical and the more heroic of the two characters (C. A. Moore: lii). Esther's great accomplishment has made it possible for people both within and outside of the text to see not her true worth, but Mordecai's.

What allows Esther into the king's court, against the law, is not a contravening law but a momentary transcendence of the law, when by the king's good grace, because of her beauty and ability to please, he extends to her the scepter. Legally, upon invitation, the women are ushered into the court by desexed men. Now alegally, Esther is ushered in by what is surely a symbol of this man's sex. The message is encoded but real: the laws diminishing women cannot be rescinded or reversed; they can only be temporarily set aside in the interests of men's sexual desire and stature.

GENDER GAMES AND GENDER WARS

Esther actually gets to write a kind of law before this story is over, and the kind of law it is is not insignificant. It is Esther who institutes Purim by giving "full written authority" for the celebration of the festival (9:29). Most scholars see this as a justification for the book's existence and presence in the canon—it serves as an etiology for Purim. But there are actually connections between the plot of this story and the celebration of the festival. Purim was historically a time when drunkenness and license was encouraged; laws were lifted, temporarily, and often acts of social reversal—including cross-dressing—were part of the festivities (James: 112; cf Frazer). Esther's law, then, is opposed to the institution of law itself, the institution by which the court wields its power.

The conclusions to be drawn from this, Esther's last, act are multiple and not necessarily consistent with one another. On the one hand, this could be read as support for the understanding of woman as the eternal outsider, the uncategorizable other, the one whose power resides in the deconstruction of the male edifice. The law Esther institutes is an antilaw, the exact opposite of the law-enforcing law about the immutability of the king's decrees. Purim is a festival, not a way of life—it is not a law in itself but a temporary glitch in the operation of laws, a moment of imbalance and lawlessness to remind the legal world that it is a construction, not a part of the planet's fabric.

On the other hand, is not a well-defined period of license conducive to maintaining the very legal system by which women are oppressed? By instituting a temporary release from the pressures of the rules, Esther may be making the rules more tenable. Men dressing as women and vice versa can be social commentary, or it can be the sort of comment with which we noticed Vashti's story attracting— an assumption that the rules of behavior for the genders and the laws regulating their relative positions in society are just a harmless game, not a deadly struggle for power.

This same tension between the apparent frivolity of the competition and the underlying deadly seriousness of the events electrified *Who Wants to Marry a Millionaire?* Here was entertainment, a game—Conger herself claims to have entered the competition just for fun, with no serious thought about what might happen if she won. This was television, after all, the American anesthetic of choice. Feminists groaned at the presentation of marriage as something all women should want, as long as the grooms were wealthy enough. The dangers of traditional marriage and the minefield it has been for women's identity seemed so successfully elided from the television screen. But in the end, they showed through for those with eyes to see. The fact that Rockwell was wealthy turned out not to be the only thing Conger needed to know. Rockwell's history of violence against women, revealed in the show's aftermath, shocked viewers and apparently the bride, precisely because the potential for violence, the seriousness of gender relations in general, had been so thoroughly elided from the show itself.

Similarly, what is noteworthy in the story of Esther is the extent to which violence is *not* presented as a factor in gender relations. The violence here—the looming gallows and the terrible question of who will die there; the planned slaughter with its parallel question of who will kill whom—arises on the issue of ethnic identity and the survival, imperiled but ultimately accomplished, of the Jewish people. Even Vashti is not killed, only pushed out of the picture, as are the many former virgins who did not succeed in becoming queen in Vashti's stead. Is this absence of a connection between violence and gender also a message? I have argued above that the text takes Vashti's challenge to the king more seriously than interpreters have done. But the fact that Mordecai's life is threatened for his rebellion, while Vashti simply disappears for hers, does leave readers with the impression that threats to the status and survival of the Jewish people are more serious, more dramatic, and finally more important than threats to the social position of women.

I am compelled to ask what *really* happens to a woman who disobeys her husband, in a society that gives the husband complete authority over his wife? What *really* happens to the girls whom the man in power considers unworthy? These questions do not belong to the text; they are mine. But their absence in the text is, I fear, an example of the reality of women's lives being written over and rendered invisible, so that our own tradition—pieces even of our own psyches—do not in this sense belong to us. The struggle for women to survive with body and soul intact is real; its history is shot through with violence and terror. But that history is not the subject of the book of Esther, nor has it yet attracted mass audiences on American television.

FOR AND WITH WHOM ARE WE READING?
WHO'S PREGNANT AND WHO'S PASSIONATE?

Randall C. Bailey
Interdenominational Theological Center

The writers of the essays in this volume were charged by the introduction to this volume to focus on the intersection of gender, violence, and human sexuality in biblical narratives, utilizing a variety of methods of analysis. This they do. They were asked to bring new questions and perspectives, ostensibly from their differing social locations and interests. The title of the volume, *Pregnant Passion,* is multivalent in this regard, in that it is to connote the birth labor as a metaphor for the work in rethinking the interpretations of the passages under consideration, while it is also to bring to mind the close interrelation of sex and violence in the biblical narrative itself. Though the introduction does not explicitly promise this, there is the expectation of a paradigm shift forthcoming in these articles in line with what Musa Dube calls "to highlight the role of literary texts in the process of domination, resistance, and collaboration" (101).

As a reviewer I find myself in a most intriguing position. As a male I cannot be pregnant; thus, at worst I am placed in the position of voyeur. At best, as a husband who coached my wife through natural childbirth, I feel myself retrojected into that role, as I review these works of my sisters. As an ideological critic, I view myself professionally as a womanist collaborator, one who learns from womanist thought, one who engages in taking seriously the experience of marginalized people and using race, class, and gender as a lens for interpretation. I also use sexual orientation and the awareness of heterosexism in interpretation as a cautionary lens.

The three articles that I am to review, "Who Wants to Marry a Persian King? Gender Games and Wars and the Book of Esther," by Nicole Duran; "Love, Honor, and Violence: Socioconceptual Matrix in Genesis 34," by Mignon R. Jacobs; and "Slingshots, Ships, and Personal Psychosis: Murder, Sexual Intrigue, and Power in the Lives of David and Othello," by Cheryl Kirk-Duggan, are in the trajectory of works such as Phyllis Trible's monumental *Texts of Terror* and Renita Weems's *Battered Love,* both of which expose biblical texts that engage and sanction violence against women. Each article uses a different methodology from the other, but in each there are the characteristics of hybridity (Ashcroft: 33–34). Yet they are still very conventional.

Duran mixes popular culture with character analysis and plot exploration as she compares the television show *Who Wants to Marry a Millionaire?* with the search to find Vashti's successor. She explores the role of ethnicity in the biblical narrative, especially as to how it brings Esther and Mordecai close to danger. Interestingly, she does not explore the ways in which ethnicity, explicitly white privilege, operates in the lessening of the danger in the television parallel. Duran wants to explore the danger, which develops as one gets close to the center of power. She challenges commentators, male and female, who do not take seriously the gender politics expressed in the book, namely, that Vashti is silenced for not cooperating with the locus of power and Esther is brought in because she is willing to cooperate with the center of power. Duran sees Esther as a rounded character developing and becoming an agent pushing the plot after her confrontation with Mordecai. While Esther becomes comfortable at the court, her challenge to the law is not one of transformation. Rather, it is one of being complicit with the gender role expected and utilizing those skills of role perfection to alter the situation.

It is intriguing that Duran's major problem is with the secondary literature and not with the text itself. On the one hand, she is correct that Esther conforms to role expectations. In the instance of the fast, which is called prior to her approaching the king, Duran seems to miss the sexual nuances of this action and the meeting with the king. While she reads the fast as a "warrior preparing for battle," the fast also enables Esther to fit into the dress that will turn on the king. The seduction is more pronounced in the Hebrew text, where the expected formula, $mṣ^{\circ} ḥn b$, "to find favor," is replaced with $nś^{\circ}h ḥn$, "favor rose up in him." He extends his scepter, and she touches its $r^{\circ}š$, its head, whereupon he offers her half his kingdom. What Duran correctly sees as a strategy for keeping the king interested in Esther being alive in chapter 8 is present throughout their interaction. Thus, it is not just the commentators who read the story with the conventions of patriarchy; this ideology is deeply embedded in the text. A key message in the text to women is to rely on their sexuality as a means of escaping the ultimate danger. Thus, to me the text is even more problematic than Duran sees it. As Itumeleng Mosala has argued, the danger in the book is that it models for oppressed women a way for them to take the risks, while the men (Mordecai) get the rewards.

Jacobs explores the ways in which the ambiguities and silences in the story of the "Rape of Dinah" in Gen 34 can be nuanced through the use of sociological methods of analysis. She gives us a close reading of the text and does an intertextual reading of the story through the lens of the law of rape in Deut 22:28–29 and the war laws in Deut 21:10–14. She argues that this is the framework through which one should read the negotiations between Hamor and Jacob regarding the postrape marriage of Shechem and Dinah and the actions of Simeon and Levi. She explores the ways in which the characters respond to the social role expectations in dyadic relationships as well as within and between groups. She places emphasis on insider/outsider divisions between the Jacobites and the Hivites, as well as to reversals within these constructs and irony, which results in the actions within a group. Jacobs also explores the ethical dimensions of the actions of the characters in terms of shame and honor and utilizes comparisons with other cultures' responses to loss of honor to explore the choices made by the characters in the narrative. She is most intrigued by the role of deception within the narrative and negotiations and the interrelationship of deception and restoration of honor. Ultimately she argues that the narrative presents three options for responding to violence. These are Shechem's attempt to seek self-gratification, the brothers' attempt to seek restitution for the violated, namely, through violence, and Jacob's attempt at avoidance.

On the one hand, Jacobs reads the narrative through the dialogue of the previous commentators, struggling to decide whether Dinah was raped or complicit in the act. She also concentrates on the negotiations and responses of Jacob and the brothers in terms of the silences in the text. Unfortunately, Jacobs does not engage feminist critics such as Esther Fuchs (2000) on the subject of the "honor" sought by the brothers. Fuchs argues that the revenge of the brothers is taken as normative and never challenged by the text, thereby suggesting the legitimacy of dismissing the victim as not worthy of engagement. In essence, the foray into the social matrices tends to blind Jacobs to some of the ideological and gendered constructs propelling the plot. In this way the analysis remains too abstract and uncentered. As Eagleton would argue, the result of the literary analysis should lead one to engagement around issues, which help one see the sociopolitical dimensions of the narrative and their consequences. He states:

> What it means to be a "better person," then, must be concrete and practical—that is to say, concerned with people's political situations as a whole—rather than narrowly abstract, concerned only with the immediate interpersonal relations which can be abstracted from this concrete whole. It must be a question of political and not only of "moral" argument: that is to say, it must be genuine moral argument, which sees the relations between individual qualities and values and our whole material conditions of existence. Political argument is not an alternative to moral preoccupations: it is those preoccupations taken seriously in their full implications. (208)

Unfortunately, Jacobs's analysis and reading of the text does not take us to these places, so as to be able to discern the power of oppression sanctioned in this text.

One instance of intertextuality that Jacobs does not explore is the circumcision narrative in Josh 5:2–9, where Joshua circumcises the warriors prior to the battle at Jericho as an initiation into warrior status. Rather, she reads the requirement of circumcision through Gen 17, which speaks to ethnicity. The ties to the Deuteronomic laws of rape and war utilized in her argument would suggest that the Deuteronomic understanding of circumcision, not the Priestly one, is the backdrop of this narrative. Thus, we end up with, on the one hand, that the ironic twist of the initiation into warrior status disables the Hivites so they can be plundered. On the other hand, exploration of this dimension of the narrative brings up the use of sexual violence against men in requiring all the men of the city to undergo the operation. The ethics question that also emerges is that of the men paying the price for the excesses of Shechem and Simeon and Levi, which, given Fuchs's analysis of the brothers, further dehumanizes the Hivites. This reading also brings an ironic twist to the story. In other words, we are taught to read with the "Israelite" characters and not see the ways in which othering takes place as a normative practice. We who are oppressed in our own lives miss the connection with the exploited in the text because we are reading with Israel (Bailey 1998).

Kirk-Duggan enters the sphere of comparative literature in her character analyses of David and Othello. She begins by contouring a womanist reading of texts and then plunges into the exploration of the characterizations of David and Othello through first introducing the reader to the plots and then exploring the marriages and responses to the marriages of the characters. She compares and contrasts David and Othello's responses to conflict and manipulation. She explores ethnicity as it regards Othello's characterization, especially as Iago and Brabantio utilize racial epithets to characterize Othello's actions and motivations. Interestingly, Kirk-Duggan does not explore ethnicity in the presentation of Uriah, Goliath, or David, though she does make Bathsheba a Hittite, in contrast to the genealogy in 2 Sam 11:3 and the role of Ahithophel in 2 Sam 16–17.

As in Jacobs's article, circumcision enters the David narrative in the characterization of Goliath as the "uncircumcised Philistine" (1 Sam 17:26). Again this is used in a derogatory way to minimize Goliath as warrior, since he could not undergo the pain of circumcision. By the same token, the mutilation of the Philistines for a bride price of one hundred foreskins continues the dehumanization of these men and leads to their sexual violation. Though Kirk-Duggan does note this latter instance, she does not explore the "pregnant passion" in this nor the homoerotic nature of the depiction of David in this activity. Kirk-Duggan does lift up the elegy of David for Jonathan in 2 Sam 1:25–26 as an indication for the homoerotic in the narrative. She does not, however, further explore this, either in terms of the presentations in 1 Sam 18–20 nor in the triangle between Saul, David, and Jonathan (Jennings: 41–42). By the same token, the repeated references to the listing of David's wives and children in 2 Sam 5:1–3 seems to serve for both the Deuteronomist and Kirk-Duggan as the straight cover to limit his designation as "possibly only bisexual."

Kirk-Duggan explores the presentation of the women in the narratives and concentrates on psychological readings of their motivations for actions. While she explores the social class of the women in Othello, she does not spend time with a similar analysis of the women in the David narratives. In this way she misses the dimension of his engagement with powerful upper-class women: Ahinoam, Abigail, Michal, and Bathsheba. Similarly, she seems to miss the similarity in these being women who are married to other men, switch loyalty from their husbands, and marry David. Rather, she embraces a victim analysis of these women. Even when they are allowed to speak, she does not explore the sociopolitical nature of their pronouncements.

I find the choice of comparison of David and Othello to be most strange. On the narrative level it appears that Othello is more parallel to Uriah, both in commitment to the military, loyalty, and naïveté. It is almost as though Othello plays the part that Uriah should have been allowed to play. Similarly both Desdemona and Bathsheba's social status as upper-class women from families that are aligned to the throne makes for interesting contrast in use of privilege.

Kirk-Duggan explores the role of scapegoating as a mechanism for short-circuiting spill over of violence in accordance with Girard's theory. What is most intriguing in this analysis is that Kirk-Duggan seems to miss that it is YHWH who is doing the scapegoating, especially in the speech of Nathan in 2 Sam 12:7–15 and in the actions that take place in 2 Sam 13–18. On the one hand, we see David, in 2 Sam 7, wanting to build YHWH a house. Nathan says, fine. YHWH then tells Nathan he got it wrong and to go back to tell David not to do it. In 2 Sam 12 Nathan pronounces judgment on David in the name of YHWH by proclaiming that his children will kill each other, his women will be raped, and the baby will die. On the narrative level we expect YHWH to come back and say, "No, Nathan, you got it wrong again. This isn't retributive justice; it is scapegoating." Instead we see the events unfold in line with the divine will. This is true horror, which could lead to spontaneous miscarriage.

Interestingly, all three of these writers do not want to engage the deity, either the one who appears in the narrative in 1 and 2 Samuel (Bailey 1995) or the one who does not show up in Gen 34 nor in the book of Esther. Kirk-Duggan to her credit does acknowledge that this could be explored but that it is outside the realm of her investigation. She continues to associate David and his advancement with the will of the deity, but she does not explore the relationship of the thuggish David to the deity. On the other hand, Jacobs does not explore the message of the absence of the deity in Dinah's plight, nor does Duran explore the implications of there being no mention of the deity in this endangering approach to the seat of power. What does it mean to be raped and have no response from God? Not only Dinah knows, but also the Hivite women, Tamar (2 Sam 13), and the Benjaminite women (Judg 21) all know (Bal 1988). But they are silenced, lest we consider the absence. What does it mean to have the power of the state against you and the deity does not speak out or intervene? Not only Esther and Mordecai know, but all oppressed peoples who have undergone oppressive violence can speak to that. But the question is never raised, either by the text, the secondary literature, or our passionately pregnant interpreters. It could be, given the dynamics of 2 Sam 13–18, that the absence of the deity is a blessing for the others.

All of these writers speak to the variable of difference in the characters and plots: the difference of gender, ethnicity, and social status. There is focus upon the ingroup/outgroup, inter- or intragroup dynamics. This is seen in many respects as the cause or precipitator of the violence. In many instances the difference is seen as stark, and lines are drawn, so that the reader will easily be able to identify with the "right party." As Wittig argues, however, "The concept of difference has nothing ontological about it, it is only the way that the masters interpret a historical situation of domination. The function of difference is to mask at every level the conflicts of interest, including ideological ones" (29). As readers we are conditioned to read with Israel and those characters who represent the nation. We are led by the narrators to accept their abuses as normative and sanctioned. We are encouraged to read with the upper classes. In so doing we fall prey to ideologies that allow us to see some actions as violence but to ignore others because they are not perpetrated on the different character. In this way, the violence against the men gets lost, because we have missed the point that

> Gender is the linguistic index of the political opposition between the sexes. Gender is used here in the singular because indeed there are not two genders. There is only one: the feminine, the "masculine" not being a gender. For the masculine is not the masculine but the general. (Wittig: 60)

Thus, the readers fall into the trap. Similarly the eunuchs in Esther are not seen as having pregnant passion, for the concern is with the heterosexual Esther. But where are Mordecai's children? Why is he alone at his age? Or are we raising the wrong issues? He did like dressing up in the royal robes. Perhaps this is the cross-dressing of Purim to which Duran speaks.

In these three articles there is exploration of the intersection of violence, especially as it relates to sexual violence and gender. It is at these points that the articles seem the least passionate. Perhaps it is the reliance on the tools of the master, which prohibit the breakthrough (Lorde). Perhaps it is not taking the cues from the common people and injecting this into the analysis (P. H. Collins). While there is questioning of the secondary literature's portrayal of the issues in the narrative, there is not enough engagement with the ideologies of the text itself to see how the intersection of the violence with power is a sanctioned and intrinsic sustainer of the culture that dominates. Unless we engage and confront these ideologies, we end up lost in the silences of the text. In this way the transformation of the culture and the dismantling of the powers of dominance, which abort us daily, will continue to harass and dislocate us. It is the passionate engagement and struggle with and against such texts that can impregnate us all with the hope to stay in the struggles.

Finally, were it not for the work of these women, I would not have been led to formulate this concern in the way that it has been put forth. I am grateful to you for the insights you brought forth and for the opportunity to rethink texts and arguments.

PART 2:

LEGAL AND REGULATORY MATTERS

Murder S/He Wrote? A Cultural and Psychological Reading of 2 Samuel 11–12

Hyun Chul Paul Kim and
M. Fulgence Nyengele
Methodist Theological School in Ohio

Was Bathsheba an innocent victim, a surviving opportunist, or a master-mind schemer? The story of David and Bathsheba has placed this perennial question before readers through the ages. To be more specific, readers have been pondering this question because the biblical story does not seem to offer an unequivocal answer (Yee: 240–42). Or does it? What really happened? Was this story no more than a story after all (Perry and Sternberg)? Or was this no less than a historiography (Garsiel: 245–49)? Or, if not either exclusively, then a combination of both that was eventually molded into what we have by the final redactor(s)?

Let us suppose the case of Bathsheba was taken to the court, say, by the state of Judah. This narrative fits within the larger framework of the Court History or "Throne Succession Narrative" (Bailey 1990: 7) in the Deuteronomistic compendium. But we are supposing a kind of modern-day court experience in the ancient case. In this modern court, the case technically would not be a trial of adultery (which would have been a legitimate case to take to the court in the ancient legal system) but rather that of murder. Although the discussion below will address the possibility of a rape case, the case filed here is that of murder. Here we have a case of murder of Uriah the Hittite along with the unidentified soldiers in the battle. One would be fairly safe in convicting David based on the textual evidence (although David did use a hit man, Joab, to execute the crime). But what about Bathsheba? Was she an accomplice to the murder? Or was she innocent?

The present study examines this story—with a special attention to the dynamics of gender, violence, passion, power, and politics depicted in Bathsheba and her surrounding characters—from multidimensional angles. As for the format of this article, we will present *both* prosecutor's *and* defendant's arguments in a simulated twenty-first-century court. Because we are not trained in the disciplines of legal practices, however, our presentations should be considered more like those of outside analysts rather than those in the actual court. And, as we present both perspectives, we invite the readers of this article to be the jury and eventually leave the verdict of this case to them, just as our biblical text does.

The study starts with a literary analysis, paying attention to plots, gaps, and several key literary features. Then it compares the societal dynamics of ancient Israel with pertinent cultural aspects of ancient Korea, and it explores those possible cultural gaps concerning gender, patriarchy, and monarchy both within the literary complexity and between the two remote worlds. From a psychological perspective, we use the frameworks of Jean Baker Miller and Carol Gilligan to analyze Bathsheba's sense of self and agency, her participation in the relational dynamics between her and David, her responsiveness to David's aggression, and the psychological underpinnings of the relational and power dynamics between the two of them (and Uriah). We also use grief theory to assess Bathsheba's emotional response to Uriah's death and the insights it provides with regard to her possible innocence and victimization.

1. AN AMBIGUOUS PLOT

Since it would be redundant to retell this story, we only point out some significant features of the literary device, such as irony, pun, wordplay, and chiastic structure. These features help us see not only the artistry of the narrator's composition but also the subtlety and complexity of diversely concatenated plots that are full of both coinciding and conflicting ironies, themes, and ideologies.

This story of the David-Uriah-Bathsheba triangle is surrounded by stories of war: 2 Sam 10 is a story of war against the Ammonites, with its resolution occurring as the Israelites defeat the Arameans, not the Ammonites, and 2 Sam 12 concludes with the Israelites' sack, finally, of the Ammonites (12:26–31). In between these wars is our story, which ironically continues the setting of war (11:1). This too is a story of war, but a different kind of war. Amid David's dispatching the army to besiege *a city* (Rabbah; often a city is personified in the feminine form), David himself engages in another battle to conquer *a woman* (Bathsheba; "bath" in Hebrew means "daughter," as in "daughter Zion"). Whereas Uriah fights hard *against the Ammonites*, David ironically fights *against only one man*, his own soldier Uriah. These ironic contrasts point to David's internal struggle with his own lust, his pursuit of Bathsheba, and his militant strategy against Uriah. Thus, this story is ingeniously placed in between the texts about real wars (10:1–19; 12:26–31), highlighting what is going on with David with regard to gender, sex, and violence.

Furthermore, there are other ironic puns and wordplays that help draw readers' attention to the subtle implications concerning the issues of agency vis-à-vis adultery and murder in this plot. First, whereas David "collects" (אָסַף) all the people to fight against the enemies in 10:17 and 12:29, in this middle narrative David, the great warrior, "collects" (אָסַף) a woman (11:27). The use of this word "to collect" in these passages offers a hint about David's skillful use of power to achieve his desire. Second, the word "send" (שָׁלַח) occurs thirteen times in 2 Sam 11 (cf. Peterson: 182–83). David *sends* Joab, his servants, and all Israel to the battle (11:1). David *sends* (11:3, 4), Bathsheba *sends* (11:5), and Joab *sends*, too (11:6). David then *sends* a letter by which Uriah and other soldiers will die (11:14). In Joab's instruction to his messenger, a woman *throws* (Hiphil form of "send") an upper millstone (11:21). This episode ends with David *sending* to "collect" Bathsheba (11:27). Yet the parable immediately starts with the report that YHWH *sends* Nathan to David (12:1). Again, in light of the frequent occurrence of this word "to send," the narrator displays subtle power dynamics among the characters, of which David is depicted as the predominant agent. However, the narrator also complicates the whole plot by depicting other characters, including Bathsheba, as agents on their own terms. At the same time, the narrator wants readers to see another agent, YHWH, although this information becomes available only after the whole incident of chapter 11. Third, another wordplay is used to address the issue of power dynamics. In 11:4, David *lies* with Bathsheba. In this affair, who is really in control, David or Bathsheba? It remains ambiguous. In 11:9, Uriah *lies* at the gate of the king's house, disobeying David's command to go home and "wash" his feet. Here Uriah's act of resistance is an expression of his own power, however limited it may be. This becomes clearer in his statement of fidelity in 11:11, as Uriah defies how wrong it is to *eat, drink, and lie* with his wife during war. Then, in 11:13, David somehow made Uriah *eat, drink,* and *lie*—a sign of David's dominance. On the contrary, Uriah lay only with other comrades, not with his wife—a sign of Uriah's defiance. Later in Nathan's parable, the ewe-lamb is described to be so dear to the poor man as to "*eat* from his morsel, *drink* from his cup, and *lie* in his bosom" (12:3). By echoing this same set of words, Nathan reminds David of the violence he has committed against Bathsheba, referred to as the ewe-lamb.

In addition, the extant form of 2 Sam 11 is composed in a rough chiastic (or symmetrical, concentric) structure, making it a composite whole and signaling many counterparts toward several punch lines:

a David "sends" Joab, servants, and all Israel   1
  b Bathsheba-messenger-David   2–4
    c A *woman* bathing   2
      d "messengers"   4
        e "at the entrance of the house of the king"   9
          f David-servants-Uriah   6–13
            g Uriah "slept" along with the servants   9
            gg Uriah went out "to lie" with the servants 13
              h *"Why did* you *not* go down...?"   10
                i David wrote a letter   14–15
              h' *"Why did* you approach so near...?"   20
            gg' Some servants, with Uriah, "fell"   17
            g' Some of the servants with Uriah "are dead" 24
          f' Uriah-soldiers-David   14–21
        e' "to the entrance of the gate"   23
      d' A "messenger"   22–25
    c' A *woman* throwing an upper millstone   21
  b' Joab-messenger-David   22–25
a' David "sends" and "collects" her (Bathsheba)   27a

As illustrated above, this text has a nice framework with its inclusio (a-a') as a unit. Some lines are clearly out of proportion. Some even correspond to more than one component, making the whole like a spider's web. Nevertheless, most components do correspond and thereby function as legitimate pillars of the whole structure, inviting readers to see and follow the intentional design that ties the whole together. This structure discloses subtle signifiers toward several key notions. For instance, David's dealing with Bathsheba via the messengers (b) coincides with David's dealing with Joab via the messenger (b'). There are not one but two women mentioned in this story, one bathing (c) and the other throwing an upper millstone (c'). Both plots are direct causes of the deaths of two men, Uriah and Abimelech (Fokkelman: 69; Bal 1987: 25). Uriah *the Hittite* is related to Abimelech, whose name makes a pun with Ahimelech *the Hittite* (1 Sam 26:6). Both plots also point to two kings, David and Abimelech (Judg 9:1–6). Bathsheba is "object of the higher-placed focalizer," whereas the anonymous woman "is the higher-placed female and [the one] who kills the lower-placed male victim, Abimelech—like David, a king" (Bal 1987: 29). Furthermore, the name *Abimelech* echoes the king Abimelech of Genesis, who, Abraham and Isaac thought, could have killed them to take their wives, had they not lied to him, saying, "She is my sister" (Gen 20; 26 respectively). Other pivotal events are described within the frameworks of the messengers (d-d') as well as the mention of the "entrance" of the palace and gate (e-e'). In between these frames is the very encounter between David and Uriah. Just as the messengers play indirect but significant roles between David and Bathsheba as well as between David and Joab, now the servants and soldiers are portrayed importantly in the words and actions between David and Uriah (f-f' and g-g'). Just as Uriah remains to "sleep" with his comrades (gg), so some of the brave soldiers "fell" along with Uriah at the battle (gg'). Last but not least, in light of this chiastic structure, a conceptual center can be found in verses 14–15, which conveys a crucial notion within the whole plot— murder David wrote.

In summary, this text is compact and condensed and thus full of gaps and many unexplained episodes. At the same time, its plot is also full of puns and wordplays. All these function as signifiers to the veiled realities within the text. These signifiers play double duty; they help connect and clarify some aspects of the plot, on the one hand, while they also cause this text to be more complicated and multivalent, on the other hand. The various components of the chiastic structure (see above), along with its regular structure (Bailey 1990: 84–85, 91–93, 99), likewise display both clarity and ambiguity.

2. Prosecutor's Reading

Having made a condensed recap of the plot, it is now in order to hear both arguments. Let us proceed then with the argumentation first from the perspective of the prosecutor.

The prosecutor accuses Bathsheba of being an accomplice in the conspiracy of Uriah's murder and presents the following reconstructions as evidence. David is a very capable man. He is charming and handsome (1 Sam 16:12; cf. 1 Sam 9:2; 1 Kgs 1:6), a valiant warrior, and a gentle poet at the same time. He is a capable leader and a gifted musician. After all, he is the king! Could it not have been possible that Bathsheba had felt lonely because of her husband Uriah's continual absence for battle and, more significantly, his increasing indifference and insensitivity toward her (Aschkenasy: 116; Rand: 91)? This brings us to pose other pertinent issues momentarily. How did Bathsheba marry Uriah? Was it an arranged marriage, possibly against her desire? Or was it a consequence of a forbidden love between an Israelite woman and a resident alien soldier? Was Uriah, and Bathsheba as his wife, an old acquaintance to David? Or was this couple never introduced to David previously? In light of some evidences (e.g., the rhetorical question, "Is not this Bathsheba?" [cf. Bailey 1990: 85]), it is possible to deduce that David and Bathsheba may have met and/or known each other earlier. If so, it is possible to conjecture that some women yearned for the power and glory of becoming the wife of a king. Perhaps Bathsheba had such a plan in mind.

Then comes the bathing episode! Whether or not David had known Bathsheba (and Uriah) before, certainly she knew who David was. Then, why was she bathing in that place at that time? Why in such a place where someone could see her with naked eyes? David clearly could see that she was "very beautiful"; was Bathsheba also able to see that David was watching her? The text remains ambiguous on this issue. However, it seems not unusual that the king would take a walk on the roof after a siesta, especially during the springtime in the desert climate (Garsiel: 253). King David is not described as taking a stroll out in the street and peaking over someone else's fence. Rather, it was the woman, though a married woman, who chose to take a bath, knowing the possibility of being seen. At that time of casual resting and roaming in his own palace, the king was confronted with the seductive scene of a woman bathing. Thus, it is an incident of a king fallen into temptation. He was seduced first, and, as a consequence, she was abducted.

A question arises as to what may have been going on in Bathsheba's mind while being summoned. The fact that "she came to him" (11:4) is not really strong enough evidence to accuse Bathsheba—which will be discussed in the defendant's section below. If Bathsheba knew why she was summoned, would it not have been more common for her to express a sign of resistance? Yet the text is silent on this issue. The narrator does not seem to be interested in that issue. But we are. The text is silent as to whether Bathsheba was summoned right at the moment of her barely finishing the bath or several days later. An ingenious literary device may give us a clue. The fact that the whole episode of this affair is narrated in only three verses (11:2–4), in contrast with the lengthier surrounding plots, is a clear evidence of the literary design for the reader to feel the high speed of the actions. This vignette is so intentionally designed that the narrator (or final redactor) inserts a note of her purification (as a proof that the child would have to be David's) in an out-of-place sentence. The lovemaking is meant to be a hasty one with full speed, minimum delay, and maximum secrecy. Clearly David controls the wheel of this wild ride. Nonetheless, we have yet to ask whether or not Bathsheba wanted or dared to resist. Whereas the text is unclear about this issue, there are biblical instances of similar cases where resistance was attempted. For example, in Gen 39:8–10 Joseph pleads his resistance against Potiphar's seductive wife. In 2 Sam 13:12–13, Tamar reasons against the lustful Amnon. In these similar narrative plots, those in danger are not silent. We then wonder why Bathsheba acquiesced.

In the ancient Korean custom, there is a strong tradition of women's fidelity. Critical to this tradition is an emphasis and exaltation that a virgin should keep her chastity and that likewise a married woman keep hers. To do so, a silver-decorated knife (un-jang-do), used for hair decoration or self-defense, was handed down from a grandmother to her mother and then to the daughter. When their chastity was in serious danger without any means to rescue, this was the final resort they could use to protect their chastity and/or fidelity, by taking their own lives rather than being attacked. Although this was considered a lofty virtue, it required an incredible amount of courage, and thus such a woman was exalted with high regard (yet often this tradition was used as a key resource for men and society to oppress women). In light of this kind of culture, the reader would still wonder whether/why Bathsheba had not resisted. The text resists offering the answer.

In 11:5, we find the most challenging literary crux. Here Bathsheba, who remains—or is made—silent throughout the entire story, speaks out, via a messenger (cf. Esth 4:5, 9, 13, 15). Without doubt, this very phrase can be the crucial key evidence of power dynamics of which Bathsheba must have been an active part (Nicol 1997: 50). "I am pregnant"—this short phrase is so brief but full of possibilities. The intention of her conveying this information is unexplained. The tone is also unsure. If this story were retold by modern-day novel writers, at least three different punctuation markers, indicating three different messages using the same three words, could be used: (1) "I am pregnant . . ."; (2) "I am pregnant."; (3) "I am pregnant!" In this usage, the first could be interpreted as an expression of Bathsheba's shock, pain, and agony; the second as an expression of the narrator's emotionless report (and this is what we have in the extant form of the Hebrew text); and the third as a sign of exuberant gain in her part.

By cultural comparison, in the ancient Korean society, for a woman to have a royal child meant a great deal of fortune. Even a maidservant in the palace might be picked by the king (which is referred to as, in Korean, "Being clothed with a saving kindness" [to serve the king at night]), and once she became pregnant with the king's child, especially a son, her status would virtually rise to second next to the queen. Certainly, only young unmarried girls were qualified for this group (cf. Esth 2:2). Yet, the important thing is that even for them the probability of receiving the royal call was low, like winning a lottery. If a woman became one of the wives of the king, then her family, relatives, in-laws, and even pertinent town would benefit by political, social, and financial gains. This also meant that often there was a lot of hidden rivalry and strife among the women toward their ultimate goal. With this view, the phrase "I am pregnant" might indicate a hidden power play by Bathsheba, who would become the real controller of the following scenes. In this context, this usage might convey a one-time affair in the attitude of this lustful, hapless king. Yet for this woman it may have been a "fatal attraction" that would lead to tangled threads of consequent power struggles and intrigue.

From a psychological perspective based on the work of Jean Baker Miller (1976; 1984) and Carol Gilligan, Bathsheba's behaviors and statements seem to point to her sense of agency and participation in the relational dynamics that establish connections between her and David. The above discussion suggests that Bathsheba may have known who David was, and we can guess that bathing in a place where someone (David) could see her reflects some intentionality, if not motivation, to get his attention.

Further, the facts that "she *came* to him" when summoned by David and that she *sent* a messenger to him saying, "I am pregnant," when she conceived a child may suggest that Bathsheba is a willing, cognizant, and self-determined person in the pursuit of her own desire to seduce him, sleep with him, and connect with him at a deeper level. All these are psychological evidences that she was proactive, self-motivated, and willing to participate in the affair between her and David. She was involved in this "relationship" from the standpoint of strength rather than weakness. She clearly has a strong sense of self (Miller 1984: 1–2) and a clear voice in the text. Her "voice" (Gilligan: x), as minimally represented as it may look, points to the sense of self and agency mentioned above. Also, she had no fear of speaking her mind. Even though she might not have had a "political voice," she clearly had a "personal voice" (Gilligan: xxii). All these aspects (agency, self-determination, choice, and voice) are psychological evidences that she was a willing participant in the relational dynamics between her and David, and, at points, an initiator of the relationship itself.

Now, the subsequent episodes in the literary plot further depict that the real controller may have been Bathsheba, in contrast with the desperate, panic-driven David. If we read the "good" David in the preceding chapters, we now read the "evil" David in a vivid exposure: once Dr. Jekyll and now Mr. Hyde. What changed him so dramatically, if there ever was a change in character? Why is it that, in contrast with the cogent decision and swift action in 11:2–4, David's tactic in 11:6–25 is full of delay, negotiation, flaws, and alterations? Who really influenced David to act out as such a cold-blooded killer? David's "insanity" can be seen in the ironic tone in his conversation with Uriah in 11:7, "Is there *peace* with *war?*" This literal translation displays a sense of paradox, a theme that continues throughout. Perhaps the narrator wants to convey a notion that this David is not so much of a winner but rather a loser, defeated by a woman's seduction and haunted by the consequence in pregnancy. This David is not the young David who defies the indomitable giant Goliath in the name of YHWH but more like "the man" who keeps on adding lies and excuses after having fallen into the seduction of "the woman" (Gen 3:10, 12). Perhaps this was a fatal attraction that led David into the resulting action. Readers may wonder why David did not care to deal with Bathsheba, in the gap between 11:5 and 11:6, by having her killed or tainting her reputation rather than sending for Uriah (Aschkenasy: 110). One might conjecture that Bathsheba may have been a part of these power dynamics. David, though the real commander of the various tactics of the external war, may well have been defeated, led, and controlled by Bathsheba, who hides as the real influencer of the internal war of the David-Bathsheba-Uriah triangle.

Last but not least, scholars have pointed out the literary parallels between the David-Abigail-Nabal triangle (1 Sam 25) and the David-Bathsheba-Uriah triangle (2 Sam 11) episodes. George G. Nicol argues that the narrator intends to establish a transformation from the former to the latter because there are shifts of character depictions: for example, from a promising king David to a corrupt king, from a disloyal man Nabal to a loyal man Uriah, and from a noble woman Abigail to a seductive woman Bathsheba (Nicol 1998: 131–40). Here readers may also find Nabal's foolish and rash actions as similar to David's (e.g., compare 1 Sam 25:2, "the man [Nabal] was very rich," with 2 Sam 12:1), not Uriah's! Whether Bathsheba makes a contrast or comparison with Abigail, it is possible that, in both cases, women do take the apex of the triangle and thereby the plot: one as the prudent problem-solver, the other as the seductive problem-maker (or as the innocent object of a wicked man's lust). These women play significant functions within the plot, though at the very margins. In this sense, it is then possible to argue that David indeed was fooled, tricked, and fell into the trap from which he could not escape. Or, alternatively, David tactfully welcomed Bathsheba in the acts of "co-partnership" of political marriage (Bailey 1990: 90, 100; Aschkenasy: 113–17).

So, could there have been a tone of betrayal in Bathsheba's solidarity toward her Hittite-Israelite husband? Possibly. Is it likewise possible that Bathsheba had the desire to be in the harem of the king? Possibly. Therefore, was Bathsheba a co-conspirator in the death of Uriah? Not impossible.

3. DEFENDANT'S READING

Now it is the defendant's turn to present an argument. In light of the narrative flow, King David's staying in Jerusalem is clearly intended as a sign that something wrong is about to occur, something wrong in a fairly tiny matter, that is, from the perspective of a powerful king. However, it turns out that something indeed went wrong that will affect so much in so many tragic ways.

One key issue the readers wonder about is when and why Bathsheba took a bath. In light of the textual evidence, it seems safe to deduce that

Bathsheba was taking a bath after the hottest time of the day, an ideal time for people to bathe while avoiding sunburn and visibility. Furthermore, there is a significant reason for her to be bathing. If this were a legal case, this information was rather inadvertently given away. Bathsheba was purifying herself according to the ritual laws (11:4; cf. Lev 15:19–24). The fact that this information is offered in an awkward place (but cf. Berlin: 80)—that is, not in verse 2 but in verse 4—certainly indicates the narrator wants to convey, first and foremost, that the child Bathsheba would conceive must be David's and not Uriah's. If this content were presented by the prosecuting attorney, even if this information was given for a different motive, a fact is still a fact. Now the readers can understand that she had every reason to be bathing, especially while faithfully observing the law of ritual cleansing. What is actually untold is the possibility that this may not have been David's first time looking down from his roof as a voyeur.

The text is also not clear as to whether someone else was present with David (Exum 1993: 175; cf. Nicol 1997: 48). What is clear is the fact that David turned to action not only secretly but also hurriedly. At the same time, though he acted secretly and quickly, he did act with power. David had been a power-hungry soul ever since he had tasted the game of power politics. As Randall Bailey argues, David's taking of Bath-sheba may have been a part of David's political marriage tactic (Bailey 1990: 85–90). However, even then, this does not establish a case that Bathsheba also planned such a political marriage. In fact, it could be argued that Bathsheba was a prey of David's political power struggle, considering that she was the daughter of Eliam, the granddaughter of Ahithophel (Bailey 1990: 87; cf. 2 Sam 23:34). In contrast with the case of Abigail, David did not wait for any doom to fall upon Uriah and then get married to Bathsheba. Rather, David went ahead and took Bathsheba. Only afterwards did David have to improvise as to what he had to do regarding Uriah.

More tangible evidence against prosecution may be found in the syntactical patterns. A major case from the prosecutor's argument resides in the narrative description that Bathsheba "came to him" and verbalized that "I am pregnant." These phrases can offer the reader every reason to speculate that she was indeed a very proactively involved actor of the whole scene. Let us consider why such may not be the case. Some scholars argue that the phrase "she came to him" (11:4) is a clear evidence of her willing participation. The narrator could have said that she *was* abducted or taken—in a passive sense. However, this phrase, "she came to him" (ותבוא אליו), occurs in the similar pattern in 11:7, "Uriah came to him" (ויבא אוריה אליו). In the case of Uriah coming to David, no reader will assume that Uriah actively came to David and therefore he must have been a calculator who planned the whole thing so that he could be brought into this scene. Actually it is quite the opposite. Uriah is clearly a subordinate subject who was summoned by David and sent by Joab (11:6), and thus he came to David (11:7). Likewise, the text describes that David, through the messengers, "took" Bathsheba so that "she came to him" (11:4). This parallel pattern clearly shows that we cannot deduce that she came voluntarily or jubilantly to the king's palace. On the contrary, it is more likely that she was taken, if not abducted, by force, indeed by the unchallengeable power of the king.

A more daunting case can be found in the phrase where Bathsheba sends a message to the king, "I am pregnant" (11:5). This is much too brief and yet most shocking. Not only does she speak out, whereas in the rest of this story she is totally silenced, but also her news of pregnancy is filled with powerful possibilities and potent problems. On one level, her telling the king of her pregnancy can be seen as a sign of a woman "devising a plan" (Bailey 1990: 89). This view is supported by similar episodes of women, Lot's daughters and Tamar, initiating illicit relations (Gen 19:29–38; 38:13–30). This is a convincing argument. However, there is a substantially significant difference in comparison. In those two episodes, Lot's daughters lost their husbands, who chose not to follow their father-in-law and thereby must not have survived the destruction (Gen 19:25, 31). Likewise, Tamar was widowed and then approached Judah (Gen 38:14). In our text, Bathsheba was still married and there is no textual indication that this couple struggled to have children (contra Klein: 53–58), in which case there was no reason for her to initiate an act for progeny. Such would only incur a case of adultery. Thus, the differences in these cases should be noted as significant. On another level, moreover, she may be directing her case to the king, who would take the jurisdictional duty (1 Kgs 3:16–28), though in this case, alas, this supreme-court judge is the very offender.

Clearer evidence lies in the strikingly identical textual pattern of report formula. The phrase "and she sent and told David" (ותשלח ותגד לדוד) in 2 Sam 11:5 is identical with Joab's report, "Joab sent and told David" (וישלח יואב ויגד לדוד) in 2 Sam 11:18. This similarity seems intentional. This intentionality may imply at least two subtle ideas. On the one hand, it implies that both cases are similar cases of simple reports. David is the center, and both Bathsheba and Joab are not the exercisers of "authority" but mere subordinates (contra Bailey 1990: 86). They had better know their places, and it seems that they did (Bergant: 264). On the other hand, there is also irony. Whereas Joab's report was something desirable to David, it seems that Bathsheba's report was something unexpected to him. The text never tells us whether or not David was actually looking forward to having a child with Bathsheba—yet what king would mind another child of his own by any means? Be that as it may, here we find similarity in the speeches of both Joab and Bathsheba; they share ironic overtones of sarcasm, defiance, and even mockery. Apparently, neither Joab nor Bathsheba but a third person is speaking these didactic messages. Joab's words are more elaborate than Bathsheba's. In 11:19–21, David was supposed to recall the story of the king Abimelech killed by a woman, which never did get across in David's words but only in Joab's. Seemingly, the reader should be invited to ponder: If King Abimelech was killed by a woman, why is it not King David but Uriah who is killed? This sarcasm may be likewise implied in Bathsheba's brief words. Here, Bathsheba is not reporting that she is having the king's child with exclamation but rather reminding King David that the king's act of adultery is proven. Even as David remains the center of action, by the same token he becomes the center of cowardice, cruelty, and crime.

In addition, the fact that Bathsheba mourned and lamented the death of Uriah (11:26–27) can be further evidence that she did not take part in David's plan to kill Uriah, nor did she expect David to take such action against her husband. Her mourning and lament, just like her report about her pregnancy, seems to bear a tone of agony and defiance—she made "lamentation for him" (11:26). Her grieving implies a woundedness of spirit and mind because of loss.

Psychological theory defines grief as "an emotional state occasioned by separation from a loved person or loved object" (Bowman: 76; Mitchell and Anderson: 54). Further, grief is understood as "a pain of mind, of soul, of spirit, or body, which comes from some deep trouble or loss and in which one's relationship to a person or thing is broken" (Bowman: 78). From the perspective of grief theory, Bathsheba's grief connotes her experience of emotional pain and deep trouble over the loss of her husband. The statements "she did lamentation for him" and "when the mourning was over" (11:26–27) indicate that her grief was real and that she genuinely suffered when she heard that her husband was dead. The defendant's argument must not ignore this experience, nor can the prosecutor's argument play down or belittle her grief. The text's mention of her lament and mourning is not by chance.

In the prosecutor's argument above, we mentioned the possible correlation between the David-Abigail-Nabal triangle (1 Sam 25) and the David-Bathsheba-Uriah triangle (2 Sam 11) episodes (cf. Nicol 1998). Here, in addition to the similarity between Nabal and David (instead of Uriah), we must also add that, whereas Bathsheba is recorded to have made lamentation, there is no report (i.e., literary gap) of Abigail's mourning for her deceased husband (1 Sam 25:39–42). Ironically, it is Abigail who is described to have "*hastened* to rise and rode on a donkey" (1 Sam 25:42)—a clear sign of willingness to enter a new royal life on a donkey as a queen (cf. Zech 9:9; Gen 49:11; 1 Kgs 1:33). In contrast, this narrator, who tends to leave so many places ambiguous, does bother to state that Bathsheba made her wailing for her husband.

From a pastoral psychological perspective, because grief is reported it must be real. Indeed, because Bathsheba grieved, there is a great possibility that she still felt emotionally attached to her husband. She still loved him. She probably did not want him to die. As grief theory suggests, "if we love deeply, we grieve deeply" (Bowman: 78; Mitchell and Anderson: 58). Perhaps her capacity to grieve indicates her deep pain of mind, soul, and spirit over Uriah's death. This capacity points to her experience of trauma (Mitchell and Anderson: 56). Her grieving could also be viewed as a psychological evidence of her victimization and, consequently, as psychological proof of her innocence.

Given such rationalization with regard to Bathsheba's innocence, we are left with evidence that seems to depict David more as a cold-blooded politician, strategist, and murderer than as a victim. David is the master-minded schemer, not Bathsheba or Joab. What little voices they raise are not so much of counterattack from the equals but rather voices of defiance against the unjust oppressor. This voice from the powerless may also be found in the very speech of Uriah. In 11:11, Uriah replies with words that seem to be coming from an elderly teacher to a young pupil, "The ark, Israel, and Judah are dwelling at Succoth, and my lord Joab, the servants of my lord are encamped out in the field, and shall I go to my house to eat, drink, and lie with my wife? By your life and by the life of your soul, I will not do this thing!" There is a double entendre here. On the one hand, Uriah may have known or sensed what was going on, possibly from his elite comrades at the palace (Garsiel: 256–58; Nicol 1998: 141–42; Hertzberg: 310–11). In this sense, this may be Uriah's cry against the iniquity and injustice committed by this king. On the other hand, Uriah may have been in an inescapable trap devised by David. In this sense, this very phrase may have been what David devised to declare to Uriah, if Uriah did go home and sleep with his wife (Bailey's translation of the word משאת המלך in 11:8 as "spy" rather than "gift" or "food" makes this view much more convincing [1990: 97–98]). Inasmuch as David may have meant to send Uriah to have intercourse with Bathsheba, it is equally possible to deduce that David was more interested in getting Uriah trapped and caught (Bailey 1990: 97–99; Anderson: 154). This becomes most evident when David sends the letter of Uriah's death warrant by the hand of Uriah (11:14–15). If Uriah opens the seal, he would incur "an act of treason" (Garsiel: 258–59). If he does not open (which was the case), he would be murdered as David wrote. In either case, it is clear that David is a master-minded planner of the perfect crime—the king takes a "beautiful" woman, conceives a child, and gets rid of the woman's husband. This becomes clearer in 12:15b–23, which depicts how David so suddenly changes from a seemingly genuine repentant to a chilling ruler. In 12:21, we find an ironic speech by the servants,

"What is this thing you have done?" They were dumbfounded by the behavior of this king, no longer a wee shepherd boy, showing obedience and humility, but now a murderer.

In addition to the above rationales, there is additional strong evidence that further clarifies Bathsheba's innocence: Nathan's parable in 2 Sam 12. In an earlier compositional stage, both chapters may have been originally independent, possibly 2 Sam 12 being a secondary addition to 2 Sam 11 (Bailey 1990: 102–13). Nevertheless, in its extant form, 2 Sam 11 and 12 are clearly meant to be read together (McCarter: 306; Garsiel: 246). Seemingly, the reader is given a midrash (or innerbiblical commentary) of chapter 11 in chapter 12. Let us examine how chapter 12 comments on 11. We shall mainly note the pertinent key issues. First, nowhere in this divine oracle of judgment through the prophet Nathan is there accusation of Bathsheba. David alone is accused (12:7). In contrast with 2 Sam 11 (in 11:27b is "the only unambiguous statement of the whole story" [Yee: 247]), 2 Sam 12 is much more transparent because YHWH is actively involved in this passage and Nathan does not beat around the bush but exclaims, "You are the man!" (12:7). If this prophet does not beat around the bush, it does not make sense why he would not condemn Bathsheba as well (Garsiel: 254). Whereas the woman is condemned along with the man in Gen 3, on the contrary, here only the king, "the rich man," David is condemned. Any interested readers should not consider as a trivial matter in this passage the fact that whereas the biblical writers/redactors tended to be male-oriented in their patriarchal culture and quick to blame or condemn women (e.g., Gen 3:12; 1 Kgs 21; Hos 1–2; Job 2:9–10; cf. Bal 1987: 33), the divine condemnation on Bathsheba is missing—absent from either the prophet or the narrator.

Second, Nathan's parable serves to fulfill many subtle rhetorical goals. For instance, this parable more powerfully succeeds in convicting David's guilt. The plot, content, and wordplay in Nathan's tale must have been so similar to what David actually did that David interrupted Nathan's solemn homily, with his outburst as a "Freudian slip" (Rand: 94). David was not so naïve as to be ignorant of who this rich man was. Rather, he must have understood it so well that he exaggerates the due punishment on this sinner (12:5–6)—this kind of crime need not be met with a death sentence (Exod 22:1). Moreover, this parable highlights one significant aspect to the point that it understates another significant aspect. The rich man should be David. Then the poor man is Uriah and the one little ewe-lamb Bathsheba. If the parable should be faithful to the episode in 2 Sam 11, then it should have been the poor man who is slaughtered and not the ewe-lamb. After all, the murder of Uriah is the case. However, the parable is pointed toward the case of abduction and rape rather than murder. Perhaps because Uriah was a resident alien or because Nathan was upset about the whole incident, this parable does not perfectly parallel the actual incident. Why that is so, we may not know. What is certain rather is the implication that this "taking" (לקח, 12:4) of the powerless woman should be seen as one of the most heinous crimes in the divine sight. This very notion is emphasized in the parable.

Third, the accusation is made on both accounts of murder and rape (12:9). In both accounts, the divine punishment entails forceful attack and humiliation (12:10–13). YHWH declares to make the divine retribution of David's "taking" (לקח) of the wife of Uriah the Hittite (12:9, 10) by the same "taking" (לקח) of the wives of the Davidic dynasty (12:11). Again, the victims are Uriah the slain and Bathsheba the abducted/raped. The accused is David. Therefore, if we read 2 Sam 11 in connection with 2 Sam 12, it becomes more evident that Bathsheba was a powerless, tragic, and innocent victim "taken" by the powerful and heartless king (McCarter: 290; Gunn 1978: 97).

Scholars have pointed out Bathsheba's resourceful and active participation in this plot based on the evidence in 1 Kgs 1–2 (Aschkenasy: 113–15; Bailey 1990: 89–90; Klein: 58–64). In 2 Sam 11–12, we see the portrayal of Bathsheba as a vulnerable, powerless young woman. In 1 Kgs 1–2, Bashsheba's depiction is strikingly changed as a powerful elderly queen who actively participates in the political affairs of legitimizing Solomon her son as the heir to the throne. What caused such a change in Bathsheba? There is only a huge gap in between these two places and not much explanation, as we would like. However, there is a strong possibility that Bathsheba took her part in the political affairs of 1 Kgs 1–2 not because she wanted to exercise her power for her own advancement but because she wanted to protect her own son over against Adonijah's attempt to claim the throne by himself (1 Kgs 11:5). The fact that it was Nathan who approached Bathsheba and initiated the counterplan to put Solomon to the throne (1 Kgs 1:11–14) strongly supports this interpretation.

From a cultural comparison, Rai Ok Choi enlists at least nine ancient Korean folktales that portray the instances of a *powerful* man taking a *powerless* woman, which he calls "Royals Taking Common Women Folktales" (91–93). In most cases the takers are kings or high nobles. Except for a few cases in which these common women are spouses of officials (i.e., a woman's husband works as a royal official and so the king would have a legitimate chance to run into her), most women are of lower classes. One condition is without exception: these women have to be beautiful and intelligent (cf. Gen 12:11, 14; 26:7; 1 Sam 25:3; 2 Sam 11:2). In most stories, surprisingly, these powerless women are either *married* or *engaged.* As mentioned in the prosecutor's argument above, due to the custom that enforces chastity, these women would either prudently run away or strongly resist. To do so under the invincible power, of course, meant a tragic end. Choi surmises the common structure of the key contents of these folktales, apparent in the questions as follows:

a. What is the status of the husband?
b. What is the status or appearance of the wife?
c. How is the common man able to marry such a beautiful woman?
d. How does that woman become noticed by the noble?
e. What is the status of the noble/king?
f. How does the king approach the woman?
g. How does the king treat her husband?
h. What is the woman's reaction?
i. What happens to the couple afterwards?
j. What happens to the king afterwards? (94–95)

To compare each element with each folktale would require another major study. We will note some significant features for the sake of our comparison. First of all, these kings are lustful takers. Some are witty and shrewd, as in the "Do Mi folktale" (a folktale during the early period of three kingdoms in ancient Korea, ca. first century B.C.E.–first century C.E.), in which the king tricks the husband, Do Mi, who is a low-class farmer, into a debate that women do not keep fidelity (Choi: 94–96). But most kings are depicted as flat-out wicked. Second, in most stories, the plot regarding how the couple falls in love with each other and/or gets married is missing or lost. Third, the husbands are clearly no match to the king and thus are persecuted. In the Do Mi folktale, the husband wins the debate as his wife does not fall into the test devised by the king. Keeping Do Mi in the palace, the king disguises one of his servants as a king and sends him to Do Mi's home, telling Do Mi's wife that he would take her as his wife. She agrees but disguises her maidservant and sends her to the king instead. This enrages the king, who then pokes out Do Mi's eyes and banishes him to a remote exile. Fourth, the women are mostly married or engaged to lowly men. Sometimes they were coaxed but mostly forced by the king or noble. This forceful power meant that if they resisted, they would meet a tragic end. In the Do Mi folktale, *after* poking out the husband's eyes and expelling him, the king devises to take his wife into the palace and sleep with her. Do Mi's wife says to the king that, now that she has lost her husband, she would no longer be able to refuse the king's request and that because she happened to be unclean, she would go, wash herself, and return. This excited king believes her. But she escapes and meets her blinded husband in another country for a new bitter-sweet life. Fifth, this king clearly has no rival when it comes to power. Unless the king himself repents and changes his mind, it is never a fair game. Sixth, whereas some later versions do have the stories of a divine retribution and/or a happy ending, in most cases, such would be only wishful thinking. The wicked king does not get punished, and the poor couple's justice would never be found. This theme is clearly representative of the agony and bitterness (which is called "han" in Korean) of the common people, for whom vindication would hardly have been possible in their real life. Although there are differences, many of the above features, especially with regard to the king's force of power against the lowly husband and his wife, are strikingly similar to our biblical narrative.

Such similarity of power abuse also continues in today's culture and society, where it is not the taker but the victim who often becomes doubly or triply victimized by the violence present within the visible and invisible social pressures, the historian's biased description, and the people's misinformed or prejudiced value judgment (cf. Exum 1993: 170–76). In the cases of domestic violence, we learn that all too often the victims become silent—that is to say, silenced—about what, how, and especially who is involved in tragic incidents. In the cases of sexual harassment, even in today's industrialized Korea, power dynamics easily overpower any possibility of resistance in the victims. If women speak out, the society tends to condemn not the men but the women. Society accuses the victims, saying "You are a loose, damaged (no longer chaste) person," "You must have asked for it" (Exum 1993: 188–90), and so on. Sadly, it is a no-win situation for women. Thus, the ongoing vicious cycle is prolonged not only by the harassers but also by the villainous society and vulnerable victims. By the same token, even in international affairs, many criminal cases (e.g., the Korean "comfort-women" during the Japanese colonization period of the World War II) have been forgotten not only by the outright denial of many countries but also by the very survivors who have been so afraid that they could only resort to hiding.

Similar dynamics of power abuse against the powerless can further be found in the psychological analysis of the inequality of status and power between David and Bathsheba (Miller 1976: 3). The factor of inequality seems to be working in favor of David's fulfillment of his sexual attraction and desire. Bathsheba seems to be aware of the power gap between her and David, and her awareness of David's status and her own status seems to have put her, psychologically speaking, in a position of weakness. Working with the assumption that one's psychological state is oftentimes subordinated to cultural and social arrangements, it seems appropriate to suggest that Bathsheba's social location undermined her possibility for resistance to David's advances. The violence she suffers is "inherent in inequality" between her and David (Gilligan: 100). Indeed, David's sexual desire toward Bathsheba is very strong. Whether seeing and pursuing Bathsheba was initially well calculated or not, what is of interest for psychological analysis is that when he was confronted with the seductive scene of a naked woman bathing, he quickly developed a very strong attraction, a sexual desire, to sleep with her. In pursuing Bathsheba, the object of his strong desire, David acts not only secretly but also quickly. He is very assertive in his pursuit. First he inquires about the woman. Second, when he identifies who she is, his actions become aggressive. He sends messengers to get her. David's assertiveness is turned into aggression. He is determined to go after the object of his sexual desire. In fact, his passionate desire, coupled with power, is turned into sexual violence—he abducts Bathsheba and sleeps with her. He goes from being assertive to being aggressive, and finally he commits a violent act by sleeping with a married woman.

Here there is a parallel process in relation to Uriah. The pattern of passion observed in his action toward Bathsheba is also present in his dealing with Uriah. David assertively calls for him to come from the battleground; he aggressively sends him to his house/wife; he questions Uriah when he does not comply with his commands to "wash" his feet and go to his wife; he designs alternative plans to have him do what he wants by making Uriah drunk. But still Uriah "did not go down to his house" (2 Sam 11:13). Without a doubt, David's actions display a lot of passion in the way he seeks to fulfill his desire and cover his mistakes. Because his wishes are frustrated by Uriah's noncompliance, his final plan turns into murder as he sends Uriah to be killed. His assertiveness and aggression turn into violence. As Miller (1976: 87) suggests, because aggression is rewarded in some measure, it can get one somewhere if one is a man. In the case of David, it gets him what he desires because of both his gender (in relation to Bathsheba) and his power (in relation to both Bathsheba and Uriah). Miller adds,

> To give [aggression] up altogether can seem like the final degradation and loss—loss especially of manhood, sexual identification. In fact, if events do not go your way you may be inclined to increase the aggression in the hope that you can force situations. This attempt can and often does enlarge aggression into violence. (1976: 87)

This is what has happened in our text. David's assertiveness and aggression are enlarged into violence toward both Bathsheba and Uriah. In relation to Bathsheba, David's status, power, and gender overpower her and, in the end, victimize her.

The psychological perspective of Jean Baker Miller also helps us see that the psychological dynamics between David and Bathsheba reveal a basic (traditional) domination-subordination model of relations between men and women (1976: 85). Here David displays what Miller has called "the set of traits held out for male identity" (88). They include, "advance at any cost, pay any price, drive out all competitors, and kill them if necessary" (ibid.). These "manly virtues" (ibid.), historically exercised by most men with power, are clearly present in David's pursuit of Bathsheba, the object of his desire. Clearly, pursuing Bathsheba does not involve a sense of advancement for David, but it surely involves passionate self-determination to fulfill his desire and wish. Anything that threatens to frustrate the fulfillment of this desire must be removed. In light of what David has done in our text, these virtues can be paraphrased as follows, "Pursue what you desire at any cost, do whatever it takes, remove anything or anybody who gets in your way or frustrates your wishes and desires, kill him/her if necessary." Clearly, David is a calculator in this scenario. He has manipulated Bathsheba and Uriah, and he has fulfilled his wishes. His aggressiveness is rewarded.

We now turn to Bathsheba. Why did she come to David when he called for her? Why did she yield to his advances? Could she have acted differently? Was she aware of her ability to exert effective action in her own behalf against David's passionate desire? Why didn't she resist David? These are complicated questions to answer. Again, from a psychological perspective, we may note that the dynamics at play between her and David are complex, probably made more complex by the interplay between David's aggressive pursuit (probably a threatening pursuit), his personal and political power, and Bathsheba's status. There may also be Bathsheba's personal factors at play as well: her husband is absent, so she probably is lonely, and this makes her vulnerable. These factors may point to her state of psychological weakness when faced with an aggressive and powerful man's passionate desire to sleep with her.

Following Miller, just as David has been described as displaying characteristics of traditional manhood, we can infer that Bathsheba might be viewed as displaying traditional notions that women are meant to be submissive, docile, and compliant in relation to men—especially when power is involved. Such cultural expectations might have impinged on her psychological state and, therefore, have controlled her behaviors and responses to David (Miller 1976: 6). The position assigned to women in the ancient world (submission, dependency, and subordination) and the cultural expectations must have influenced the psychological structuring of life and, therefore, made it difficult for Bathsheba to resist David's advances (28).

In her discussion of domination and subordination, Miller notes that subordinates are always "described in terms of, and encouraged to develop, personal psychological characteristics that are pleasing to dominant groups" (7). She further adds that "if subordinates adopt these characteristics they are considered well-adjusted" (ibid.). This might have been the case with Bathsheba. She must have been operating under these cultural prescriptions and psychological forces that made her respond in the way she did—compliance. If we follow Miller's perspective, we may suggest that since women lived under the major prescriptions that they please and serve men, they were predisposed psychologically to be victims of desires such as David's (33). As Miller argues, dominant groups (and persons) "usually impede the development of subordinates and block their freedom of expression and action" (7). David's aggressiveness and power, combined with cultural prescriptions, psychologically speaking, overpowered Bathsheba and rendered her unable to resist David's advances. These forces silenced her and deterred her from acting in defiance of David's moves. These psychological forces, amid cultural dynamics and expectations, limited her possibilities and controlled her behavior. As Miller comments on contemporary women's situation of subordination,

> In a situation of inequality the woman is not encouraged to take her own needs seriously, to explore them, to try to act on them as a separate individual. She is enjoined from engaging all of her own resources and thereby prevented from developing some valid and reliable sense of her own worth. Instead, a woman is encouraged to concentrate on the needs and development of the man (18).

We wonder if these dynamics are not operative in Bathsheba, in relation to David's pursuit of her. We must ask, though, What if Bathsheba refused to comply with these aggressive advances? What if she resisted him? What would have happened? What would have been the outcome of David's wishes and desires being frustrated? Although we do not know for sure, we can speculate. Having the situation of Uriah as the only source for our psychological reflection, we can suggest that what happened to Uriah, or some version of it, would have happened to her as well. Uriah's noncompliance with David's suggestions, commands, and manipulations cost him his life. Perhaps Bathsheba was very much aware of this possibility, and the rootedness of her psychological state in the aforementioned dynamics made her opt for the course of action and response we have in our text. Because she could not move out of her psychologically restricted place, concern for "survival" (Miller 1976: 10) led her to the course of action she took. Both Carol Gilligan (110) and Jean Baker Miller (1976: 10, 93) have noted how women victims of male aggression and violence tend to pull back from resistance and how, even when they have attempted to resist, in the end refuse to follow through on the course of resistance. Concern for survival makes them choose a different course of action.

Indeed, Bathsheba is a victim of David's aggressive desire, his personal and political power, cultural forces, and their psychological underpinnings on her. She is not a willing participant in her dealings with David, nor is there evidence, on the basis of the above psychological analysis, that she participated in the plot to kill her husband. Therefore, she is an innocent victim.

4. PREGNANT PASSION AND PASSIONATE READING

As the above study illustrates, we have two theses (*both* prosecutor's *and* defendant's arguments; cf. Kim 2001)—rather than one thesis. This would not be considered a good scholarly piece of work because it ought to stick to one "coherent" view. But does our biblical text really contain an unequivocal, coherent view? Was the narrator of this passage so concerned about being "logical" throughout? Or, alternatively, does this text display many "ambiguous" plots and notions as well as not display any at all? Certainly, we do not claim that this text is full of chaos (nor do we claim that all biblical texts or concepts are ambiguous). Rather, it is full of an ingenious artistry of literary puns, catchwords, and chiasm. At the same time, it defies succumbing to *our* own desire for coherence or logic. Hence, the issue is again not only a textual problem but more importantly a "*sextual* [both social—gender-specific—and textual] problem" (Bal 1987: 36), full of "ironic tension" (Yee: 250–51), and "politics … written on the bodies of women" (Fewell and Gunn 1992: 159).

This text is ambiguous—both compact and complex; its conceptual brevity and diversity can both fascinate and frustrate the interested readers. Why is it so? Because it is pregnant. The text itself is pregnant with many plots, ironies, and implications. This text starts with pregnant passion in a man watching a woman washing. This passion leads to the pregnancy of the woman. This pregnancy engenders the subsequent plots, pregnant with coaxing, suspense, fidelity, betrayal, and death of another man and many other men. Characters are pregnant with complicated and conflicting depictions. We focus on one example, Bathsheba: her bathing, her cry that she is pregnant, her absence, her silence, her reappearance, her mourning, and her pregnancy of two children in sequence. These depictions of one character create ripple effects on others in many divergent directions.

Reading from a psychological perspective, we may see Bathsheba as having a strong sense of self, displayed through her sense of agency, choice, voice (though minimally represented), and self-determination. In this sense, she willingly and proactively participated in the affairs between her and David. Using the same psychological approach, however, we may also clearly find that, from the standpoint of inequality of status and power between her and David, she is a powerless woman who was victimized by the conglomeration of David's power, gender, and violence. Reading from a Korean perspective, the text's ambiguity causes readers who are familiar with the ancient Korean cultural dynamics to ponder the possibility that she welcomed the opportunity to have the king's child and thus become a queen (Klein: 54–55). However, from the same perspective, a careful reader who remembers the ancient folktales that depict the ongoing injustice and violence committed by the evil kings will empathize with Bathsheba's fate of innocent suffering.

So, was Bathsheba an innocent victim, an opportunist, or a willful schemer? If we adopt the U.S. legal system, the above study will infer that she is innocent, that is, until proven guilty beyond reasonable doubt. To ponder differently, suppose we have a jury composed of six male and six female Bible-literate persons. Would we then have a hung jury? Will we ever know the truth about Bathsheba? Or is it legitimate or worthwhile to raise this kind of question after all? We cannot but get passionate about all these issues. Amid deliberate ambiguity, for the strong chance that she was really innocent, this text of pregnant passion beckons readers to be passionate, discerning, and ethical about the potential use of our own power, abuse, hope, violence, and silence.

CRY WITCH! THE EMBERS STILL BURN

Madeline McClenney-Sadler
Duke University

When Osama bin Laden effectively cried "witch!" against the United States, he declared our allegiance with evil and sanctioned the attacks that occurred on September 11. In light of that day—the day four commercial airlines were hijacked, the World Trade Center and Pentagon destroyed totally and in part respectively, and thousands of lives maliciously destroyed—an academic and religious vigil against modern-day witch hunts seems an exceedingly urgent project. Modern-day witch hunts are multifarious. Rhetoric concerning the destruction of the infidel, the evil foreigner who threatens the status quo, is commonplace from Kabul, Afghanistan to Capitol Hill, Washington, D.C.

In the United States, the most recent form of the witch hunt is characterized by racially profiling Arab Americans. Abroad, witch hunts have been characterized by Taliban executions (beheadings, beatings, and acid baths) of improperly behaving or improperly dressed women, girls, and men. In the Christian church, witch hunts are characterized by the gross maltreatment, ostracization, and intimidation of women, girls, the homeless, and nonconformists who conduct themselves improperly according to traditional standards. Each of these hunts is in a slightly different stage of development, bearing fruit appropriate to its stage—some fruit more repulsive and deadly than others. Nonetheless, each hunt brings an assault of some kind on the human body, psyche, and soul.

The gains that women have made in the United States ought not to be taken for granted. The ingredients for a reversal in our own country already exist. One imagines that a severe economic downturn, the rise to power of Taliban-like extremist Christians, and people of good will who keep silent unable to recognize the danger on the horizon could trigger a paradigm shift. At the least, we must learn from September 11 that when we continue to participate in or ignore modern-day witch hunts, whether local or global, we may do so at the expense of our own liberty.

In my essay, I use witch hunts as an analogue to explain the dangers of contemporary persecution in the church. I am not offering a history of the witch-hunt craze; rather, I am offering a hypothesis concerning the origin of what I have witnessed, experienced, and what has been reported to me in relation to contemporary churches. I propose that witch hunts proper are a thing of the past in the United States *de jure*; however, their impact continues to be felt *de facto* in the form of what I call purity trials, which I will define later in the discussion. First we review religious and philosophical tradents that fueled the search for witches and wizards during the pre-Enlightenment period in Western history. Second, because women were the primary targets for witchcraft accusations, we take note of the fifteenth-century handbook on witchcraft that defamed women and associated them with witches. These precepts heightened and continue to be used to heighten the rejection of women. Third, we review the case of the famous Virginia Witch, Grace Sherwood, and the significance of seventeenth-century sumptuary legislation to witch hunts; that is, legislation that attempted to control the conduct—diet, dress, and drinking habits of citizens. These laws reflected early modern Europe's paranoiac obsession with being able to look at a person and determine religious and class status and thus contributed to the witch hunt craze. Sherwood's case is used to illumine contemporary analogies. Fourth, we spend a significant part of the discussion exploring the contemporary panoramic of church witch hunts, which have been renamed *purity trials,* in recognition of the contemporary context in which persecutory behavior continues in Christian practice not only as a function of a desire to control women but also as a way to manipulate already-despised groups. Fifth, a structuralist reading of Deut 22:5 and 2 Tim 2:9 illumines weaknesses in modern biblical interpretations that punctuate purity trials. Alternative interpretations will be proposed with the aim of reducing the justifications for purity trials and increasing opportunities to create just and loving communities of faith.

In Search of the Witch: Strategies of Rejection/Exclusion

We can best understand the local context for contemporary persecutions in the church by understanding the ideological stem cells from which they gain life anew. I am employing the expression *ideological stem cell* as a description of the organic elements of ideals and to convey that these organic elements can be used to *re-create* dead or dormant ideals in other environments or time periods. In the case of modern-day witch hunts in the Christian church, the ideological stem cells of the early European witch hunts are used to give life to traditional theological beliefs. The ancient Christian belief or ideological stem cell that all evil is caused by the devil, the archenemy of God, provided one of the rationales for witch hunts, trials, and executions in Europe. Thus, anyone who practiced witchcraft was a heretic, and heresy was punishable by death (Exod

22:18). According to some records, the last execution for witchcraft in England took place in 1685 (Bostridge: 3), only a few years before one of the most famous witch crazes hit United States colonial soil in Salem, Massachusetts. Estimates of the number of people accused of witchcraft from the fourteenth to the eighteenth centuries range from a modest 100,000 to eight million (Ochshorn: 94).

According to early Christian demonology, the devil controlled witches and wizards, who were endowed with demonic power to move from one place to another in an instance. Witches (women) and wizards (men) could be distinguished by unusual marks on their bodies and unusual attitudes and perspectives. Medieval Christians believed that Satan's consorts met in nocturnal assemblies called sabbats, and their primary activities were reproducing with the devil, feeding imps, and leading Christians astray.

This essay neither calls into question the dangers of the occult, nor does it suggest that every single witchcraft case adjudicated was unfounded. Like many others, I call into question the use of religious purism as a pretext to persecute groups of people already hated by a society. That women were charged and executed at a rate of four to one is not simply a matter of coincidence. Nor is it coincidental that the vast majority of witchcraft accusations were made by people who had had disputes (usually relating to borrowing or sharing household items) with the person against whom they lodged a witchcraft complaint (Willis). Those typically accused of witchcraft were characterized by one or more of the following traits: poor in relation to their accuser, female, a widow, and/or nonconformist. The relevance of the witch hunt to modern churches is that their ideological stem cells live on in another form of persecutory behavior that I call the purity trial. The purity trial is a modern-day witch hunt similar to the witch hunts of old. Purity trials use religious dogma as pretext to expel a congregational nuisance, someone already disliked or hated or someone subconsciously labeled unclean by virtue of behavior, mannerisms, or attire.

The historical documents of early Western Europe are replete with examples of moralizing discourses that justify the need for witch hunts and trials. Reduced to their lowest common denominator, the justifications for witch hunts and trials are attempts to distinguish between the clean and the unclean. Given that religions and cultures everywhere maintain the social order by identifying clean and unclean objects and behavior, it is no surprise that the fundamental motives for ending witchcraft are consistent cross-culturally. At best, the aim is to bring unclean (antisocial/harmful) behavior to an end; at worst, the aim is to keep hegemonies intact. On a regular basis, the boundaries between the best and worst motives for witch hunts are blurred, resulting in exclusionary social practices and outright persecution. Consequently, where witch hunts continue around the globe, those who threaten the status quo are at risk for being identified as witches and wizards (M. Douglas: 723–26). The attempt to keep hegemonies intact will be the focus of this examination inasmuch as the ruling elite define the determinants of cleanness and uncleanness and use these to justify witch hunts.

In early modern Europe and the U.S. colonies, a simple syllogism guided the justification of witchcraft accusations: the unclean are possessed of mysterious undefinable powers to contaminate and destroy; people who have mysterious undefinable powers to contaminate and destroy are witches or wizards in league with the devil; witches and wizards must be exiled or destroyed (Cohn: 11). One purpose of this examination is to use some of the data that we have on the early European and colonial witch hunts to identify the lingering ideological stem cells that revive specious accusations and persecutory behavior in the life of the church today.

In a cross-cultural examination of witchcraft and leprosy, anthropologist Mary Douglas refers to an attempt to manipulate or ban an unclean person from the community as a *strategy of rejection* (M. Douglas: 723). That is, those in power use that power to expel anyone who threatens the status quo. As previously noted, the rejected persons often fell into a few categories: poorer than the accuser, female, widow, and nonconformist. Witchcraft was understood as a tool for retaliation after losing an argument (Willis: 29). Ordinarily, the person accused of witchcraft or wizardry had been involved in a dispute with her accusers, who blamed a recent sickness, loss of property, or death on the use of witchcraft for payback. In addition to accusations hurled between warring neighbors, many accusations were made by the church and the state against specific citizens. When used as a strategy to reject enemies of church and state, witch hunts received additional validation in the philosophical and theological traditions of the West. A brief review of a few of the concepts representative of the Western philosophical and theological traditions evinces the worldview that a person accused of witchcraft faced.

First, based on Aristotelian logic, the average European Christian believed that inequalities in society were naturally occurring and divinely preordered. According to Aristotle, "Again, the male is by nature superior, and the female inferior; and the one rules and the other is ruled; this principle of necessity, extends to all mankind" (Clark 1999a: 41). Likewise, the hierarchical relation between slave and master or rich and poor was considered a condition of birth. Second, evil and suffering were the consequences of demonic powers (Kors and Peeters: 43). Third, the ancient patristic concept that women were more susceptible to the temptations of the devil than men survived during the pre-Enlightenment period (Tertullian: 117). In his treatise on how women should dress themselves,

Tertullian exclaimed, "the sentence of God on this sex of yours lives on even in our times and so it is necessary that the guilt should live on also. You are the one who opened the door to the Devil.... all too easily you destroyed the image of God, man" (118). Fourth, failure to conform to the status quo indicated rebellion against the natural order, implying rebellion against God and alliance with evil (Cohn: 15). Although the Western philosophical tradition is not responsible for the witch hunts, in the volatile crucible of church politics the aforementioned precepts were easily drawn upon to justify witchcraft accusations. For example, in 1022 several clerics were burned at the stake for rebelling against the religious status quo. They were "denying that the body and blood of Christ were really present in the Eucharist, they denied that baptism with water has any supernatural efficacy, they regarded it as meaningless to invoke the intercession of the saints ... and they claimed to receive the Holy Spirit by laying-on of hands" (ibid.). Thus, religious purity became the handmaid of religious tyranny, and executions were used to stamp out the early formulations of what would become mainline Protestant theology.

Witchcraft accusations were initially handled in ecclesiastical courts, and in later years they were turned over to secular courts, which handled executions or imprisonments. However, prior to the twelfth century, sorcery and witchcraft were tolerated in Europe; it was understood that witchcraft could be used for good or sinister purposes. According to Cohn, there is little documentary evidence that anyone really cared about the existence of witchcraft prior to the eleventh century. What caused the change in viewpoint? At the point the ecclesiastical authorities connected witchcraft with devil worship, witchcraft became associated with heresy, and heresy was a contamination of the body of Christ that had to be extracted.

Despite attempts to protect the church from the devil's devices, the witch hunts amounted to little more than what Mary Douglas describes as a *strategy of rejection.* As the cases themselves demonstrate, for the average person a witchcraft accusation was a way to counteract suspected bewitchment from a hostile neighbor (see Gibson; Hill). Thus, witchcraft accusations may be understood as ideological disputes between the clean and the unclean: the rich and the poor, the bishops and the local clerics who challenged papal authority, the city people and the village people. What the movement needed was a system of thought to organize its operations.

THE HAMMER OF WITCHES

In 1487, Dominican inquisitors Jacob Sprenger and Heinrich Kramer produced a handbook called the *Malleus Maleficarum* (*Hammer of the*

Witches) (Kors and Peeters: 176). Almost overnight it became the authority on witchcraft: "it was precisely those characteristics of witchcraft to which the *Malleus* paid most attention that [suddenly] appeared all over Europe during the sixteenth and seventeenth centuries"(ibid.). The *Malleus* delineated the ways in which witches could be "found, convicted and executed."

Prefaced by Pope Innocent VIII's bull *Summis desiderantes*, the longheld belief that the average woman could easily be an agent of demons was rearticulated in the *Malleus*. With the pope's preface, the *Malleus*'s view of women received additional sanction. Kors and Peeters note that the influence of the *Malleus* can be accounted for by its comprehensive nature (177). The *Malleus* provided a historical summary of witchcraft and synthesized prevailing views and perspectives while offering its own prescriptions on how to abolish it. If the majority of people tried and executed for witchcraft were women, then the chief heretics and thus devil worshipers were women, and someone had to answer why. In answer to the question, "why is it that Women are chiefly addicted to Evil superstitions," the *Malleus* drew upon ancient theological discourses to explain:

> Now the wickedness of women is spoken of in Ecclesiasticus xxv: There is no head above the head of a serpent: and there is no wrath above the wrath of a woman.... All wickedness is but little to the wickedness of a woman. Wherefore S. John Chrysostom says on the text, it is not good to marry.... What else is woman but a foe to friendship, an unescapable punishment, a necessary, evil, a natural temptation, a desireable calamity, a domestic danger, a delectable detriment, an evil of nature paint with fair colours! (Kors and Peeters: 182)

The historical significance of the *Malleus*, Aristotelian logic, and the Western philosophical and theological traditions cannot be underestimated. Almost two and a half centuries after the *Malleus* and a continent away, Grace Sherwood had to answer for the suspicions that these tradents perpetuated.

GRACE SHERWOOD: THE VIRGINIA WITCH

Grace Sherwood is commonly known as the Virginia Witch. The lore surrounding her trial continues to enliven Virginian historians. Utilizing court records and oral histories, every year in Williamsburg, Virginia, the trial of Grace Sherwood is reenacted on stage. In 1999, while attending a play about Grace Sherwood's trial known as "Cry Witch," I reflected on how frequently homeless people in Washington, D.C., cited feeling demonized, rejected, and unwelcomed in churches as a reason for failing to seek assistance from Christians. While attending the play, I was also experiencing a strategy of rejection in my own church, although I would not have identified it as such at that time. Because of my own trial and the play that unfolded before me, I was understanding on a personal level what had been told to me in the late 1980s by the people I sought to serve in the Community for Creative Non-violence homeless shelter on Second and D, who often exclaimed, "church people treat us like dirt!" As I watched the play and considered my own experience, I understood the lamentations of my homeless friends on a deeper, visceral level. As the reenactment of Grace Sherwood's trial unfolded, the theological and political processes enmeshed in witchcraft accusations seemed to be close cousins to the theological and political processes that excluded the homeless in the District from places of worship. In each case, the lowest common denominator was a fear of contamination, a fear of the unclean.

Amazing Grace

The commonplaces of early modern European and colonial thought on class, status, and gender are clearly evinced in the court records of colonial Virginia's most famous witch. We should at least note the following details compiled from court records transcribed in the *William and Mary College Quarterly Historical Magazine* and the oral record presented in the trial reenactment "Cry Witch." Grace Sherwood and her husband were upwardly mobile, hard-working people. In the absence of evidence that they owned slaves, it may be presumed that they were not among the most wealthy of the landed gentry. However, James Sherwood's attempts to defend his wife's honor clearly demonstrate concerns about status in the community and perhaps a desire to spare his wife the fate of the Salem witches (1692). Ms. Sherwood herself came from a land-owning family; furthermore, it is clear that she and her husband knew at least some of their rights within the court system, and they were not too intimidated to avail themselves of its powers of mediation.

As previously noted, those accused of witchcraft were most likely to be poorer than their accusers, female, widowed, or nonconformist. Although we do not know her status relative to that of her accusers, Grace Sherwood fits into all of the remaining categories. Sherwood is described in the official Virginia Beach web site history as "strikingly attractive, strong-willed, and a non-conformist" (http://www.vabeach.com/history.htm). According to a cryptic note in the court records: "one writer thought that she was a member of the despised free negro class, while she was, in fact, the daughter of a substantial mechanic and small land owner"(*William and Mary College Quarterly Historical Magazine* 3 (1894): 96 n. 1). The author of the note has not accounted for the fact that being a Negro and a daughter of a small landholder are not mutually exclusive. If both female and Black, Sherwood possessed two traits considered characteristic of those familiar with witchcraft. One early twentieth-century historian noted that Blacks were prone to utilize witchcraft (Cross: 270–87), and in some accounts, the devil appears as a Negro to new initiates (Cohn: 8). In fact, any group of people or phenomenon that was poorly understood was vulnerable to being associated with the demonic. Interesting to note, the wizard's powers were often considered good. Wizards were men who used magic to "counteract the evil of the opposite gender" (Cross: 224).

Notwithstanding questions about her racial identity, Sherwood had been accused of using witchcraft for at least seven years before her trial, and the evidence suggests that there was a preexisting dispute between Grace Sherwood and several of her neighbors, who accused her of witchcraft. We have no idea what those disputes might have been. In the Hills' case, the dispute came to physical blows. Grace was assaulted by the Hill couple and blamed for the loss of their child. The records reviewed confirm the death of cattle only; however, the play draws upon the oral history associated with Ms. Sherwood. In the reenactment of her trial, she was accused of murdering the Hills' baby. The fear of maternal instincts gone awry or "malevolent nurture," as Deborah Willis calls it, and its association with witches appear in many witchcraft cases, and it is reflected in English literature. Willis notes:

> In Shakespeare's plays witchcraft is clearly intertwined not only with treason but also with gender transgression. Shakespeare's witches and the women associated with them, often endowed with masculine traits, regularly step out of place and become usurpers of the male role. Paradoxically, because they act like men, they also become associated with mothers: they recall that period of life when women dominate the lives of their male children, when the gender hierarchy of the adult world is inverted.... For Shakespeare, typically the witch or witchlike woman is one who can make the adult male feel he has been turned back into a child again, vulnerable to a mother's malevolent power. Witches were women, I believe, because women are mothers: witchcraft beliefs encode fantasies of maternal persecution. (6)

In an examination of witchcraft accusations between 1563–1611, Willis compares and contrasts witchcraft accusations made on the English village level with those made on the gentry level. On the village level, the witch's malevolent maternal features figure prominently; on the gentry level, the witch loses "some but not all associations with the malevolent mother; she is featured rather, as an enemy of God, and a rebel against the state, and her crime is betrayal rather than magical harm" (Willis: 14). On the gentry level, an accused witch had behaved in a manner unfitting for her place as a woman in society. According to Willis, the typical village accusation began between an older (post-menopausal) woman and a younger woman who had had words with each other. The older woman was poorer, and she had sought assistance from a younger neighbor who refused her request. The older woman would then go away swearing. When suffering (sick child, death of cattle or loved one) of any kind came upon the neighbor who refused to offer assistance to the older poor woman, the older woman would be suspected of witchcraft because she walked away swearing (32). In fact, her behavior had already suggested that she had witchlike tendencies. Begging to borrow something in itself was suspicious because it was known that witches would use objects belonging to others to curse the owner of the object, or the object could be used to remove a protective spell invoked by the owner and a wizard. As one historian noted, "wizards were men supposed to possess the same mischievous powers as the witches; but they were seldom exercised for bad purposes. The powers of wizards were exercised for the sole purpose of counteracting the malevolent influences of the witches of the other sex" (Cross: 224). Thus, the male witch's behavior was sanctified and the female witch's behavior demonized. Both men and women internalized the suspicion of women inherited from Western philosophical and theological thought as represented in the *Malleus.* They also inherited an obsession with outward appearance as a marker of worth, value, and familiarity with evil.

During the pre-Enlightenment period, behavior as well as attire were considered reliable indicators of goodness. We are particularly interested in the witch-nonwitch dyad. Specific guidelines governed these areas. If a woman looked and acted like a witch, it would be fair to make such an accusation. However, the definition of acting like a witch was not static and often included any behavior considered unbecoming to the "natural" behavior of women. The use of behavior and apparel as signifiers of identity was reinforced by sumptuary legislation or conduct codes enacted in England in the period from 1337 to 1604 in order to control the private life of citizens: dress, diet, and drunkenness (Rose: 27). Although these statues were repealed in 1604, the notion that one might look at another person's behavior or attire and determine something about that person's status and background was firmly rooted in English and colonial worldviews and persists today.

In a study on the "Use and Abuses of Apparel in Early Modern England," Margaret Rose Jaster notes that "no matter what other rationale exists for attempts to enforce sumptuary regulations, the dominant motivation is to inhibit class mobility, and that this aim of the regulations is furthered by texts that are informed by sumptuary codes" (26). Here Jaster is referring to pamphlets and sermons that were published in order to propagate the message of conduct codes. When sermons addressed women's attire, women were told that their need for apparel caused their husbands to become involved in bribery, extortion, and deceit. Again, we note the influence of the perspective of women as temptresses conveyed in the *Malleus*. Furthermore, says Jaster, "Williams [a preacher] mentions women who distract church services because they become prodigious monstrosities by their half-male, half-female apparel" (57). One of the greatest fears lying behind the introduction of apparel codes was the fear of disguise. Class and gender distinctions were supposed to be readily observable, and one who dressed in a manner unfit for his or her place in society was considered abominable (59). Expressing honor and reputation through attire became paranoiac obsessions. According to Willis, during the latter part of the sixteenth century, slander suits increased considerably as people attempted to clear their good names in secular and ecclesiastical courts (Willis: 40). Thus, as we examine witch hunts and purity trials, we must keep a historical perspective in view on the following psychosocial concept that makes persecution possible: gender, attire, conduct, status, and ethnicity signify degrees of piety. The closer one appeared to be at the bottom of the Aristotelian hierarchy, the more susceptible one became to a witchcraft accusation.

Although the respective ages of Grace Sherwood and her female accusers are unknown, we have already noted several risk factors that lead us to predict that she would be accused of witchcraft. She was female. She was outspoken. She was a self-assured litigant with or without her husband present. She became a widow, thus, a woman no longer under the authority of a man. According to oral history, she wore pants and danced in the field, thus defying the unwritten conduct codes that continued de facto after they were outlawed. In addition, she may have been a free Black woman. Sherwood's circumstances begged the question: Under whose authority was she operating? Her connection to an evil poltergeist would be a looming suspicion in the early eighteenth century. Although Ms. Sherwood was subjected to the ducking trial, bound up in the nude and thrown in the river, she survived. Under normal conditions, only a drowned victim was declared innocent of witchcraft. The person who swam did so with the aid of the demonic. Thus, a good swimmer survived in order to be hanged. Fortunately for Sherwood, the witch hunt was going out of vogue, and the educated elite thought them irrational. The records show that she lived well into her eighties and left 144 acres to her sons.

The hermeneutical commonplaces of contemporary Protestant preaching suggests that many Christians today would read the details of Grace Sherwood's case and render judgments similar to those of her accusers. This is due in part to the fact that the rules about attire, status, piety, and goodness that the state abandoned as unjust the church has continued with vigor. Modern-day "witch hunts," that is, attempts to cast out so-called uncleanness, dirt, and heresy continue to enliven the saints of the church. In appeals to godliness, holiness, and tradition, church authorities sanction new and archaic strategies of rejection under the pretense of religious order and purity. With uncanny similarity, contemporary strategies of rejection in the church have descended from the same ideological stem cells as the witch hunts of England and early modern Europe, pitting the rich and the middle class against the poor, men against women and girls, women against each other, and the conformist against the nonconformist. I call these ecclesial strategies of rejection *purity trials*.

Purity Trials

As with the witch hunt, women in general and certain classes of men (those with felony records, those considered effeminate, or those with drug addictions) are the primary targets of purity trials. Appropriating Mary Douglas's analysis of strategies of rejection in light of ordinary church politics, I offer the following definition of a purity trial. A purity trial is a strategy of rejection that occurs in four progressive phases: (1) an accusation of minor moral weakness is made; (2) the accusation progresses to the full imputation of filthy living; (3) the candidate is accused of causing *insidious harm* so severe that he or she can be classed as a public nuisance by consensus of the congregation or its authorities; and (4) actions are taken to prevent further damage or to exorcise the target from the congregation. Douglas's explanation of *insidious harm* is instructive as it relates to my concept of the purity trial:

> Awareness of insidious harm arouses public concern on behalf of the public good.... a successful accusation is one that has enough credibility for a public outcry to remove the possibility of repeating the damage. The preventative action will entail degrading the accused. However, though anyone may accuse, not all accusations will be accepted. To be successful an accusation should be directed against victims already hated by the populace. The cause of the harm must be vague, unspecific, difficult to prove or disprove. The crime must be difficult to deny, even impossible to refute. (M. Douglas: 726)

Drawing upon twenty-first-century commonplaces in Christian religious life, I now describe strategies of rejection that have either been directly witnessed by me or reported to me in the context of doing ministry. The purpose is to deconstruct the symbolic and psychic "witch hunt" invoked in strategies of rejection to exclude the following classes of people from full participation in the church: the poorer[1] and homeless, nonconformist women and girls, homosexuals and men with earrings, and unwed pregnant women.[2] As Douglas notes, accusations against them are successful because they are already disliked, hated, or viewed as suspect.

The Homeless

For the homeless person, dress codes, like those outlawed in the seventeenth century, are clearly operative in some churches. They lead to a purity trial. In the first phase of a purity trial, the minor moral weakness commonly imputed to the homeless or poor working person is slothfulness or laziness. An industrious person would not be in such a situation: dirty, unkempt, vagrant. A common refrain becomes more common: "A little sleep, a little slumber, a little folding of the hands to rest, and poverty will come upon you like a robber, and want, like an armed warrior" (Prov 6:10–11 NRSV). Even the most socially critical and informed minds resort to accusations such as "he did it to himself." The Aristotelian hierarchy of status becomes operative, and, similar to the way the panel of women searched Grace Sherwood, the elite act as if it is their God-given right to begin a search for evidence of uncleanness and demonic influences.

In the case of the poor or homeless person, the second stage of a purity trial, an imputation of filthy living, is reached almost immediately. After the imputation of filthy living has been made, the trial moves to stage three and the poor or homeless person becomes a public nuisance to the congregation. Complaints are made to the governing authorities, and various strategies of rejection are employed: if the homeless population is large enough, separate worship services are established to the "benefit of all." In some cases, the risk of contamination becomes so great that the entire church moves to a new location in the suburbs; in other cases, the homeless person or poor person is *offered* an opportunity to receive new clothes and "clean up." The *offer* of help is often a veiled way to coerce conformity to middle-class tastes. We can be sure of this by examining a popular response to refused assistance. When a working poor or homeless person is pleased with her industrious use of thrift-store or secondhand clothes, it can be an insult to her faith and intelligence to suggest that God requires new attire for worship. However, her adamant refusal to receive help (change attire) is frequently

---

1 It appears that congregations view poverty and class relative to the average income of members.

2 The targets of strategies of rejection however are not limited to those listed.

viewed as unappreciative, rebellious, disobedient, and/or contentious—additional indicators of "demonic" influences. A homeless person who acquiesces and changes under these coercive conditions knows intuitively that something is inherently unchristian about purity trials; however, the need for community acceptance is a compelling reason to keep silent. Silence is rarely the response given by the next group of targets. It is precisely their failure to keep silent that makes them suspicious. What is true for the homeless person is equally true for others who fail to meet the unwritten rules of middle-classdom.

Nonconformist Women and Men

Nonconformist Christian women and men are people who define themselves in relationship to themselves and God only. They usually seek neither to control or be controlled but simply to be who they are in Christ. They are usually transparent, speak what they believe without apology, while at the same time valuing the thoughts of others as well. This kind of confidence can be unnerving to women and men who have built personal identities around overly submissive adherence to church doctrine, dogma, and tradition. Men are typically rewarded for nonconformity, for sounding a trumpet as a lone warrior in the wilderness, unless they are sounding trumpets on behalf of female nonconformists. For this reason, their plight is considered similar to that of nonconformist women. Their association with such women is often treated as a form of contamination. An accusation of unsaved, liberal or licentious, is the beginning of the purity trial for such persons in the average Christian church.

If a nonconforming woman adopts traditional attire, she may be able to delay the onset of a purity trial; however, eventually, if she asserts her spiritual views often enough, she will be lumped together with the women who wear short skirts, low-cut tops, or pants in worship. Like Sherwood, by refusing to accept preestablished cultural conventions, women such as these have crossed the boundary put in place by the Aristotelian concept of a natural hierarchy and God-ordained order. Like Sherwood, she is out of order. Like Sherwood, when she became a widow, a nonconforming woman is a threat because she is no longer under the authority of a man. With respect to attire, the obvious must be noted. Attitudes toward attire are relative. What is short in length to one person is acceptable to another, what is low-cut to one person may be tastefully fashionable to another. In one case, a pantsuit may be evidence of fully covered modesty; to another, it is evidence of cross-gender attire. A man in a suit without a tie is considered dressed up in one instant and disrespectful in another. Yet the absence of a consensus does not hinder the purity trial.

Slowly and then with rapid speed, concerned members begin to express their distaste for the opinions or attire, as the case may be, of nonconformist women and men. Failure to comply with conduct codes betrays an inability to accept the will of governing authorities, and the collective consciousness of the congregation considers, but rarely utters, its belief that the target is influenced by rebellious spirits. A wizard is needed to counteract the bewitchment. The leadership may use its wizardry as a part of the process or sit silently by as others manage the trial. Nonetheless, when the target's beliefs or behavior is unaltered, what began as curiosity and intellectual engagement becomes outright ostracization and gross maltreatment. Fear is the motivating factor in these scenarios. The forces of change appear to be on the horizon, and those with entrenched religious dogmas view the forces of nonconformity as fundamentally "sinful" and "unchristian," code words for a lexical field that includes out of bounds, dirty, improper, sinful, disobedient, offensive, pagan, and evil. As Douglas points out, in strategies of rejection and exclusion, the offense must be difficult to deny and impossible to refute. When a woman is charged with "offending" or "leading women astray" by wearing pants or "enticing men" by wearing a low-cut shirt, she cannot argue against what other's claim to *feel* due to her attire.

The nonconforming person is thus identified as a public nuisance in the third phase of the purity trial. Unwanted stares, harassing comments, religious indignation, judgment, and persecutory name-calling figure prominently in this period. The fourth and final stage approaches at which point official statements are adopted by the leadership or a small group of the congregation to undo the bewitching that has occurred as a result of nonconformist behavior. Indeed, many are bewitched. The feelings described by offended parties resemble descriptions of bewitchings. They lack control of visceral reactions to outward appearances or spiritual difference. "It hurts me to see that" or "that music he plays is offensive" is a common refrain; the obsession turns to a possession. A demonic influence must be involved. In traditional churches, the teachable moment gives way to a witch hunt. Action must be taken to stop the spell that has been cast before further insidious harm is done by the congregational nuisance. A contamination has occurred, and the dirt must be removed or exorcised before everyone is bewitched—even if only a few care at all. The offended parties are convinced that their coercive instructions fall under the category of religious instruction aimed at the good of the target; all the while, they are tearing down self-esteem and confidence. The damage can only be seen in the long term, when young targets mature, when the adult target receives affirmation in other worshiping communities, or when church attendance falls off. Like the witch hunts, few recognize purity trials for what they are and challenge them, and like our sisters in Afghanistan,[3] failure to recognize, identify and challenge persecutory behavior can easily lead to an erosion of the God-given liberties that women and men generations before us fought for on our behalf in the body of Christ.

My personal experience of a purity trial came as a result of wearing a pantsuit to church and submitting a grievance about a sexual advance from a deacon. The full case will be presented in a separate article on sexual harassment and the Black church. In summary, a sexual harassment complaint was deemed suspect (I was told) because I lodged a verbal and written complaint against a conservative ruling on church attire. In the first phase of the trial, an accusation of minor moral weakness was made: "she wears pants to church." We then entered the second phase of the purity trial. An explicit imputation of filthy motives was made against me because I asked if the person who had made a sexual advance toward me had anything to do with creating the official dress code (since he had also been harassing me about my attire, arguing that I was "leading women astray"). The imputation of filthy motives was used by the pastor and some members of the deacon board to impugn my character and discredit the timing of the sexual-advance grievance. In the third phase, my grievance and inability to acquiesce to the dress code caused insidious harm to the congregation. I was treated as the stereotypical scorned female compelled to rebellion by forces beyond her control—certainly nothing holy. Actions had to be taken to prevent further damage—phase four. The pastor wrote to me stating that in order to submit the grievance on sexual harassment I had to give assurance in writing that I would "give up all ministerial privileges" while wearing pants and promise to stay away from serving at the communion table. I was also required to "affirm in writing that the sexual advance grievance was not for the purpose of rescinding the dress code." I was utterly baffled and disquieted. After all, if I were dishonest, I could lie about my motives, and no minister served at the communion table or in any other capacity unless called upon to serve. What was the point? Initially I did not recognize this as a witch ducking. Yet to comply with this request meant that I would have to sink (give up ministerial privileges) to prove I was not a witch. Refusing to give written assent to the pastor's demands would require swimming, an indication of witchcraft. I complied and, like the witches of old, drowned to prove my innocence. At that time, I still trusted the pastor, and I assumed he was being forced to make those repulsive requests. Refusing to live beneath the veil of abusive power, a

---

3 The organization RAWA (Revolutionary Association of Women in Afghanistan) is an exception.

burka of silence, and for the sake of justice, my own well-being, and the well-being of the women in the church, I gave up all ministerial privileges and made all assurances in writing as requested so that the grievance could move forward. As the imbroglio unfolded, I discovered that another female minister and many other women had lodged complaints over an eight-year period against the same deacon, and the pastor and many members knew it also. I made reference to this ongoing issue of harassment in my grievance and asked the board to take "substantive action." The pastor and board ruled that my sexual-advance grievance was "too subjective" and dismissed it. I resigned from the staff a month later after learning that the pastor would do nothing to investigate other allegations of impropriety against the same deacon. After a year of conversations with the pastor, hoping to find a reason to trust the leadership enough to continue submitting to their authority while serving the congregation, I left with my spouse. I have learned, if nothing else, that purity trials are effective strategies for rejecting congregational nuisances who refuse to live beneath veils of abuse and oppressive traditions.

Eight months after our departure, the congregation conducted its own investigation and removed the deacon from the board during a church conference. Unfortunately, most purity trials in churches do not culminate in justice being served. This congregation was an exceptional one. Yet, with Taliban-like legalism, the dress code for men and women remained in effect. In cases such as these, God's love is obscured, and purity trials are bound to continue. In other cases, God's love is rarely even feigned, especially if the target is suspected of homosexuality.

Homosexuals and Men with Earrings

The connection between homosexuals and men with earrings is not common enough to make the rule, yet for many the two go hand in hand. It begins with slander. In the case of bewitchment by homosexuality, the simple assertion that someone is "different" functions as an imputation of minor moral slackness—phase one. At this stage in a purity trial, people presumed to be homosexual are then classified as either too effeminate if male and too masculine if female. As with eighteenth-century witches, body language, outspokenness, and dress habits are given extraordinary amounts of attention. In colonial North Carolina, ageism and a fat phobia characterized witch identifications: "her breasts [are] situated under her arms and the skin about her neck resembles a collar" (Cross: 229). Today, for gender transgressions, a single painted pinky finger, long nail, or clear polish or color-painted nails on a man or for women an extremely low haircut in the absence of other feminine traits such as makeup and earrings usually provide fodder for the inquisition in the early stages. This is followed by an informal inquiry about the potential candidate's comings and goings, who his or her most intimate friends are, marital and/or dating status, and level of spiritual development.

Once sufficient evidence has been mounted, the accusation of minor moral weakness grows to one of filth, and filth implies cursory or direct contact with evil. The notion that such a person will contaminate the congregation often grows in proportion to his or her actual involvement in the congregation. Direct questions are asked of the potential candidate in order to justify continued scrutiny. If the answers are unsatisfactory, the candidate is accused of causing insidious harm and therefore becomes a nuisance within the congregation, an eyesore, a weed that needs to be pulled. In the fourth and final stage, actions are taken to prevent or offset damage caused by the candidate. The preaching becomes acerbic and even toxic when issues of homosexuality are addressed. Handshakes are not extended as warmly or are withheld altogether. Since filth has been imputed to the target, a fear grows that anyone can be infected by his or her homosexual lifestyle, yet as Douglas points out, there is no way to prove or disprove that such infection is an actual threat—or not unlike other threats. By this time, the potential target has usually succumbed to the rejection and departed from the church, changed outward appearance in order to become more acceptable, or tried unsuccessfully to defend his or her position (like Grace in her countersuits) and thereafter has been directly asked to leave or convert and be saved. After all, the acceptance of the homosexual, like the acceptance of the witch, is heresy. Symbolic duckings are common. The target is theologically stripped naked in public, right thumb tied to left toe and left thumb tied to right toe and thrown into a watery abyss. Soon to be ducked after the homosexual is a man with earrings.

Men in earrings are public nuisances who cause insidious harm to those with more traditional attitudes about men and jewelry. Adherence to codes of conduct similar to those that were outlawed in the seventeenth century underlie discrimination against men in earrings. The status of men in earrings is thus treated with suspicion. Young men who wear earrings are often heckled and harassed by older men in traditional churches, where strategies of rejection are commonplace. On occasion, the filth imputed to a young man wearing an earring(s) can be counteracted by his academic achievement, musical ability, a girlfriend, or a feared and influential parent or guardian who comes to his defense. Thus, despite the earring, such a person may be sanitized and taken from the list of contaminating young people or adults. Yet if he is poor, has a criminal record, or defies the lead judge of the purity trial, that is, the senior deacon or deaconess who has instructed him that "men don't wear earrings," his treatment will be much like that of the person treated as a homosexual. He is likely to be written off, imputed as filthy, excluded from pulpit duty, and overlooked for participation in church functions, since, after all, "he might wear that earring." At the root of this strategy of rejection is a fear that other young men will be bewitched by the one who wears the earring and begin to wear earrings themselves, thus becoming gay, prison bound, effeminate—or all three. A man with an earring is an embarrassment not unlike another target of purity trials—the unwed pregnant woman.

Unwed Pregnant Women

The same processes involved in purity trials for the homeless, nonconformists, and suspected or actual homosexuals apply to unwed pregnant mothers. For all the revelatory advances we have made, the purity trial that an unwed mother faces in some churches is both mystifying and horrifying. Even progressively centered churches resort to the purity trial to exorcise a bewitchment of the pregnant fornicator. Evidence of the illegitimate sexual encounter is viewed as a danger to younger people and other singles. An unmarried woman's pregnant presence is treated as a contaminant in the church service. The evil that possessed her may latch on to others. At the very least, she is ritually unclean. There is no minor moral lapse; she is obviously a fornicator. An assumption of malevolent nurture, as Willis calls it, is made. The unwed mother is blamed for harming her unborn child by not having secured a committed father. In a rape culture where one out of two women are raped or victims of attempted assault, few consider that she could have been coerced/raped or incested or that she should not have to disclose the circumstances of her pregnancy. If she is assaulted, the denial of the attack serves a purpose for a while in her recovery. Whatever the circumstance, she is urged to explain all. Hence, the second stage of a purity trial begins. She is imputed with filthy living.

In the third phase, she too is a congregational nuisance causing insidious harm in the worship service. In nine months, one pregnant woman is expected to do what millions of unwed parents and several liberal revolutions in thought have not been able to do in two thousand years of Christian history: convince everyone that premarital sex is acceptable. Her mysterious powers to pollute the church have to be stopped, or the devil will take over and other girls will become pregnant. In the final phase of the purity trial, the church leaders must take steps "gently" to ban her from the choir, pulpit, and other positions of visibility until the pregnancy has ended. In one case, a young woman in a small West Indian town was so overcome by the negative attention she received— banishment from the choir and other activities—that she had a miscarriage. When she threw herself on the altar wailing her lamentation, no one comforted her. Her purity trial had ended. Whether she continued to sin or not, she was welcomed in the choir again, because at the very least she did not appear to be bewitched anymore. The feared heresy that she might spread—that fornication is acceptable—had been stopped. The belief that single unwed mothers contaminate and cause harm in the church is especially curious to me as a person who saw more than one single pregnant teenager or adult woman sing in the Baptist church choir of my youth, yet I (like others) still chose celibacy until marriage. I believe the only spirit that possessed our church during their pregnancies was the one my pastor's loving position invoked—the Holy Spirit.

What's Going On?

Influenced by the Western philosophical and theological tradition and presumed to be supported by Scripture, middle-class values are deemed representative of Christian piety and lend authority to purity trials. Two biblical passages are critical to understanding the scriptural impetus for purity trials: Deut 22:5 and 1 Tim 2:9. Although its historical setting cannot be harmonized with Paul's travels in the undisputed letters, 1 Tim 2:9 is part of a larger discourse addressing the author's need to challenge heretical practices and to provide order to the practices of the churches in Ephesus (Marshall: 359). New Testament scholars are not in agreement on the exact nature of the heretical practices opposed in 1 Timothy, but false teachings are widely presumed to be one of the author's main concerns (Bassler: 29).

With respect to purity trials, 1 Tim 2:9 is a key prooftext used against nonconformists and the poor: "women should adorn themselves modestly and sensibly in seemly apparel, not with braided hair or gold or pearls or costly attire" (NRSV). The widest application of this verse is utilized. Although it is explicitly gender focused, in traditional Christian rhetoric today its instruction is presumed to be equally applicable to men, and although it proposes modest dress as a standard, it is often used to make a case for middle-class dress styles as well. The strictures of this text is indicative of multiple tensions in the early Christian church, between men and women and the wealthy and the poor (L. Brown: 487).

Keener provides an excellent explanation of the class issues that likely influenced this epistle and its dictates on dress. The expectation in 1 Timothy was that Christian women would emphasize spiritual virtues rather than physical virtues and distance themselves from the ostentatious practices of some wealthy women (Keener: 105). One can easily imagine that the desire to imitate the rich in the first century is not too far

removed from a similar cultural ethos today. The popular African American and Southern maxim that "everything that glitters ain't gold" is a
contemporary expression equivalent to the truism that 2:9 seeks to
convey: core values cannot be represented in externalities. A wealth of
the material is not indicative of a wealth of the spiritual—implicitly, we
may add, especially with reference to the homeless, a lack of the material
is not indicative of spiritual lack. Interpretations of 1 Tim 2:9 are often
derived through eisegesis. The Greek terms for modesty, decency, and
propriety (κοσμίῳ, αἰδοῦς, σωφροσύνης) are exploited to make cases for the
class and personal preferences of the purity-trial interlocutors. The fundamental assumption of a purity trial is that the more in conformity the
outward appearance, the more in conformity with piety—the Christian
wearing the attire. This is the exact opposite of what the pericope in
which 1 Tim 2:9 appears is meant to convey. The real issue is not dress.
The pertinent issue in the pericope is accented in 2:10 "women should
adorn themselves ... with good deeds" (Dewey: 355). In its general application, the instruction was for men as well.

With respect to apparel, Deut 22:5 also shapes purity-trial discourses,
particularly those directed at outward appearances; its presumed thrust
is used to bolster teachings on middle-class standards of behavior and
dress.

לא־יהיה כלי־גבר על־אשה ולא־ילבש גבר שמלת אשה כי תועבת
יהוה אלהיך כל־עשה אלה:

A woman shall not wear a man's apparel, nor shall a man put on a
woman's garment; for whoever does such things is abhorrent to the
LORD your God. (NRSV)

Traditional readings of this verse have been limited to the understanding that women must wear dresses at all times and men pants. In its
widest application, it applies to behavior. Women must act like women,
and men must act like men. Such a reading fails to account for cultural
diversity within the worldwide Christian community. What qualifies as
women's and men's apparel and male and female behavior is culturally
patterned, having no transcendental value or immutable biological quality. For example, in Scotland men wear kilts, the equivalent of skirts, and
in the Arab/Asian world men wear tunics, the equivalent of long dresses.
Even though there are behavioral traits particular to men and to women,
we cannot escape our fundamental sameness or that our socialization
determines how differences in male and female behavior are manifested.
Our attempts to limit and rigidly define ourselves border on sacrilegious,
given the claim that the Divine intended for individuals to be unique.

More important, the limitations of uncritical interpretations of Deut 22:5 place Christians in precarious ethical positions.

One can only imagine the exclusionary practices that would arise in a multicultural Christian service where bare-breasted Christian women in West Africa, stomach-showing Indian Christian women, and tunic/dress-wearing Arab Christian men meet American deacons and deaconnesses. The kingdom could not come. The beloved community would self-destruct. A popular defense to the theological dilemmas that this multicultural scenario unveils is that Christians only have to follow the conduct codes for their culture of origin. Yet to suggest a relative interpretation for Deut 22:5 cross-culturally is also to suggest its relative meaning interculturally, thereby deconstructing the merit of the literal interpretation of this passage that so many uphold. Ironically, by conceding the relativity of its meaning, one comes closer to its historical and theological import.

A historical-critical structural reading of Deut 22:5 illumines its meaning in its literary context. Key terms and parallelism are instructive. The first key term is כְּלִי, which is translated by the NRSV as a man's "apparel." In biblical Hebrew כְּלִי has a wide lexical field and may signify equipment, vessels, and utensils of many kinds. In Deut 22:5, it appears in the construction כְּלִי־גֶבֶר, literally "utensils of might," that is, weapons. This construction may also be translated "vessels belonging to powerful/mighty men." The parallel clause that follows provides a clue for an interpretation of the verse: "and a man shall not put on a woman's *garment*." The second key term, שִׂמְלַת "garment," stands in opposition to כְּלִי, suggesting the comparability of the prohibition for women and men and yet complicating its thrust, since כְּלִי has a much broader semantic range. On November 24, 2001, CNN telecasted part two of the documentary "Behind the Veil." Journalist Saira Shah interviewed an Afghani male holding a gun; she asked, "You grew up with guns?" Her interviewee replied, "Our guns are to us like a veil is to a woman." His response is illuminating and exemplifies the Deuteronomic association of weapons and attire with gendered identity. We can safely assert that Deut 22:5 instructs that *something* particular to men that defines male identity and *something* particular to women that defines female identity is not interchangeable. Biblical scholars agree on this much at the very least.

According to Harland, Deut 22:5 is designed to keep distinctions between males and females intact. Specifically, it may be intended to proscribe women's participation in military operations and prevent disguises that could lead to treason or espionage. Weinfeld, Craigie, and Braulik view this as a ruling against transvestism. Cairns sees a relationship between Deut 22:5 and the condemnation of fertility rituals rather than transvestism. Given that Israel's neighbors observed fertility rites involving transgender performances, Cairns states that this verse has "nothing to do with unisex jeans, but aims to preserve the purity of Yahwistic faith by checking the encroachment of such distortions as manipulative fertility rites" (Cairns: 194).

A more valuable tool and the key to understanding this verse is to analyze its meaning in relation to other verses like it. As Weinfeld notes, the motive clause in Deut 22:5 "it is an abomination to the Lord your God" is used here and in other places only in reference to behaviors that are "two-faced": idolatrous images, child burning, sacrifice of blemished animals, transvestism, remarrying one's divorced wife, and falsification of weights and measures (Weinfeld: 268). If abominable acts are behaviors that betray a fundamental trust and communal ethic (true worshipers do not use idols, parents do not kill their children, priests do not offer blemished sacrifices, merchants do not cheat customers), then Deut 22:5 is better understood as a prohibition against men and women betraying the trust of others through the manipulation of externalities. However, Deut 22:5 is not concerned as much about what men and women actually carry or wear. The text aims to prohibit socially conditioned practices from being exploited by those who would intentionally act to deceive. Consequently, the application of Deut 22:5 is best determined individually. Like the prohibition of false weights and balances, which assures honesty in commerce, Deut 22:5 governs interactions between an individual and her or his neighbors. Men and women are expected to represent themselves with integrity.

Because the apparel that defines identity for one male may seem transgendered to another and the apparel that seems feminine to one female may feel masculine to another, modern interpreters who rely on biblical texts to shape Christian ethics will have to determine when a transgression of Deut 22:5 occurs based upon self-knowledge and contextual reference. This Deuteronomic precept advises its students to adorn themselves in ways that will prevent betraying the trust of the community. The same latitude used in applying Deut 22:4—"you shall not see your brother's ass or his ox fallen down by the way, and withhold your help"—must apply to Deut 22:5. Just as there are many other proprietary interests of a neighbor that one might be required to protect besides an ox or ass, there are many ways cross-culturally and interculturally for women and men to clothe themselves without misrepresenting themselves or deceiving others. There is no one standard, and Deut 22:5 is not an attempt to convey a standard of dress.

Consequently, this verse is marginally related to attire. Because the Deuteronomist's linguistic signifiers for difference are limited, the Deuteronomist uses attire and gender as metaphors for identity. To paraphrase in a way that moves beyond a wooden translation and takes into account the *Tendenz* of the Deuteronomist, I offer the following paraphrase:

> a woman shall be true to herself, not to a man's self, and a man shall be true to himself and not to a woman's self; for whoever is untrue to himself or herself insults the Lord your God.

To be untrue to oneself and so deceive a neighbor is to be two-faced. This reading goes beyond the assertion that transvestism is problematic. According to this reading, transvestism is problematic when it involves deception. In the past thirty years, the numbers of people born hermaphrodites (or intrasexual) have risen dramatically in the United States. For many Christians born with male and female phenotypes, transvestism may be the only way to adhere to this Deuteronomic ethic of personal integrity. The paraphrase above captures the thrust of the verse: exist in the community in a way that is truthful. If Deut 22:4 prohibits pretending that you did not witness your neighbor's property in distress, Deut 22:5 prohibits pretending to be something that one is not.

Ironically, a purity trial is a process of coercion that often leads its target to transgress Deut 22:5. In a purity trial, one Christian asks another Christian to misrepresent herself or himself by changing appearance or behavior to suit a tradition or cultural pattern preferred not by Scripture but by the interlocutor. The homeless person must change outward appearance, and the single unwed mother must behave as if being pregnant is a sin and a contaminant to the congregation. Purity trials steer away from the command to love and accept one's neighbor and drive head on into frivolous judgments.

In defense of purity trials, many parishioners and ministers contend that they do not impose their personal preferences on others and do not really believe that demonic influences control nonconforming behavior. Rather, the underlying concern is that others know what is expected of them in community and abide by those expectations. Defenders of purity trials maintain that modesty and temperance is the concern, not uncleanness or impurity. Yet if the targets are in need of coaching, they are free to request our opinion. Such is not the case in a purity trial. In a purity trial, unsolicited criticism is launched under the assumption that we are capable of discerning what another person's attire signifies about them. An observation of West Coast Christian attire and East Coast Christian attire should rid us of the presumption that specific articles of clothing or jewelry signify the same thing at all times and on all wearers. Purity trials teach their targets that outward appearances are reliable signifiers of inward conditions.

They increase the likelihood of narcissistic manipulation and scape-goating (Kirk-Duggan 2001b: 119). At the very least it is curious that a spiritual community whose Savior descended from an unwed mother would expel unwed mothers from choirs. Ultimately, purity trials, like witch hunts, have little to do with casting out evil (Gaskill: 268).

As previously noted, before the Enlightenment conduct codes were strategies of rejection used to ensure easy distinction between insiders and outsiders, rich and poor, common folk and landed gentry. Conduct codes before the Enlightenment sought to restrict upward mobility and to prevent the lower classes from conforming to the upper echelons of society. The purpose of conduct codes today has been inverted in the church; they ensure upward mobility—but only as long as one conforms. The purity trial has been the primary way that churches have perpetuated conduct codes in a historical period and region of the world in which they have been outlawed. We need to ask ourselves if we are unnecessarily driving people away from the church with our persecutory practices that lead many to feel unwelcomed in the house of God. Is it true that a person's saintliness can be judged by outward appearance, whether homeless, nonconformist, homosexual, or single and pregnant? There was a first-century prophet, to some, Messiah, who would answer, "No . . . absolutely not."

Conclusions

Christian churches are everywhere and at every time preaching the pregnant passion to love the Samaritans in their midst, to accept the lepers and eunuchs, to embrace young girls, women, and men tradition-ally viewed as suspect, yet purity trials undermine the delivery of that love. A purity trial is an unjust strategy of rejection used in contemporary churches to maintain the pretense of righteousness and the orthodoxy of hegemonic forces. A purity trial is a strategy of rejection against a member or visitor in a congregation who fails to conform to traditional conduct codes; it occurs in four progressive phases: (1) an accusation of minor moral weakness is made; (2) the accusation progresses to the full imputation of filthy living; (3) the candidate is accused of causing *insidious harm* so severe that he or she can be classed as a public nuisance by consensus of the congregation or its authorities; and (4) actions are taken to prevent further damage or to exorcise the target from the congregation.

If people *look right,* it is presumed that they are righteous. If people *look* as if their lifestyle contaminates, it is presumed that it does. Purity trials are prompted by pretense, characterized by unconscious fears of contamination, and justified by appeal to spiritual warfare, conduct codes, moral superiority, or tradition. To be ethical, strategies of rejection need first to be self-critical. A purity trial, however, is never ethical in a Christian context because it relies on an irrational perception of personal or communal harm attributed to a person we refuse to accept fully because of what he or she appears to have done to himself or herself outwardly. Purity trials honor local traditions at the expense of honoring the commandment of God—to love.

Some strategies for rejecting immoral behaviors are necessary, even desirable, when establishing Christian communal ethics—but they must be highly self-critical and justified. Although I would not support this strategy of rejection, it would seem much closer to something relevant to Christian practice if we admitted single pregnant women to the choir and rejected people from the choir who failed to bring a homeless person into their homes (Isa 58:7). What a purity trial amounts to is the gross maltreatment, ostracization, and intimidation of people that the Divine has called near. In effect, our critical response is—"go away and come again when you clean up."

The purpose of this essay was neither to challenge the notion of existential evil nor to question vigilance against occult movements. My aim was to identify the purity trial for what it is: antithetical to core Christian values. I offered my perspective on these processes and an alternative exegesis of two of their Scriptural roots, thus laying the groundwork for future research and reflection on the relationship between the witch-hunt craze of the past and purity trials today.

I conclude that current sumptuary rules in churches cloak class and tradition preferences and interpersonal power struggles at the expense of achieving the spiritual goals of righteousness, holiness and love (see Hill; Moessner; Poling; Skaine; Wartenberg). If there is any doubt that middle-class hegemonies have overridden core Christian values, one must simply ask why it is that we never see a church run by homeless people ostracizing the middle class. Current sumptuary rules in the body of Christ revive the ideological stem cells that undergirded the European and colonial witch hunts. Albeit they are dressed up and redesigned in the name of *purity*, but no less with a stake at the center. We must reread Deut 22:5 and 1 Tim 2:9 from new lenses and appreciate their fundamental instruction to live authentically, which also means allowing others to live authentically. What a person's outward appearance and idiosyncratic behavior signifies cannot be known through mere observation. Nonetheless, interlocutors presume to know and judge accordingly.

Consequently, I am certain that demonic forces are involved in purity trials whenever they occur. For this reason, wherever She is in our communities, we ought to defend Grace and duck ourselves until we have been exorcised.

Sex, Stones, and Power Games: A Woman Caught at the Intersection of Law and Religion (John 7:53–8:11)

Barbara A. Holmes
Susan R. Holmes Winfield

Then each of them went home, while Jesus went to the Mount of Olives. Early in the morning he came again to the temple. All the people came to him and he sat down and began to teach them. The scribes and the Pharisees brought a woman who had been caught in adultery; and making her stand before all of them, they said to him, "Teacher, this woman was caught in the very act of committing adultery. Now in the law, Moses commanded us to stone such women. Now what do you say? They said this to test him, so that they might have some charge to bring against him. Jesus bent down and wrote with his finger on the ground.

When they kept on questioning him, he straightened up and said to them, "Let anyone among you who is without sin be the first to throw a stone at her. And once again he bent down and wrote on the ground. When they heard it, they went away, one by one, beginning with the elders; and Jesus was left alone with the woman standing before him. Jesus straightened up and said to her, "Woman where are they? Has no one condemned you?" She said, "No one, sir." And Jesus said, "Neither do I condemn you. Go your way and from now on do not sin again." (NRSV)

THE GAME

In John 7:53–8:11, we encounter a milling and jostling crowd. A woman is being shoved from hand to hand toward the center of the gathering. If their faces were not so serious, if the stakes were not so high, one might assume that they were playing the children's game of "hot potato."[1] Too hot to handle, too dangerous to hold, she is hurled into the

---

1 The children's game of hot potato is played in a circle. The children stand close together, without touching. When the music plays, the children pass an object. They pretend

dusty semicircle. There is no escape and no point in denial. In an instant, she is dragged from passion to public sentencing. Jesus is there, and so are we.

When the dusty, frightened woman is hurled at his feet, Jesus is in the temple compound preparing to teach. Assessing the intent of the crowd is not difficult. Jesus can see that the woman is alone and that her partner in passion is nowhere to be seen. He also knows that if he scans the faces in the crowd, he will recognize the glint of familiar eyes. The religious authorities are here, and the tension is palpable. This will not be the usual morning Torah study.

In this pericope, gender and violence are layered over institutional power and religious authority. We argue that, despite outward appearances, the real issues underlying this crisis have little to do with the morality or criminality of the woman or, for that matter, her missing male partner. We also conclude that the narrative raises issues that far exceed the boundaries of the death penalty and punishment debate.[2] Instead, we examine how issues of alleged sexual impropriety and immorality are used as a smoke screen to mask power struggles.

In this critical text, power seems to be vested in the religious authorities. In fact, 8:6a seems to portray them as negative protagonists and a legalistic and conspiratorial religious order that harbors the intent to entrap and stone. Biblical scholar Brad Young argues that just the opposite is true. His thesis is that originally this story did not include the "testing" verse. He contends that its later insertion was influenced by Luke 6:7; John 6:6; and Matt 22:15 (Young: 2-4).[3] We will examine his arguments in the latter section of this essay. For now, it is enough to say that if we could ask the religious authorities and the indignant accusers of the woman about their motives, they would probably say that they are acting for God, in God's name, and to keep God's laws from becoming besmirched.

Moreover, they would probably say that the authority to act "for God" emanates from a special covenant with a relational deity. Men of

---

that it's a hot potato, and move it quickly so that they don't get burned. Without warning, the music is turned off. The person holding the hot potato must leave the game.

2 At the start of this writing project, we presumed that death-penalty issues would be central and critical to our analysis of this text. They are not, despite the obvious issue of whether the woman should be stoned and the correlation of her plight with that of so many others on death row throughout the ages. Instead, issues of delegated power and the corrupting influences of unbridled authority became more meaningful to our analysis and discussion.

3 Young credits the scholarship of Professor David Flusser of Hebrew University of Jerusalem for the development of this argument.

these times presumed that the mandate to exercise dominion/domination carried with it the right to enforce laws and punish the lawless. Such control is not a new phenomenon. For as long as people have gathered in societies, it has been presumed that armies, courts, and execution squads are necessary to the well-being of the wider community. Most societies delegate the responsibility of inflicting sanctioned violence.[4] They delegate to the civil government and even to the private realm control of property as well as interpersonal and familial matters. The same is true in this ancient society. Yet in our text, neither civil nor formal religious options will be needed, for the men in power are taking the accused woman directly to Jesus. The indictment of sex, sin, and condemnation becomes the basis for a confrontation of "the powers that be."[5]

According to the text, a woman has been caught in the very act of adultery. Biblical adultery is defined as sexual relations involving a man (whether married or single) and a married or betrothed woman (Lev 18:20; 20:10; see also Boaz). Religious mandates and cultural practices allowed a man to have illicit and even extramarital affairs as long as his paramour was single. However, a "woman committed adultery if she had sexual intercourse with anyone other than her husband" (Toensing: 107). The definition assumes that adultery is not only a sexual offense but also the violation of a husband's property rights. Because these rights were considered sacrosanct, violators could be stoned to death (Deut 22:22). Accordingly, adultery was a murky and dangerous charge even when witnesses emerged to say that they were qualified and prepared to testify against the accused. But in this case, the crowd does not want a trial or they would have brought the woman caught in adultery to the Sanhedrin. Since the woman does not deny the accusation, the only matter before Jesus should be a pronouncement of guilt or innocence.

So why is the game of hot potato being played in earnest? Is the woman being passed to Jesus like a "hot" property because the accusers have a hidden agenda? Clearly there is more to the story than is readily apparent in the text. This drama is unfolding in the midst of an important narrative intersection. The woman caught "in the very act of committing adultery" is also caught between major christological declarations and clashing Jewish and Roman religio-legal forces.[6] One cannot help but

---

4 For a comprehensive global review of societal reactions to the death penalty and other punishments, see Walsh.

5 See Walter Wink's books on the powers entitled as follows: *Naming the Powers* (1984), *Unmasking the Powers* (1986), *Engaging the Powers* (1992), *When the Powers Fall* (1998), and *The Powers That Be* (1999).

6 For a discussion of the conflicting Jewish and Roman laws pertaining to capital crimes, see below.

pause at this juncture of law, religion, gender, and violence to consider the identity of this woman.

WHAT'S IN A NAME: THE IDENTITY OF THE WOMAN

When we were growing up, children engaged in conflict with their peers would chant the refrain, "Sticks and stones will break my bones but names will never hurt me!" This chant naïvely denies the power of verbal abuse. If we did not understand it before, we are learning from the children who shoot their classmates that taunts destroy self-esteem and fuel anger in teens who are labeled nerds, outcasts, or merely "different."[7] In North America and in other global communities, some teen subcultures embody a shame/honor ethos reminiscent of early Christian communities. In a shame/honor culture, naming is important. Naming conveys identity and reveals relationships and potential avenues of control.

The woman caught in adultery is not named. A clandestine relationship makes her the focus of textual attention. As is the case with many women in the Bible, the writer of this narrative has relegated her to anonymity. What we know about her must be gleaned from the social and religious circumstances that surround the text. She suffers a similar fate at the hands of latter-day theologians who question the validity and sequence of the story.

Although some biblical scholars contend that this story does not appear in any Gospel text until the fourth century, others, such as New Testament scholar Bruce Metzger, note that the story has a ring of authenticity about it that marks it as a part of the oral literature and Jesus tradition that emanated from the first-century church (Metzger: 220; Burge: 141–48).[8] In fact, debates about the textual authenticity of the story

---

7 In October 1997, Luke Woodham killed his mother, then murdered two students and wounded seven others at Pearl High School in Hattiesburg, Mississippi. Two months later, a fourteen-year-old boy, Michael Carneal, shot and killed three people and wounded five others at his school (Heath High School) in Padukah, Kentucky. In March 1998, Drew Golden (eleven) and Mitchell Johnson (thirteen) pulled a fire alarm at their Westside Middle School. As students poured out of the building, they shot and killed five and wounded ten in Jonesboro, Arkansas. In the same year, Kip Kinkel, a fifteen-year-old student at Thurston High School in Eugene, Oregon, killed his parents, then shot two people at his school and wounded twenty-six others. In April 1999, Eric Harris and Dylan Klebold shot and killed fifteen students and teachers at Columbine High School in Littleton, Colorado. Seth Trickey, a seventh grader, wounded four people when he shot at a group of students at his middle school in Ft. Gibson, Oklahoma. In March 2001, fifteen-year-old Charles Andrew "Andy" Williams shot two and wounded thirteen other students at Santana High School in Santee, California.

8 It is interesting to note that Ambrose (d. 397), Pacian of Barcelona (ca. 350), Augustine (d. 430), and Jerome (d. 419) were familiar with the narrative. Also, a similar story is found

may mask ecclesial discomfort with issues of sexuality. Burge says, "the patristic fathers were unequivocal in their judgment on adultery.... Jesus' refusal to condemn the woman would have stood at odds with the mainstream of Church teaching" (Burge: 147). Because of this discomfort, Burge opines that the church hierarchy would have deemed it to be in their best interest to omit the text from the emerging canon.

Women biblical scholars acknowledge the textual authenticity issues but tend to focus their attention on the unique juxtaposition of the characters in the narrative.

> Jesus' focus is not on the woman alone but is evenly divided between the scribes and Pharisees and the woman.... what is striking about this story is that Jesus treats the woman as the social and human equal of the scribes and Pharisees.... Jesus invites both the scribes and Pharisees and the woman to begin life anew in the present moment. They are invited to give up old ways and enter a new way of life. (O'Day: 297)[9]

This approach emphasizes the didactic relevance of the story. Accordingly, we will not argue the authenticity of the text. Now that the story is included in John, the woman can no longer be ignored. Even without a name, she becomes one of the women of the New Testament who have a critical encounter with Jesus.

In the New Testament, the women who interact with Jesus are for the most part family members, disciples, commissioned as "evangelists" who "go tell," or recipients of God's direct healing grace.[10] The nameless woman caught in adultery is different. There is no indication that Jesus knows her. She does not ask for any help, healing, or mercy. There is no reason that Jesus should mediate the brewing dispute, except for the fact that they are both on trial, and in each instance the potential for the death penalty looms large.

On the surface of things, it seems that the woman is completely marginalized. Her name is not recorded. She had no voice in the development of the laws that now ensnare her. She had no ability even to carve out a moment of privacy to engage in a very private act, and she

---

in the *Didascalia Apostolarum* (2.24), a third-century document written originally in Greek but now surviving only in Syriac.

9 Holly Joan Toensing (96) argues that the pericope challenges "the escalating self-aggrandizement of most of the Jewish leadership in terms of Scripture or the Law and how they use it to judge others."

10 Compare Jesus' mother, Mary, the woman with the issue of blood (Mark 5:25–34), Lazarus's sisters, Martha and Mary (John 11:1–27), the Canaanite woman whose daughter was possessed (Matt 15:21–28), and the woman who washed Jesus' feet with oil (Mark 14:3–9).

has no advocate at the public hearing. Yet, arguably, she evinces a remarkable strength and resilience in an untenable situation. In the same way that Jesus will later refuse to participate in his rigged trial, she also keeps her peace.

During his trial, when Jesus refuses to accede to the renegade questions of a system of laws and religious presuppositions that have run amok, he is not deemed to be powerless and marginalized. Instead, it is presumed that Jesus is exhibiting character, strength, and faith in God. The same argument can be made for the alleged adulteress. She is silent either because her protestations were not deemed worthy of inclusion in the text or because she made none. In any event, there is no reason to assume that she is powerless simply because there is no evidence of her denials, no pleas for her life, and no attempt to blame her lover, as Adam did in the garden. ("Lord, it was that woman that you gave me!" [Gen 3:12]).

We rely on the work of women scholars from the two-third's world to support the argument that the woman caught in adultery retains personal choices and modalities of resistance even when she seems to have no options. A recent example comes to mind. Soon after the tragedy of September11, 2001, grainy videos were smuggled out of Afghanistan. A woman wrapped in her burqua was hurled into a dusty soccer field. She crouched silently on the ground surrounded by her accusers.

She did not speak, was not named, and did not struggle. Her crime was uncertain; her fate was not. As unlikely as it seemed at the time, the videotape of her death was seen around the globe. The brutality shocked the conscience of the world community and exposed the cruel treatment of Muslim women by the Taliban regime. Although the women seemed powerless, womanist/feminist/mujerista theologies suggest that power emanates from the ability to sustain a liberative moral vision despite oppression.

Womanist ethicist Marcia Y. Riggs suggests in her analysis of socioreligious praxis as the crux of a liberative moral vision that women who hold an alternative vision of reality may find themselves in conflict with domination system. This alternative view may differ significantly from the normative vision that is premised upon ideologies of domination (Riggs: 97). Riggs's suggestions for womanist liberation include renunciation, inclusivity, and responsibility (ibid.). However, this model assumes that the victims of institutionalized oppression have the means and power to seek their own liberation. The alleged adulteress may not have those options, but she does have the choice as to how she will respond to her accusers.

Mujerista scholar Ada Maria Isasi-Diaz refers to issues of choice as "living into our preferred future"(Isasi-Diaz 1999: 153–57). She says "our preferred future breaks into our present oppression in many different ways. We must recognize those eschatological glimpses and rejoice in them and struggle to make those glimpses become our whole horizon" (Isasi-Diaz 1996: 101). Her challenge to Hispanic women is to embrace the role and priorities of the "biblical remnant" and to oppose the systems of domination that threaten peace and justice (1996: 88). In essence, Isasi-Diaz recognizes the power of social, religious. and experiential interconnections.

The woman caught in adultery seems to be ensnared by these same intersecting forces. In silence she waits, perhaps with faith, perhaps out of fear, perhaps in defiance. We cannot know her state of mind, but it certainly seems as if she will not play their game. And in the end, without begging for mercy or reprieve, she is not executed.

The Case/Caught in the Very Act

Make no mistake about it, this is potentially a death-penalty case, at least under prevailing Hebraic law. According to Lev 20:10 "if a man commits adultery with the wife of his neighbor, both the adulterer and the adulteress shall be put to death" (see also Deut 22:22). The charge against the woman is adultery. To be more specific, her accusers allege that she has been caught in the midst of a tryst. The reader senses a suppressed lasciviousness and glee in the narrative. Sexual sins have always intrigued and incited the righteous, yet history records that religious and legal attempts to control, limit, and proscribe human sexuality inevitably fail.[11] It is ironic that when the forces of domination try to hinder, denounce, or condemn human sexual energy, powerful subliminal forces are unleashed, which divert and distract the faithful from their main purposes. The reality is no different in this pericope.

Note that the discourses of sexual condemnation usually operate on more than one level. In this text, the rhetoric of accusation is faith-based, egalitarian, and shaped by shame/honor, while the rhetoric and practices of constraint and punishment inevitably invoke hierarchical, patriarchal, and provincial presumptions. In matters of sexuality and gender there are great disparities between faith discourses of love and inclusion that contrast with actual practices of exclusion, fear, and rejection. Unfortunately, religious, legal, and even medical attempts to regulate gender and sexual differences tend to be both malignant and hysterical. In many

---

11 There is hardly a religion or society in history that does not define and condemn myriad sexual offenses, including varying degrees of rape, incest, bestiality, fornication, adultery, indecent exposure, corrupting a minor child, sodomy, prostitution, and sexual assault.

instances, ritual practices, laws, and social conventions exert power over female bodies, homosexuals, transgendered people, children, and minorities in ways that are detrimental to the physical and emotional well-being of the whole community.[12]

Sex is complicated business in religion and in society. Because men and women are attracted and repelled by expressions of passion, sex becomes a prioritized and selectively punished "sin," this despite the fact that neither divine nor legal realms elevate sexual infractions above any other. The belief that humankind is made in the image of God (*imago Dei*) tends to be restricted to spiritual, intellectual, and soul affinity. If the physical/sexual aspects of humankind were deemed integral to this divine image, perhaps we could see sexuality as sacred and good. C. S. Lewis says this about our conflicted approach to sexuality:

> If anyone thinks that Christians regard unchastity (sexual sin) as the supreme vice, he [or she] is quite wrong. The sins of the flesh are bad, but they are the least bad of all sins. All the worst pleasures are purely spiritual. The pleasure of putting other people in the wrong, of bossing and patronizing and spoiling sport, and backbiting; the pleasures of power, of hatred.... That is why a cold self-righteous prig who goes regularly to church may be far nearer to hell than a prostitute. But of course it is better to be neither! (Lewis: 81)

The woman caught in adultery is neither a prig nor a prostitute. The inference is that she has flaunted both public and private laws of morality. Because she has been "caught in the very act," she is not subject to the trial by "water of jealousy" referenced in Num 5:11–31. This was a remedy for a jealous/suspicious husband who lacked proof of his wife's infidelity. A suspected woman would be taken before the Sanhedrin to answer charges. If she denied them, she would be forced to drink a "guilt cocktail" composed of the dust from the sanctuary floor mixed with holy water and the ink from curses written on a scroll and dipped into the cup. The priest would recite:

> If no man has lain with you, if you have not turned aside to uncleanness while under your husband's authority, be immune to this water of

---

12 Any number of countries in Africa, the Middle East, and parts of Asia, and immigrant communities in Europe and North America, continue to subject young girls to the ritual practice of female genital mutilation. Practitioners argue that excisions are necessary to make the girls marriageable and economically secure. The fact that this effort destroys any opportunity for sexual fulfillment and pleasure is not an important consideration. Western cultures use similar operations to "normalize" transgendered (intersexed) children, with the same detrimental effects. See Rahman and Toubia; Walker, Parmar, and Austin-Smith; and "Female Genital Mutilation" at http://www.amnesty.org/ailib/intcam/femgen/fgm1.htm.

bitterness that brings the curse. But if you have gone astray while under your husband's authority, if you have defiled yourself and some man other than your husband has had intercourse with you let the priest make the woman take the oath of the curse. (Num 5:19–21a)

Then the priest would say, "the Lord make you an execration and an oath among your people, when the Lord makes your uterus drop, your womb discharge; now may this water that brings the curse enter your bowels and make your womb discharge, your uterus drop!" And the woman shall say, "Amen. Amen" (Num 5:21b–22, 23–31). It was assumed that, if the woman were guilty of sleeping with a man other than her husband, the water would cause her to suffer severely as her abdomen swelled from the water and the curse. If she were innocent, presumably, she would suffer no ill effects at all (Num 5:13–31).

Although this rather unusual ritual option was authorized, there are no recorded instances of its use. Brad Young argues that Johanan ben Zachai "canceled the use of the bitter waters" (Young: 5; Toensing: 109 n. 29).[13] Young relies on this cancellation and a comparative analysis of the reluctance of the Pharisees in other instances to impose the death penalty to support his theory that the Pharisees were not genuinely seeking the execution of the woman caught in adultery.

It is important to note that under Roman rule the Jewish people did not have the right to execute those who violated their laws. Rome retained that right. In John 18:31, the Jewish authorities acknowledge, "we are not permitted to put anyone to death." But if the authorities were not seeking her execution, why were they there?

Young argues that the Pharisees were seeking a *responsum* rather than retaliation. He describes the *responsum* as formal discussion with a learned teacher. The teacher is asked to resolve a confusing matter of religious law and application (Young: 65–66). But this is not a confusing matter; it purports to be a straightforward case of adultery until the case begins to unravel. The case unravels because there are matters of purity and holiness with respect to the witnesses that could disqualify them. There are embarrassing questions about who saw what and how they acquired such an intimate vantage point (cf. Deut 17:6; 19:15). Also, the selective accusation of the woman and not her partner specifically contravenes the law.

As in many colonized states, there are several layers of law operating at the same time in Jerusalem. There is the original Hebrew law of

---

13 Toensig cites Adriana Destro, *The Law of Jealousy: Anthropology of Sotah* (BJS 181; Atlanta: Scholars Press, 1989), 181.

Moses, which includes such provisions as the *lex talionis* ("eye for an eye"; Matt 5:38–39; Exod 21:24). The Mosaic code (as much religion as legislation) is the revered law of the land among the subjugated. Under this law, it is written that all who are convicted of adultery—both the adulterer and the adulteress (see Wegner)—are subject to mandatory sentencing (Lev 20:10; Deut 22:22–24). The guilty must be stoned (David-off: n. 13).[14] There is no discretion. Yet the man in this incident has been released or was never caught.

Superimposed on the law of Judea is the law of the Roman government. Under this colonial system, the death penalty could not be imposed for any crime by any Hebrew authority. This penalty could only be imposed by Roman authority, either *sua sponte* or as referred by a Hebrew magistrate. The Roman law, moreover, eliminated certain crimes, including adultery, from the roster of capital offenses.

> When Augustus enacted the *lex Julia de adulteriis coercendis* in 18 BCE, he sought to shift much of the power to prosecute adultery from private vengeance to public judicial process.... The law established a *quaestio perpetua* for the hearing of accusations of adultery.... The husband was required to divorce his wife as soon as he found out that she was adulterous, or he would himself be liable for prosecution for pimping. (Toensing: 112–13)

Under this system, the woman could not be tried until her male partner was convicted. Punishments in the Roman empire were meted out according to class distinctions. Upper-class adulterers might be exiled or lose property. The lower classes were subject to physical labor (ibid.). Curiously, by the time the hapless woman is allegedly caught in adultery, she is actually not at any serious risk of being put to death under either system. This is because, despite the unequivocal mandate in the Hebrew code that calls for her to be stoned, the de facto Hebrew system and the de jure Roman laws methodically thwarted the imposition of the death penalty for most crimes. The Roman system was by all accounts less strict (some would argue less moral) than the ancient law of Moses. But even the Hebrew authorities had by then constructed an elaborate network of procedural barriers to the imposition of the death penalty.

---

14 There were four methods of carrying out capital punishment in Jerusalem: stoning (Deut 22:24), burning (Lev 20:14), decapitation (Exod 32:27), and strangulation or hanging (2 Sam 21:6, 9). Davidoff cites Samuel Mendelsohn, *Criminal Jurisprudence of the Jews* 45 (1991). In his article, Davidoff reports that capital punishment could be imposed by means of stoning or strangulation. Davidoff also claims that the penalty for adultery with anyone other than the daughter of a priest was strangulation. In the latter case, the punishment was burning.

In a comprehensive article on this aspect of the Judaic system, Steven Davidoff cites the myriad procedural rules that were designed to restrict imposition of the death penalty (Davidoff: n. 22, 101–2).[15] As examples, capital punishment could not be imposed on the word of a single witness.[16] The testimony of multiple eyewitnesses could not conflict in any way. If it did, the accused would be spared. Women were not qualified to be witnesses at all, even if they agreed in their testimony, eyewitnessed the event, and numbered in excess of two (Num 35:30; Lev 17:6; Gleicher: n. 71).[17] Thus, men were the only members of the community with the power to impose the death penalty.

The death penalty, moreover, could not be imposed on circumstantial evidence or on a confession by the accused. It therefore did not matter that the woman did not deny her complicity. Even had she confessed to the crime, this could not have been used against her. Perhaps the most onerous of the prerequisites to capital punishment was the requirement that the accused be forewarned by at least two witnesses of the consequences of the wrongful conduct (*Code of Maimonides* 14, *Judges* 34:12-1,2; Davidoff: n. 22, 102). Also, the accused had to acknowledge the penalty before the crime was committed. Thus, an adulterer would have to be warned of and acknowledge the stoning penalty before committing adultery in order to be lawfully executed. These last two requirements taken together were sufficient to eviscerate the penalty altogether. But there is more. The accused could only be put to death if convicted by fewer than all twenty-three of the members of the Sanhedrin (*Encyclopedia Judaica*).[18]

Ironically, if there was a unanimous vote to convict by the twenty-three trial judges, the accused was by law entitled to an acquittal. Some

---

15 This article relies on numerous sources, including the Talmud and the *Code of Maimonides*.

16 See Num 35:30. "If anyone kills another, the murderer shall be put to death on the evidence of witnesses; but no one shall be put to death on the testimony of a single witness." See also Deut 19:15: "A single witness shall not suffice to convict a person of any crime or wrongdoing in connection with any offense that may be committed."

17 Gleicher cites ancient texts as the origin of this prohibition. He cites "a somewhat dubious reading of Deuteronomy 19:17—'And the two men, between whom the controversy is, shall stand before the Lord, before the priests and the judges.' Talmud Shebu'oth 30a; Talmud Baba Kamma 88a" (n. 71). According to Gleicher, rabbinical law allowed for a woman to testify concerning the death of another woman's husband in order for the woman to remarry (*b. Rosh HaShanah* 22a).

18 The Sanhedrin was the "great council" of Hebrews priests. The Sanhedrin functioned in some respects like our own Supreme Court to the extent that it was the supreme Jewish court of justice that determined the laws for the society. The high priest was the president who presided along with seventy other priests appointed for life. Twenty-three of the priests served as criminal judges who heard all capital cases before the Romans stripped the Sanhedrin of its power.

one of the judges had to disagree with the decision of the others before an accused could be executed. Finally, the pronouncement of the death penalty could properly take place only when the Sanhedrin met within the temple. After a time, the Sanhedrin moved its deliberations permanently outside the temple, in part to avoid the imposition of the penalty. Thus, a death knell to capital punishment had been skillfully and meticulously crafted to avoid, but neither defy nor repeal, the written law of Moses (see also Rudolph). This solution of sorts creates a pregnant pause between accusation and judgment. Clearly, crime and its punishment, passion and its suppression creates a quandary for those invested with the power over life and death.

WHO IS IN, WHO IS OUT: CRIME AND PUNISHMENT

To appreciate the complexity of the intercourse of power and punishment, we have to step outside the circle of accusers briefly to review the origination of crime and punishment in religious history. From the standpoint of Judeo-Christian narrative, it all begins with God. God has power and authority over all things and shares with no one. Exercising complete autonomy, God ejects Adam and Eve from Eden, spares Cain, and floods the earth. Yet in negotiations with Abraham over Sodom and Gomorrah there is evidence of either an erosion of divine ultimacy or a sovereign decision to self-limit. Abraham is empowered to challenge and contest a God-given edict, and Jacob is allowed physically to contend with God's angel (see, e.g., Gen 6:5–9, 29; 18:16–33; Sanders: 108–13).

From this point on, human-divine relationships become overtly covenantal with mutual obligations. Moreover, God continues to self-limit and restrict divine power (Fretheim). At the same time, the besieged Hebrew community accepts its God-given responsibility to enforce the laws in its fledgling society. Presumably, the authority is God-given because Moses brings laws to the people that are purportedly written by the very hand of God.

At first, the entire system of rules and procedures is entrusted to the priesthood. The scribes, Pharisees, and Sadduces, each from its own perspective, kept, enforced, and taught the extensive body of law to the common people. Later, in response to demands of the people, magistrates and judges were installed and empowered to enforce laws and impose punishment when required. Eventually, societies began to develop civil codes to further regulate human behavior.[19] This power to

---

19 Several authors argue that the purpose of the Judaic law of "an eye for an eye" and the many prescriptions for the death penalty was to control the natural tendency of a wronged

decide life and death, to mete out punishment, and to execute is weighty and uncomfortable. Out of necessity, in an increasingly complex society, and out of an implicit discomfort and desire to maintain both order and "clean hands," community members delegate responsibility to institutions, tribunals, and courts. The intent is to invest the authority to impose punishment, to guide and correct, and to seek vengeance through agencies that are distanced from daily life.

The story of the woman caught in adultery is a story of how members of the society try to complete the circle of divinely delegated power by bypassing authorized hearing tribunals and laying the decision at the feet of the Teacher. Instead of taking this matter to the proper authorities, this man who alludes to messianic authority will be sought instead. From God to humankind back to this Son of Man/God, the social "hot potato" of sentencing and punishment is being tossed back to its divine origins. The woman is literally caught in the center of this circle of transferred power. She is an ideal vehicle through which the competing societal forces clash. The crisis is local as it relates to the woman and the particular facts of the case but of cosmic proportions as it relates to the power struggles that ensue.

Violence, Power, and Gender

In societies, ancient and postmodern, power seems to be parsed out among those (historically men) who in exchange for the protection of the whole agree to control and govern smaller units of families, villages, and tribes. One presumes that the ultimate authority, other than the power of God, belongs to the body politic. The "nation," in turn, delegates its power to subsidiary units that may be regular, standing municipalities, militias, and courts. These arrangements seem to work well enough until the people no longer see delegations of authority as enactments of their will, then ad hoc groups, vigilantes, and mobs emerge.

These ad hoc groups form to channel, direct, and violently assuage the corporate angst that erupts over intermittent social crises great and

---

individual or victim to exact vengeance. See Nygaard; Jones. According to these articles, in ancient societies before the codification of the Mosaic law, the practice was to exact "blood revenge" in response to a homicide. Blood revenge authorized the next of kin of the victim to kill the murderer with his or her own hand. This "right" of revenge was practiced in an effort to avoid mass lawlessness, anarchy, and tribal or family wars. Thus, it does not appear that the law of Moses was so much a command to kill as an authorization for punishment in a restricted, regulated, systematic manner. As Jill Jones put it: "[T]he Old Testament scriptures endorsed blood vengeance and the principle of 'an eye for an eye' only as civil rather than moral principles" (140).

small. These implicit delegations of punishment to fringe elements of society includes the power to enforce latent societal desires for punishment or vengeance with unchecked malice and violence.[20] Violence tends to be an equal opportunity option. The man who slaps his wife and the woman who abuses her child are both on an interlocked continuum of violence with the child soldiers who shoot other children in the name of nationhood, and the teens who kill the classmates who taunt them.

New Testament scholar Walter Wink explores the effects of redemptive violence in purportedly civilized societies (1992:195–257). Societies seem to accept violence as an endemic and pervasive reality until its mimetic efforts boomerang into the community and the lives of its people. Although the myth of redemptive violence pervades most societies, on occasion, the profoundness of the power to punish overwhelms the people entrusted to wield it. An example in modern times occurred when then Governor George W. Bush was confronted with the cries for mercy for convicted pickax murderer, Karla Faye Tucker, from many in the religious and secular communities.

After struggling with the decision whether to grant a reprieve to a professed born-again Christian prisoner sentenced to die, Governor Bush stated: "I have sought guidance through prayer. I have concluded that judgment about the heart and soul of an individual on death row are best left to a higher authority." With that, Bush declined to grant Tucker a reprieve from the penalty (Graczyk: A1; see also Jones). Was the issue really about Tucker and whether she was worthy of a pardon or reprieve, or was it a power struggle between religious and political forces?

The woman caught in adultery is caught in the midst of a serious power struggle. Bolstering those who confront Jesus is the power derived from gender bias. In this early Mediterranean society, men were invested with power simply because they were men. The men who confront Jesus are husbands, fathers, brothers, and sons who controlled all matters within the domestic life of the family and, by extension, the community. What we now call domestic violence was merely the right of the patriarch to govern and control his family.[21] Whether it was the wife, the children,

---

20 The work of these functional fringe elements is pervasive. Billie Holiday reminds us in the song she popularized, "Strange Fruit," of the too-common practice of vigilantes who lynched and burned Black men in the U.S. South for even a rumored sexual glance at a White woman. In other times, women have worn the scarlet letter of social ostracism for no more than acknowledging their own passions.

21 See Rapaport. The patriarchal franchise to inflict violence seems to have roots in the Hebrew Bible. God is depicted as one who inflicts and sanctions violence (Exod 4:24–26), but God also identifies with the victims of violence (Mic 4:2–4; Isa. 19:19–25). See further discussions of violence in the biblical perspective in Wink 1992.

the siblings, or livestock who were out of control or wayward, it was the prerogative and civic duty of the dominant male to determine and mete out correction when needed (Toensing: 107).[22] Within reason, the patriarch could employ violent means to maintain control and to keep the peace within his family.

The patriarchal franchise served as the basic common denominator of the civic order. Even today, in our legal institutions (of delegated authority) the crime of manslaughter stands as a historical artifact of this idea of entitlement. Today a spouse may kill the other spouse upon becoming impassioned by witnessing his or her act of adultery. The perpetrator does not escape punishment altogether, but the act is not deemed to be murder: it is the lesser crime of manslaughter. No matter how vicious the act of homicide, passion trumps intent, reducing a violent and cold-blooded act to a lesser charge. The "domestic discount" serves as a concession to gender authority (Rapaport). In the simplest of terms, the law says that if you "heat my blood" and incite my passion, I may kill you with certain legal impunities (Coker). Passion is the litmus test that on occasion gives its imprimatur to violence.

The potential violence in this narrative stands in stark contrast with the image that we have concocted of Jesus. For our own sakes, we have turned Jesus into a gentle pacifist. Scripture gives us a more conflicted image of a God/man wise beyond his earthly years, whose insights into the human condition never fail to startle. Here, Jesus is confronted by an assembly gathered to give vent to their frustration and anger. Minimally, they may be angry with the woman for violating the social mores. But the woman could have been easily dispatched forthwith at the scene of the adultery had her accusers elected to do so. More is at stake.

As Matthew Schneider notes, the crowd of witnesses is angry, not just with the woman caught in adultery (and potentially all women who may abrogate marital property rights), but also with the Romans, who have already usurped their power as men and who now threaten to destroy their culture (Schneider 1997: 3–4). Ultimately they are confused, frightened, and angry with Jesus, too, because he promises a kingdom, but one with no armies and no sovereignty. Moreover, Jesus, with his enigmatic sayings and healings, threatens to bring the wrath of the Roman government down on their society.

---

22 Toesing says that the authority of men over a household is "implicit in the Hebrew word for husband *ba'al* (master) or *adon* (Lord)." Today, in the United States, the Bureau of Justice Statistics reports that a woman is beaten in the United States approximately every fifty-two seconds (Bureau of Justice Statistics; U.S. Dept. of Justice, "Female Victims of Violent Crime" 13 [1991]).

In this text, Jesus challenges the dominant forces with innocence rather than violence. The implications are far reaching. As Old Testament scholar Walter Brueggeman notes: "Jesus has become for us the lens through which we reread power, social relations and formal policies.... Jesus' innocence is an exposé of and a threat to every other kind of power" (1996: 108). Brueggeman lifts up innocence as the unlikely weapon that will defuse this situation. An interesting thought in our own culture. Applying this theory may mean that the right to indict others depends on our own willingness to court holiness and pursue innocence with all of the energy that we have previously invested in mammon.

But to return to the dusty circle, for the time being, this crowd remains unified by a singular purpose. They are satisfying overt and subliminal desires to maintain power over women, religious doctrine, and purported messiahs. If they can secondarily bolster their own sense of authority, it is all to the better (Schneider 1999). But why do they choose a teacher to settle their dispute?

Let the Teacher Decide

Interestingly, in the narrative the scribes and Pharisees call Jesus "Teacher." This is the only reference in the Fourth Gospel to Jesus as "teacher." He is not there as a magistrate or civil judge with discretion to refer the capital case to the Romans. Neither is he a member of the Sanhedrin or the Roman government. He therefore does not have the civil authority to pronounce sentence on the woman under either governmental structure (Davidoff: n. 22, 102). Although he certainly can speak from a teaching perspective, he cannot recuse himself or decline the test for lack of jurisdiction, because to do so would be to deny his moral authority.

Jesus responds to the crisis with a single sentence that encompasses both the law and moral accountability, while deftly escaping the entanglements of both operative legal systems. Jesus avoids but does not defy the penalty required by Mosaic law; he does not deny the Roman mandate, and he concedes ultimate authority to neither. Essentially, he accepts the crowd's assertion that the woman has been caught in the act. Without saying a word as to whether or not the woman should be stoned, Jesus moves right to the matter of determining who should be the first stone throwers. Simultaneously, he accedes to the Roman proscription against the imposition of the death penalty by a Hebrew authority. For Jesus neither commands the woman's execution nor qualifies her executioners. In effect, he has announced a new standard and a different use of power. In so doing, Jesus nudges the laws of Moses and Pilate toward a hermeneutic of grace.

The lesson is about how and when to exercise the power and authority to punish. Jesus teaches by juxtaposing legal inconsistencies with questions of honor and personal accountability. As to the claims of the religious authorities that they caught the woman in the very act of sin, Jesus realizes that there are only two possibilities: either they did witness the adulterous act or they did not. If they did, the question arises as to how these men were situated so as to witness such an act of intimacy? If this occurred in a brothel, why were they all there? Or were they there at all? If the crime took place in a private place, from whence were they peering? Are they without sin in witnessing what they say they saw?

If they did not witness firsthand what they claim, have they then borne false witness against the woman?[23] Is this not a sin worthy of equal punishment? Either the accusers sinned by being in a place that allowed them to witness the intimacy. or they are lying about what they saw, which is also a sin. How can this band of scribes and holy men have brought the woman to Jesus for punishment without risking assessment of their own transgressions of purity and holiness? The answer will not be written on a scroll or pronounced for all to hear; instead, it will be written in shifting sands.

WRITING IN THE SAND

One of the most intriguing passages in the New Testament refers to Jesus writing in the sand. Although scholars have pondered what he wrote, "the important point is that he did write" (Baylis: 179).[24] Charles P. Baylis notes that the text makes specific reference to the fact that Jesus uses his finger. "This alludes to the fact that the Law was written by the 'finger of God'" (Deut 9:10). One could infer that the act of writing is in fact a pronouncement, a messianic claim. Jesus may be saying, "How can I go against the Law of Moses? I wrote the Law of Moses" (180). If every nuance of the legal enactments of Mosaic law has been given by God, the circle is complete, for the one who claims to be from God now writes in the sand.

This act of writing is reminiscent of the passage in Daniel where the finger of God writes under equally enigmatic circumstances. In Dan 5, King Belshazzar is holding a feast during which he calls for silver and gold goblets that had come from the Jewish temple in Jerusalem. Belshazzar

---

23 Exod 20:16: "You shall not bear false witness against your neighbors;" Prov. 19: 5 "A false witness will not go unpunished, and a liar will not escape."

24 Some scholars suggest that Jesus may have been writing the secret sins of the accusers, Deut 22:22–24 on stoning, or Deut 19:16–19 on bearing false witness.

intends to fill the holy vessels with wine and spirits. The narrative says that God was offended by this degradation of the holy artifacts and began to write with a divine finger on the walls where the feast was being held: "MENE, MENE, TEKEL, and PARSIN." As Daniel explains to the frightened king, the words mean "you are weighed in the balance and found wanting" (Dan 5:25–29). Because the king disappointed God, the days of his life and kingdom were numbered.

There is a symbolic progression in the examples of divine writing in biblical text, from stone tablets to walls and now to sand. At first glance, Jesus' writing does not bear any of the markers of divine immanence. There are no thundering mountains, no glowing face of a receiving prophet, no flame-scorched wall. Amid grains of sand, the impermanence of it all is apparent. One wonders whether Jesus was considering the power of a divine decree written in sand, whether the words that he traces are condemning, questioning, or didactic. Even in sand, when the God-man writes there is a sense of prophetic finality. Certainly his own days on earth were numbered by this time. Likewise, if the witnesses accept the challenge, the woman's days soon would be at an end.

You without Sin

As the crisis builds, Jesus masterfully diffuses matters in unexpected ways. Schneider suggests that he accomplishes this feat by merely suggesting that the group screen itself into just two segments: those with sin and those without. Jesus further stratifies the group into the "first" to cast a stone followed by the others. In these few words, Jesus destroys the anonymity of the group. Each person is now bound to look not only within for sin but also at the corporate culpability. No longer are they an amorphous assembly poised to victimize the woman as object. Instead, they are exposed individuals known to each other and perhaps to the woman as well.

If the crowd can maintain their unity and purpose, the woman who is the catalyst for this psychodrama will be sacrificed on the altar of religious power and intrigue. If the woman is bait with which to trap greater prey, those assembled are unable to spring the trap because they make the mistake of succumbing to mob mentality. The group, like any mob, acts as one unit. They feed off each other's passion for vengeance and action. Besieged by external forces that threaten to erode their cultural identity, they focus on the "law of Moses" as a quintessential point of communal connections.

Schneider contends, and we agree, that what foils this group is the very weakness of any mob. In order for a group to function as a mob there must be "anonymity of unanimity." No one member acts as an individual. Each is a nameless, sometimes faceless part of a whole. There is "group think" and "group action." There is no division among the members of the group and no differentiation or conscience that constrains the group as a whole.

Under the law of Moses, those witnesses whose testimony produced the conviction were obliged to cast the first stones.[25] But first, the accusers must withstand a gaze into the rhetorical mirror that Jesus holds up. What manner of witnesses are they? Their sensibilities will become apparent after the question is posed, "Let anyone among you who is without sin be the first to throw a stone at her." At that moment they are compelled to judge themselves, each other, and each other's assessment of one another. The light of this self-examination destroys the life of the mob, restoring conscience in each individual. Without responding to the question, the crowd elects instead to disperse. By their disappearance, they answer the question as to whether the stoning sentence is indeed mandatory. The text says that the crowd disperses "one by one" (John 8:9a).

When no one but Jesus is left, the woman finally speaks. When she does, one wonders whether the role of teacher has been reversed. When asked if anyone remains to condemn her, the woman caught in adultery says "no one." This "no one" includes Jesus. She seems to share a common understanding of Jewish law that requires more than one witness to trigger an execution. Moreover, if Jesus is totally human, totally divine, he cannot condemn her. No human can fulfill the laws of holiness perfectly so as to cast the first stone. No God who preaches grace and mercy can accede to her execution. And so Jesus says, "neither do I condemn you."

Summary

The unnamed woman who is caught in the very act of adultery is an important but elusive figure. She is caught in the pregnant pause of time—as the law of Moses and the law of Caesar clash around her. She is caught in the passionate arms of a forbidden lover. Yet she is almost lost among the issues of gender and sexuality, power and the authority to punish. During this analysis, her identity and individuality kept eluding our critical grasp. And yet, though we often averted our analytical attention to the men who are deciding her fate, she emerges as a presence that cannot be ignored. At a crucial moment, she provides Jesus with an opportunity not only to teach but also to confront sexuality, passion, sin, violence and redemption.

---

25 Deut 17:7: "The hands of the witnesses shall be raised against the person to execute the death penalty, and afterward the hands of all the people."

The lesson is only superficially about the imposition of capital punishment. The woman's guilt or innocence—both legal and moral—seems not to be of primary concern to Jesus. The issue is not that the guilty should not be caught, tried, or punished. Instead, what is important is that those who lay claim to "righteousness" should be certain that their use of power is rooted in humility and truth. The power to punish is an awesome responsibility that must be permeated with wisdom and grace.

This textual excerpt offers a standard of grace that might ameliorate the rancor among people of faith over current issues of sexuality and authority in the church. The scenario speaks to the necessity of self-examination before the judgment of others. Perhaps for persons marginalized because of ethnicity, gender, age, or sexuality, who bear the brunt of the domination system's assessment of their worth, the first step is a liturgical phrase taken from the text. Even for those who execute, condemn, and abuse, a simple phrase may begin the process of reflection and transformation. The phrase that embodies all of the grace of God and speaks to those who inflict suffering and those who suffer is ... "neither do we condemn you."

Terrorization, Sexualization, Maternalization: Women's Bodies on Trial

Gina Hens-Piazza
Jesuit School of Theology at Berkeley/Graduate Theological Union

More than ten years ago, a leading feminist lawyer and author of legislation against pornography, Andrea Dworkin, wrote, "The circumstances of women's lives [are] unbearable" (1989: 65). Here she was referring not so much to the conditions of women's lives per se; instead, she was reflecting upon the circumstances of women's lives in relationship to the law and their inability to get adequate assistance from the legal system. Indeed, the myriad of crimes against women, coupled with their inability to procure a fair trial against their abusers, is beyond belief. Feminists practicing law, along with those documenting the social and legal status of women down through the ages, could only agree. The catalogue of violence that has become commonplace in women's lives registers as legion. The rapes, forced childbearings, wife beatings, medical butcherings, forced prostitutions, sex-motivated murders, and sadistic psychological abuses that go unpunished are so frequent as to define them as the very condition of women's lives. The gravity of these circumstances is only surpassed by the failure of legal systems to render justice in these circumstances. Writers on feminist jurisprudence note that not only is the occurrence of these crimes defining the condition of women's existence persistent but so also is the difficult time women have had getting the law and/or the courts to come to their aid. It seems almost impossible for women to communicate their situation.

However, the lack of solution stems not from a lack of attention to the problem. Endless state, national, and international commissions have studied and reported on both the abuse of women and the gender bias present in the legal system. Moreover, there is great consensus in these findings. The enduring outcomes of these investigations consistently conclude that the most significant problem of women regarding the law and in relation to the courts is their lack of credibility. Again and again, women deserving to have their case tried before courts often find themselves and their credibility on trial.

WOMEN ON TRIAL

The three preceding essays are joined together by their common attention to legal and regulatory matters in regard to women. In each instance, a violation of a law or a code of behavior has occurred. Bathsheba is accused of murder as David's accomplice in his crime against Uriah. Women in some Christian churches today are accused of transgressing dress and behavior codes. A nameless woman in John's Gospel has been caught in adultery, a transgression of Jewish religious law. Attention to the potential crimes and conviction of these women obscures the concomitant abuse and malignment of women that should also be documented here. As we will see, in each instance women's bodies are being assigned a meaning that becomes an occasion for violence. However, instead of receiving a fair hearing for such abuse and harassment, women themselves are on trial in all three situations. Moreover, as we examine each study, we will see that what is really at stake in the legal machinations is not what is stated. Issues of gender, sex, and violence, as well as the preservation of control over the meaning of women's bodies, are everywhere present when women try to get their day in court. Laws governing society and even regulatory statutes of religious organizations are not objective templates committed to maintaining moral order. Rather, they disclose themselves to be sites of power—power determined to control matters of sex, gender, and meaning as well as power willing to resort to violence to maintain this control. While appearing as statutory attempts to curb violence, to protect the common good, and to keep people safe, laws and their adjudication in regard to women often result in the production of violence.

On Trial before a Jury of Readers

In the first essay, "Murder S/He Wrote? A Cultural and Psychological Reading of 2 Samuel 11–12," Hyun Chul Paul Kim and M. Fulgence Nyengele put Bathsheba, wife of King David, on trial before the jury of readers. Yes, that's right, Bathsheba, not David, is on trial in this article. Moreover, she is not being tried for adultery, as those familiar with this story might at first assume. Rather, she is being tried for murder. Working off the little evidence the text yields in this matter as well as the abundant silences of the text, Kim and Nyengele explore up front the question of a woman's credibility and culpability that commentaries often hint at in the unconsciousness of readers. Is Bathsheba a key accomplice with David (who has already been indicted by Nathan the prophet), or is she innocent in the matter of Uriah's death?

While the setting of this case presumes a law court in Judah, the legal argumentation is that of our own contemporary judicial system. In the course of juridical arguments, Kim and Nyengele expose the issues of gender, sex, and violence operative in the literary poetics of 2 Sam 11–12 and in the interpretations these elicit. Their study, richly interdisciplinary, draws upon cultural comparisons with Korean customs and folklore, the psychological theory of Carol Gilligan and Jean Baker Miller, along with contemporary grief theory.

As introduction to the story, the authors first offer a brief literary analysis that discloses the complexity and density of this tale. Though structurally conforming to a rough chiastic framework, their analysis reveals a plot riddled with ambiguities. Gaps, unexplained occurrences, and dissonances across this familiar tale all "function as signifiers to the veiled realities within the text" (99). However, as the format of the article reveals, how one fills in these missing pieces and construes the missing evidence determines the verdict on Bathsheba. Every time readers come to this story about David's crime, the ambiguities of the tale put Bathsheba on trial and readers sit in judgment.

In the first half of the essay, the prosecutor culls evidence from the text in arguing the case against Bathsheba. A reconstruction of the events makes her an accomplice with David in Uriah's murder, motivated as she must be by a desire for the power and glory. All would be hers if she could secure a place at the side of the king. The silence or lack of report of any resistance on the part of Bathsheba when brought before the king draws a ring of suspicion around her. In scheming her own promotion to this royal position, the prosecutor argues that she ensured that David saw her bathing. Following the affair, her message to the king claiming "I am pregnant" can be interpreted as a sign of exuberant success and gain on her part. Finally, the fact that David determines to cover his adulterous tracks by having Uriah rather than Bathsheba killed raises a further question that casts a shadow over Bathsheba. Was David himself being led and controlled by Bathsheba? When taken together, the tally of evidence gathered from the silences in the text argues the possibility that Bathsheba could have been a co-conspirator, if not a primary instigator, in the death of Uriah.

In these ancient patriarchal environs, women are often seen but not heard. They rarely are the dominant character in stories. Nor do they often have the power and privilege of speech. So while Bathsheba is not explicitly accused in the story, because of her silences in the text a case is made against her that puts her on trial for murder before the jury of contemporary readers. The lack of any statement of resistance on her part, her failure to deny playing a part in this coverup plan, and her lack of any expression of fondness or love for her husband Uriah all become the "silences" upon which the prosecutor builds a case. While women like Bathsheba are kept silent both in the patriarchal world and in patriarchal narrative, it is upon such required silences that a prosecutor's case can be crafted against them.

Next, Kim and Nyengele offer a defendant's assessment. The defendant crafts a powerful rebuttal that appears much more dependent upon what is said rather than upon silences in the text. Bathsheba's bathing was purposeful, as indicated in 11:4. Faithfully fulfilling the law of ritual cleansing, she was carrying out an act that she could not schedule on her own. That Bathsheba "came to him" (11:4) indicates nothing about cooperation with David. In fact, when taken together with other similar texts, it could signal the opposite. The defendant notes that in 11:17, "Uriah came to him [David]." If you are among the king's officers, soldiers, or subjects, when the ruler summons you, you come! Hence, that Bathsheba comes to the king with no hint of resistance is a sign of her subordinate status rather than an indication of her willingness to satisfy his lustful longings and advance her own status.

Of special importance in forwarding Bathsheba's innocence is her expression of grief upon news of her husband's death. She made "lamentation for him" (11:26). Drawing upon grief theory, the authors view her grief as a real expression of genuine suffering when she receives the news of her husband's death. Moreover, her grief is "psychological evidence of her victimization and consequently, psychological proof of her innocence" (107).

Perhaps the most compelling evidence marshaled here in support of Bathsheba's innocence is Nathan's parable in 2 Sam 12. Nowhere in this divine oracle of judgment delivered to the king by the prophet Nathan is Bathsheba accused. Only David is indicted. Hence, there is ample evidence in what the text says and what it does not say to defend Bathsheba's innocence.

How is it that in response to a story about a powerful man's lust, passion, and crime, a woman ends up on trial? Will indicting her serve to diminish David's guilt? Or what's worse, will making her the one controlling David (as the prosecutor does) serve to exonerate David all together and render her the criminal?

What Kim and Nyengele's study really demonstrates is how the legal system itself can be put to work in the interest of various forms of social domination. Laws, litigation, and the legal process itself participate in a discourse of power that can readily do violence in the name of justice. The radical indeterminancy lodged in every literary text and its interpretation also takes up residence in legal texts and their interpretation. Evidence and arguments marshaled in favor of one position can just as readily be used in support of its opposite. Moreover, the presumed lack of credibility that surrounds women in relation to the legal system makes such machinations possible and dangerous.

Conditions are ripe here for violence rather than for justice. When a woman such as Bathsheba, subjected to a voyeuristic gaze, potentially the victim of rape, impregnated against her will, and then widowed by the actions of a man's covering his adulterous tracks, ends up accused of murder, the system shows itself for what it is. Here the notion of law as maintaining the well-being of society camouflages the reality. Law is a discourse of male power. Moreover, the legal system as objective process rendering just judgment and punishment shows itself to be a cover for a violence that maintains male domination. Here the investigation of a woman on trial exposes the interplay of violence and gender in texts and in culture. At the same time, when abused women such as Bathsheba who deserve a hearing end up on trial, the alliances and kinship between the courts and the abuser make themselves known.

On Trial before an Ecclesiastical Jury

In the second essay, "Cry Witch! The Embers Still Burn," women are on trial again. This time however, the accused is not a female character in a biblical story. Instead, women down through the ages are on trial, subject to carefully formalized strategies of containment and rejection. Their lack of conformity in dress and behavior explains their lack of credibility and dependability. Author Madeline McClenney-Sadler argues that semblances of the seventeenth- and eighteenth-century European witch hunts are not confined to the obsessions of that time and place. Her historical investigations as well as her own experiences argue that the witch hunts live on in the prosecutory practices of purity trials carried out in some Christian churches today. Across her study, McClenney-Sadler makes a compelling case demonstrating that, like the witch hunts of the past, these purity trials are pregnant with the violence and evil they propose to uproot. As they seek to weed out persons (women in particular) who cause scandal to the community by violating regulatory food, drink, dress, and behavior codes, these proceedings are nothing more than a pretense of righteousness. Hidden behind these purifying exercises motivated to protect the faithful are the forces of social domination that run these ecclesiastical institutions.

Developing her thesis across a five-part study, McClenney-Sadler's investigation of the contours and the ethos supporting witch hunts of pre-Enlightenment Europe discloses them to be alive and well today. First, she rehearses the religious and philosophical tradents that fueled the search for so called "witches" during this time period. Next, she studies a fifteenth-century handbook on witchcraft that defamed women in general and associated them with witches. In the third part of the discussion, she spotlights the well-known case of Grace Sherwood, the famous seventeenth-century Virginia witch. Here the legislation used to hunt down witches reflects early European and American determination to define and control the diet, conduct, and dress of women. As modes of external restriction, such legislation also made it possible to judge women's religious or class status simply by looking at them and their behavior.

Fourth, McClenney-Sadler explores the horizons of contemporary churches' witch hunts currently disguised as purity trials. Here she speaks from her own experience and the experience of other women who have been subject to these proceedings. Like witch hunts, these purity trials function as a mode of control over women and their conduct, clothing, and speech. These trials also serve to manipulate already-despised groups such as lesbians, gays, ethnic minorities, and even the homeless. By means of these proceedings, distinctions between men and women are carefully preserved, defined, and kept intact. Gender itself is behaviorally defined and institutionally controlled.

Finally, she wrestles with two key biblical texts that often play a role in these purity trials. As prooftexts, Deut 22:5 and 1 Tim 2:9 are the frequently cited biblical grounds supporting conformity to dress, behavior, and speech codes. Hence, in keeping with the early church, contemporary ecclesiastical institutions see fit to define and maintain their established codes of dress and behavior by which a narrow understanding of men and women can be safeguarded and readily identified. McClenney-Sadler offers a sound exegesis (though not a structural analysis, as she claims) of these verses, arguing the opposite. She reads the text as a prohibition against men and women betraying the trust of others through manipulation of externals such as dress, speech, behavior, and diet.

On this basis, McClenney-Sadler concludes that purity trials and the codes upon which they are founded encourage women to change or misrepresent themselves in conformity not with Scripture but with the interlocutor. As strategies of containment, purity trials threaten to constrain women and their identity. As strategies of rejection, they tease out those who might blow the cover on the pretense of righteousness and the orthodoxy of hegemonic forces that are behind this engine. When by their behavior, dress, words, or deeds women threaten to upset this well-hewn manipulation and control of an individual's identity and self-understanding, they will find themselves on trial.

On Trial in the Biblical Story

In the third essay, "Sex, Stones and Power Games: A Woman Caught at the Intersection of Law and Religion (John 7:53–8:11)," Barbara A.

Holmes and Susan R. Holmes Winfield excavate the complex of gender, power, and violence in this New Testament tradition. Once again, a woman is on trial. However, this time the jury is not made up of readers or the authorities of ecclesiastical institutions. Rather, the trial and the jury constitutes the story itself. The familiar Gospel story of a woman caught in adultery is shown here to be caught up in other clashes as well. The unnamed woman is ensnared in religious conflicts between Jesus and the Jewish officials. She serves also as a point of controversy between Jewish religious authorities and the Roman governing forces of state. The authors' illuminating close reading demonstrates just how marginalized this unnamed woman is in regard to the legal system as well as how she is utterly stripped of any kind of credibility in such circumstances. Certainly she has no say in the composition of the laws that ensnare her. She has no voice in the trial. She evidently had no ability to protect herself during this private sexual act. And she has no advocate or lawyer at this public hearing. Thus, we can only read her silence. Moreover, we can recall from the study of Bathsheba just how dangerous the silence surrounding a woman in a trial can be.

Holmes and Winfield do their own reading of silences in the text, but this time the woman and the absence of any utterances from her are not the focus. Instead, they raise the questions about some unexplained circumstances regarding the witnesses. How was it that these men were able to witness such a private act? If it occurred in a brothel, why were they there? If the act took place in a private setting, how was it that they could observe such activity. "Are they without sin in witnessing what they say they saw?"(159).

When their investigation turns to the woman, Holmes and Winfield's analysis make a further disclosure. They demonstrate that while she and her adulterous deed appear on trial for her transgression of Jewish law, her case is actually only a cover behind which the competing societal forces jockey for power. Jewish law required the woman to be executed for adultery. By contrast, Roman law made it all but impossible to execute such persons. The crowd of witnesses is angry, but whether they are angry with the woman or with the Roman forces who have usurped their power as men to punish women is unclear. Roman law that prohibits Jewish authorities from punishing women threatens the marital property rights of Jewish men as well as the stability of patriarchal culture.

The crowd may also be angry with Jesus. After all, he had been preaching and promising a kingdom with no armies or structures of sovereignty. How could the social framework of patriarchy be maintained in such a place? His message seemed an affront to the kind of expectations those Jewish officials had who longed for the restoration of the days of old. Given the deeper issues and conflicts between the governing forces involved in these judicial proceedings, the prospects of this woman getting a fair trial are rather bleak.

Jesus delivers the woman from these straits. In place of the issues of sexuality, passion, and sin, Jesus moves the discussion to the matter of exercising authority and the power to punish. In place of the all too familiar scene of a woman on trial, he shifts the places of the players and ends up putting the men witnesses on trial. His writing in the sand joins him in the symbolic progression of divine writing of the law down through the traditions. Hence, as enactment of Mosaic law, Jesus' pronouncement that sends the would-be executioners on their way is portrayed as authorized by God.

The legal proceedings and laws at work in the first two studies—that of Bathsheba and of the women judged in the purity trials—showed themselves to be nothing more than the discourse of male power and domination. In this study of the adulterous woman in John's Gospel, the same forces rear their heads again. The question these studies parade before us is whether or not women can ever get a fair hearing. Again and again, the real issues surrounding the achievement of justice in regard to the accused are lost to the privileged and more urgent crisis of power and the authority to punish. In all these instances, women on trial turn out to be sites of power struggles—struggles over issues of sex, gender, and control. Further, these power struggles are not only about the control of woman per se but about the control of meanings about women, in particular, the meaning of women's bodies.

Legal Discourse and the Meaning of the Female Body

For a long time now there has been a growing acknowledgment that differences between the sexes is not biologically engineered but rather "socially constructed." These social and cultural forces weigh in on the construction of individual identity as well as upon what is socially understood to compose the "female" and the "male." These assumptions about sexual differences affect everything from representation in the media to decisions about the way monies are allocated in government programs to the curriculum children are taught in schools. When a woman encounters "the glass ceiling" in men's workplaces, experiences a lack of collegiality, or even finds herself subject to harassment there, it is not because she is naturally or biologically unsuited for "men's work." Feminists' lawyers and those involved in writing legal reform have been working to change laws or write new legislation that challenge or overturn some of the social forces and practices that promote these constructed differences, especially where they oppress, violate, or undermine women's potential. The underlying assumption of such efforts here is that law can mitigate these cultural forces and thus can eventually dismantle the social constructions that promote these differences.

However, amidst such efforts, what has become apparent to feminists about law and legal discourse itself is disquieting. Law, its practice, the courts, and legal discourse itself are responsible for assisting in the construction of these differences. Even in its reformed state, law often contributes to the production of differences that coheres with what is thought to be biological or "natural."

It turns out that the three preceding essays, all having to do with legal or regulatory matters in regard to women, actually share a further commonality. In each case, a woman was on trial. In the case of Bathsheba, readers were asked to consider the evidence and judge her culpability in the matter of the murder of her husband, Uriah. In the second study, we considered the witch-hunt trials of women that continue today in the form of purity trials in some Christian churches. From Grace Sherwood to the author herself, woman have been tried and judged for their violation of behavior, dress, and foods codes that they have had no part in composing. Finally, in the third study, we watched the informal trial of the unnamed woman caught in adultery and now on the brink of execution. But there is more that weaves these three different studies together. In each case, the circumstances that put these women on trial stem from issues having to do with women's bodies and the meaning assigned therein. The murder charge against Bathsheba stems from what happened to her body. The echoes of the witch hunts in contemporary purity trials grow out of women's violation of codes regulating how they dress their bodies, feed their bodies, and conduct their bodies. Finally, the body of the nameless woman brought before Jesus has been seen and thus accused by witnesses of participating in a private sexual act forbidden by their law.

As feminists today wrestle with the role law and regulatory codes play in assigning particular meaning to the female body, they demonstrate how such meanings are created by legal discourse, by the reason and manner by which women are tried, and by the cultural mores that become regulatory over their bodies. Mary Joe Frug has identified at least three meanings that such forces in our contemporary world assign to women's bodies, namely, the terrorization, maternalization, and sexualization of the female body (129). It is no surprise, then, that across our three studies all having to do with women's bodies these same meanings appear to be either embedded or cultivated by the laws, trials, regulatory codes, and cultural mores that we find there. Hence, not only in contemporary legal traditions but also in our religious traditions and in legal proceedings conducted down through history in regard to women do we find the female body being constructed with these same debilitating and subjugating meanings.

Bathsheba and Terrorization of the Female Body

The laws, the courts, and the nature of legal discourse itself often promote and even encode within their statutes the terrorization of the female body. This occurs by a combination of incongruous provisions and practices. On the one hand, the laws exist that purport to protect women, though often inadequately, from any kind of physical abuse. When women suffer such violence to their bodies, they are encouraged to seek compensatory refuge from such crimes by reporting them to the authorities and pursuing an indictment in court. However, as we are all too familiar, women pursuing a hearing often end up on trial themselves. How frequently do we hear of women who have been raped being further violated when they turn to the legal system for justice. They are vilified or rendered not credible. Hence, one meaning the legal system assigns to the female body, then, is a body in terror. Frug describes this body as "one that has learned to scurry, cringe, and submit" (129).

While law in ancient Israel forbade adultery, it did not adequately protect women, as we can clearly see in the story of Bathsheba. The text explicitly reports that when David inquired about the woman he watched bathing, he was told she was the wife of Uriah the Hittite. However, this knowledge of her status as the wife of another man did not dissuade him from satisfying his lustful longings. Nor did the Israelite law prohibiting adultery protect her or dissuade him. Bathsheba was looked at, sent for, slept with, and impregnated. The story gives no indication of her consent to any one of these actions upon her. As a wife in a patriarchal society, she was subjected to her husband. As a woman subject in a monarchial society, she was subjugated by the king. Before a husband and a king, hers was a body dominated by men.

First her body is terrorized by a king. Then, as prop in David's deceptive scheme, her now-pregnant body becomes the instrument enlisted to cover up this king's violation of the law. The expectations of her husband Uriah's sexual needs and gratification upon returning home from battle impose and imply the obligations upon Bathsheba. However, David's problem-solving scheme gets complicated when Uriah refuses to go to his wife and seek such satisfactions. When the meaning assigned to men's bodies (in this case Uriah's) regarding urgent sexual needs and prowess cannot be counted upon, the network of meanings assigned to male and female body is threatened. Hence, as David's situation becomes more desperate so too do the consequences for Bathsheba and her body. Uriah must be done away with so that David can legitimately take her as his wife. Now the terrorization of Bathsheba's body takes on another dimension. Legally and with no indication in the text of her desire or consent, she will become the wife of the man who has already terrorized her. As his wife, her physical, economic, emotional, and sexual dependence upon him only rises. As her subordination to him increases, so too does his domination of her increase. Hence, the meaning ascribed by the laws, customs, and practices operative here in regard to Bathsheba is that of a body in terror.

The Sexualization of the Female Body in Legal Codes and Institutional Practices

We have seen how laws and codes promote the terrorization of women's bodies. In addition, they also contribute to a second dimension of meaning: the sexualization of women's bodies. The right to sexualize the female body in the media, by business practices, and by means of the manufacture of certain products is protected and thus promoted by the law. The sexualization of women's bodies has been commercialized, commodified, exported, and exploited in innumerable ways—ways all deemed legally protected and legally defensible. Protected by the legal system, the image of women's body as highly sexualized becomes encoded in the culture. As this network of meanings mutually reinforces one another, they collectively convey the message that women's bodies are desirable, women's bodies are for sex, and women's bodies want sex.

At the same time, the legal system that protects this freedom of speech in constructing and communicating a message about women's bodies also prohibits rape, physical abuse, and harassment of women's bodies. Yet it is precisely these behaviors against women that are often prompted or encouraged by the very sexualization of women's bodies in culture, a sexualization protected by the law. Moreover, when a woman is raped, abused, or harassed, her protection by the law in the face of such crimes depends a great deal on the legal system's assessment of her own contribution to the promotion of the crime. Was she acting or dressing "sexy" when the crime occurred? The more "sexy" she is assessed to look or act, the less protection she is likely to be afforded by the law. A double standard seems to exist here. While cultural institutions are protected when they sexualize women's bodies, women themselves are not protected if they act according to these sexualized images. A conflict of interests appears embedded in law codes in what they protect and in what they resist protecting. The legal system protects institutions and businesses in culture that sexualize women's bodies but recoils from protecting women's bodies if they are judged to be highly sexualized by women themselves.

This same sexualization of the female body assumes a more subtle form in regulatory codes or institutional laws that govern how a woman must act, dress, speak, and even eat. This is precisely one of the dynamics at work in the church codes prompting the purity trials that McClenney-Sadler investigates. Such regulations, intended to obscure the female body from its "natural" sexualized meaning and the misconduct it might promote, typically take the form of prohibitions against certain kinds of dress and conduct. A simple ascription of meaning to the female body lies at the heart of these codes. In its unregulated state, the female body is assumed to be "naturally" sexy. If not constrained by a dress code, it dresses sexy. If not confined by a code of behavior, it walks and acts sexy. And if not curtailed by a code of speech, it is bound to talk sexy. Hence, not only is the female "protected" by such codes but so also are those who might be tempted or, worse yet, succumb to the incredibly strong natural attraction that such a sexualized body promotes.

At first glance, these regulatory codes of some Christian churches appear at odds with civil law governing society. The laws governing and protecting the practices of commercial enterprise and social institutions seem to protect and promote the sexualization of the female body in culture. By contrast, the laws of some church institutions intend to obscure or hide the female body assumed to be highly sexualized. Yet when the cultural impact of the governing forces of church and state weighs in, the outcome is the same. In what they permit and in what they prohibit, they both inscribe sexualization as the meaning of the female body.

McClenney-Sadler's study of contemporary purity trials within some Christian traditions corroborates such meanings. As an analogue to the witch hunts of seventeenth-century Europe, purity trials function to control women as well as other despised groups. As strategies of containment and rejection bent upon rooting out demonic influences and all uncleanliness that makes public this highly sexualized body, women who "wear short skirts, low-cut tops, or pants in worship" (129) are targets. Moreover, the dress code defining what is appropriate for a woman's body is tied to spiritual values and virtue.

But McClenney-Sadler's investigation exposes other damning implications of this subtle sexualization. For example, as the author herself experienced, women who wear pants or are thought to dress like men threaten to upset the implied depiction of woman's bodies as sexualized. When one dresses outside the categories of what is institutionally or even culturally defined as virtuous or promiscuous, the meaning of the female body as sexualized resists its "naturalness." If one dresses in such a way that does not allow the institution to confine it to these two categories, the meaning of the female body gets confused and cannot be controlled.

When women—or, for that matter, men—dress in a fashion at odds with these artificial and culturally constructed meanings, then control over those meanings are threatened and in danger of being lost. One becomes a congregational nuisance that causes insidious harm by upsetting the representation of reality, the reality about what constitutes men and what constitutes women in a particular community. Moreover, the very notion of women's bodies as "naturally" sexualized and thus needing to be constrained is threatened. When these churches, their codes, and their trials seem determined to "keep the wraps upon" women's bodies, not only do they communicate their assumption of women's body as highly sexualized in its natural state, but, paradoxically, their resistance to women dressing like men argues in favor of their own desire to preserve this sexualized meaning.

The Adulterous Woman and the Maternalization of Women's Bodies

Like the terrorization and sexualization of women's bodies, laws can also function to consign women's bodies to the role and function of motherhood. Many laws function directly and indirectly to maternalize women's body. This occurs when provisions exist that reward women for having children and for assuming responsibility for childcare in the years that follow. For example, in our own American system, provisions that assign a proportionally larger responsibility for childcare to women or rule in favor of women in custody hearings contribute to this meaning. As the same time, laws that undervalue or even penalize women for labor market work, for sexual activity outside the codes of marriage, or for sexual activity not directed at the purpose of childbearing also contribute to the maternalization of women's bodies. Laws regulating prostitution and abortion or laws that prevent or hinder birth control all contribute to the conscription of the female body into service of maternity.

Marriage itself and the laws governing this institution also contribute to such meaning making. Marriage is considered the legal site for sexual activity by many societal and religious institutional codes. Many of these regulatory codes link sex to reproduction. Sex motivated by pleasure is replaced by sex directed toward reproduction. Hence, a woman's decision for marriage automatically maternalizes her body. At the same time, these same institutions tend to criminalize sexual behaviors located outside the bonds of marriage or those that transgress the marital confines.

In the case of the adulterous woman brought before Jesus in John's Gospel, the question that puzzles this reader is: Where is the man? If she was caught in adultery by witnesses, where is the one with whom she was caught? Jewish law punishes both men and women for sexual behavior that transgresses the matrimonial bonds. However, women do receive the harsher sentence. This likely stems from that fact that an adulterous woman is not only engaged in sexual misconduct but also offending the property rights of her husband. In concert with Holmes and Winfield's argument, the adulterous woman is less of a threat to sexual mores than her behavior is to the rights and privileges of Jewish men that are being curtailed by the Roman culture and law under which they now live. As property of a man and for his pleasure, a woman's body may be terrorized as we saw in the David and Bathsheba story, but that is not all. As property, a woman's body produces offspring for a man. Hence, the meaning of her body is extended to include maternalization. She is to birth, nurture, and raise his children. In patriarchal Israel, barrenness was an abomination to a woman because it threatened the one avenue by which she had identity and value as a person. Adultery, on the other hand, threatens to expand the meaning of a woman's body as possession and for maternity only. For a woman to exercise her sexuality outside matrimonial boundaries threatened to upset or even overturn the claim men had on women's bodies and the confines of maternity by which they guarded their possession. Hence, the adulterous woman's actions, along with the Roman law that prevented her execution, constituted an affront to men's property rights and to the conscription and confinement of woman's body as meaningful as defined by maternity.

The Violence of a Double Assault

The separation of church and state is a common precept governing our society and way of life. Given the existence of political watchdog groups and formally appointed committees whose work is to ensure these separations, we count on its ongoing implementation. Assisting this separation, laws exist to protect and ensure the churches' self-governance. Churches, in turn, are exempt from civil obligations that would make them party to laws and practices that they cannot support (birth control, abortion, etc.). Moreover, churches, with their religious traditions and sacred texts, are often viewed as alternative to the violent vestiges of society and even bill themselves as refuges of comfort and healing from the tribulations of the world.

In these three studies of law and regulatory practices—in regard to Bathsheba, the adulterous woman, and women subject to purity trials in some Christian churches—the distinctiveness of civil and religious law and practices as well as the separation of church and state seem less clear. The meaning assigned to their bodies by the governing apparatus of religious law, regulatory codes, and practices appear glaringly similar to that which has been detected in the legal system governing civil society. Feminists working in jurisprudence have shown how law itself can be implicated in the production of meaning about woman's bodies—meanings that terrorize, maternalize, and sexualize woman's bodies and associate these meanings as "natural." However, an assessment of these three investigations suggests that religious texts and their interpretations, as well as the practices of religious institutions, promote the same meanings. Moreover, the meanings they produce are not distinct or separate from the practices and outcomes of legal discourse. Cunningly disguised as fostering virtue or obedience to a higher law or code of behavior, these vestiges of religion and its sacred texts contribute to the production of the same demoralizing meanings about woman's bodies that legal discourse promotes. Both legal and religious institutions are shaped by as well as give shape to culture. It is no surprise, then, that they appear much more as partners than as separate and distinct parties in the production of meanings.

The separation of church and state appears not so separate here in regard to women and their bodies. Working hand and hand, both civil laws and religious texts and codes not only assign the same meaning to women's bodies but also put them on trial, as a result of these meanings. The force of this double assault doubles the force of the violence therein. Culture is the carrier of meanings of its governing institutions and their practices. When the legal system and the religious institutions inscribe women's bodies with meanings that denigrate and invite abuse while at the same time continually put women on trial as the result of these assaults, the outcome is twofold. Not only are women in danger, but culture itself is pregnant with violence.

PART 3:

TYPES, STEREOTYPES, AND ARCHETYPES

Some Place to Cry: Jephthah's Daughter and the Double Dilemma of Black Women in America

Valerie C. Cooper
Wake Forest University

The story of Jephthah and of his daughter, which is found in Judg 11, has both intrigued and perplexed commentators. Over time, the narrative of the nameless daughter of Jephthah the Gileadite has been reinterpreted endlessly and the characters appropriated as tools and symbols of the interpreter's social context, message, and philosophy. From Pseudo-Philo or Shakespeare to the works of modern feminist and womanist exegetes, the story of Jephthah's daughter has served as an archetype, tragic myth, or cautionary tale of man, woman, and nation. In my essay, I examine some interpretations of the story and then propose a womanist understanding of it in terms of the reality of contemporary life for African Americans.

My essay is womanist in that it considers the influence of race upon issues of gender and class. Gender is not the only identifier of importance in the lives of women of color (Barkley Brown).[1] Evelyn Brooks Higginbotham agrees, underscoring the role of race as identifier and arguing that scholars need to "expose the role of race as metalanguage by calling attention to its powerful, all-encompassing effect in the contruction and representation of other social and power relationships, namely, gender, class, and sexuality" (Higginbotham 1995: 3–4). According to Higginbotham, race functions as metalanguage through which other identifiers such as gender tend to be interpreted. Together, race and gender have worked to produce a kind of double jeopardy for African American women, who suffer the consequences of racism and sexism. It is one aspect of such double jeopardy that I intend to explore in this essay.

---

1 Indeed, the emergence of *womanist* as a category of inquiry and study separate and distinct from *feminist* points to the concern of many scholars that gender analysis alone is insufficient without taking into consideration the significant, and complicating, effects of race.

In Judg 11, Jephthah sacrifices his only daughter in order to secure a military victory. Jephthah's impetuous and ill-advised vow, to offer "whoever comes out of the doors of my house to meet me" (Judg 11:31 RSV) as a burnt offering to guarantee triumph in his battle with the Ammonites, results in disaster when it is his daughter who greets him upon his return. Historically, exegetes have read his actions in keeping his vow and sacrificing his daughter as either heroic or tragic; frequently, the light in which Jephthah's conduct is seen also illuminates the status the interpreter's society accords women or the controls it imposes upon them. Parallels between the story of Jephthah's daughter and the near sacrifice of Isaac by Abraham highlight the ambiguities of theodicy in the drama. Why was Abraham's son spared but Jephthah's daughter allowed to be killed?

My essay considers Jephthah's actions and his daughter's responses in the context of contemporary African American society. Just as Jephthah's lack of political and economic security made his daughter doubly vulnerable to the vagaries of his position, so the interlocking rings of racism and sexism function to increase the stresses between Black men and women and within Black families. Here the essay will consider the ways that Black women are sometimes sacrificed as Black men seek to shore up their places in a still-racist, still-patriarchal society.

RECENT SCHOLARSHIP

Recent years have resulted in a wealth of scholarship concerning Judg 11. The paternalistic, androcentric viewpoint of the text is universally deplored among feminist and womanist exegetes, as is the fact that the woman is nameless, although her father's name is recorded. As a solution, several commentators have resorted to calling her "Bat-Jephthah." Some propose that she be called "Bat-Jephthah" from the Hebrew for daughter, *bat* (Bal 1989: 212; Gerstein: 176).

A number of scholars have condemned the general violence of the entire book of Judges (Bal 1989: 211; Sigal: 9). However, others have suggested that murder was not committed in this particular case; they reason that Jephthah's daughter was not actually killed at all. Given the ambiguity of the text, some exegetes postulate that her sacrifice may have been to remain a virgin all of her days (Landes: 28–42; Fuchs 1989: 35; Marcus). Others, having accepted that the woman was killed, have questioned the text's silence over the ritualistic sacrifice of a human, especially in light of Abraham's case: Why was this sacrifice allowed but the sacrifice of Isaac prevented (Gen 22:1–19)? Phyllis Trible suggests that the difference lies in the motivation of the father. "Jephthah is not Abraham; distrust, not faith has singled out his one and only child." According to Trible, Abraham was responding in faith when he offered up Isaac, but Jephthah was reacting with fear by offering his daughter. However, Trible states, after Jephthah has spoken his vow, "neither God nor man nor woman negates it" (Trible 1984: 101, 105). Landes also argues that the vow should have been released as inappropriate under Jewish law (Landes: 31). Mieke Bal argues that Jephthah simply does not understand God. His rash vow is unnecessary because God has already given "the spirit of Yahwah" to enable him to defeat the Ammonites (Bal 1989: 213).[2] Jephthah's vow seems rooted in his own insecurity and ambition; he seems to be over-compensating for his ignominious birth and tenuous position in society (Bal 1989: 213; Weems 1988: 55–56; Webb: 34–43).

Several commentators discuss the ambiguity of the Hebrew term "whosoever" or "whatsoever" that describes the first creature to meet Jephthah at his door (Fienberg: 131; Trible 1981: 61; Landes: 30).[3] Would Jephthah have completed the sacrifice had the first thing to approach him been an unclean animal? Nona Fienberg notes the irony of Jephthah's "anger that he must sacrifice" his daughter because she has joyously greeted his return "with dance and music." Because of his daughter's delight at his success, she is the first to meet him. Of Jephthah's anger at this, Fienberg observes, "the oppressor blames the victim" (Fienberg: 132; Judg 11:34).

Several feminist scholars have examined Bat-Jephthah's status as an unmarried woman. Anne Tapp sees her virginity as an idiom of her powerlessness; she is available for barter because she is unmarried. She suggests that "'sexually ripe' women who have yet to have their fertility exploited by husbands enact an ambiguous role in patriarchal (that is, paternally oriented) societies" (Tapp: 172). Mieke Bal and Peggy Day both argue that the text indicates that Jephthah's daughter is not a virgin but a nubile young woman undergoing a rite of passage between childhood and adulthood (Bal 1989: 213–20; Day: 60). Cheryl Exum counters that "as a sacrificial victim, Jephthah's daughter must be a virgin for reasons of sacrificial purity" and notes that a proclamation of her status ends the text's discussion of her in Judg 11:39 (Exum 1989: 30).

---

2 See Judg 11:29: "Then the spirit of the LORD came upon Jephthah, and he passed through Gilead and Manasseh. He passed on to Mizpah of Gilead, and from Mizpah of Gilead he passed on to the Ammonites."

3 See also Judg 11:30–31: "And Jephthah made a vow to the LORD, and said, 'If you will give the Ammonites into my hand, then whoever comes out of the doors of my house to meet me, when I return victorious from the Ammonites, shall be the LORD's, to be offered up by me as a burnt offering.'"

Were she a virgin, Jephthah's daughter's virginity would have meant many things. First of all, it would have meant that she was childless in a culture that placed a high premium upon procreation. Exum notes that Jephthah's daughter's childlessness meant that she had no way of being remembered, nor had she anyone "to stand up for her, no *go'el* to plead [her] case." Second, she is "denied not just motherhood, the patriarchal mark of female fulfillment, but also the pleasure of sex, the right of passage into autonomous adulthood that opens the eyes with knowledge" (Exum 1989: 30–31; cf. Gen 2–3).

For many modern scholars, the acquiescence with which Jephthah's daughter accepts her father's vow is troubling (Fuchs 1989: 44) That same submission that ancient writers such as Origen commended, for example, in his *Commentary on St. John's Gospel* (Hanson: 298), modern writers such as Exum have condemned. While many commentators are troubled by Jephthah's daughter's calm acceptance of her fate, others question whether or not she had any real alternative. As an unmarried, childless woman in a patriarchal society, did she have any real options other than surrender to her father's will? (Could she have survived, economically, for example, outside of her father's household?) Bal states that Bat-Jephthah probably knew that, given her status, protest against her father or his vow was useless (Bal 1989: 218). Renita Weems argues that Bat-Jephthah may not have acquiesced quietly but that her protests simply may not have been recorded by the male narrator; further, she commends the daughter's choice of a ceremony to commemorate her death (Weems 1988: 57).

According to Judges, Bat-Jephthah requests two months' reprieve before she submits to her father's vow. During this period, she will "wander on the mountains, and bewail [her] virginity" with her women friends (Judg 11:37). After these two months of mourning, she will return to be sacrificed. Fienberg describes the pathos of this time, stating that Bat-Jephthah's "community of women friends" is gathered for the purpose of "lament[ing] her powerlessness in the patriarchal world" (Fienberg: 132). Several others suggest that the text of Judg 11 is an attempt to explain the origin of a female rite of passage regularly celebrated in Israel (Exum 1989: 31; Judg 11:39–40), but Exum refutes this. "It has been frequently suggested that the story of Jephthah's daughter is aetiological, aimed at explaining the women's ritual. There is, however, no evidence of such a ritual apart from this story" (31).

Two recent studies have closely examined allusions to Jephthah's daughter found in literary sources. Both studies highlight themes linking female sacrifice and statecraft: at the heart of the story of Jephthah's daughter, they suggest, is the idea that sometimes male political power comes at the price of women's lives. Nona Fienberg's excellent work explores William Shakespeare's relatively obscure reference to Jeph-thah's daughter in *Hamlet.* Fienberg argues that this allusion to Jephthah's daughter underscores Ophelia's ambiguous and complex role in the drama and, ultimately, the ambiguous and complex place of women in Hamlet's Denmark and Shakespeare's England. According to Fienberg, while pointing to similarities between the political instability of Israel in the time of the judges and Hamlet's Denmark (as well as that of late-Elizabethan England), the allusion to Jephthah's daughter also indicates the role "of the female sacrifice [in] consolidating the state" and the regulation of female sexuality upon which the consolidated patri-archy will rest. Ophelia, like Jephthah's daughter, "becomes a pawn of her father's ambition and of the male competition for power," and her death foreshadows the "regulation of female sexuality," which is charac-teristic of an era of state formation. "In Judges, a time of political confusion follows closely upon the conquest of Canaan. Jephthah's vow, then, can be seen as a bargain with God to confirm patriarchal power through female sacrifice (Feinberg: 131). The political machinations that collude to make Ophelia "no loved one: o-philia" and "no daughter: o-filia," echo those that have rendered Jephthah's daughter nameless through the ages. Here Fienberg makes a play upon the name Ophelia, suggesting that it might derive from the negation of either the Latin for daughter, *filia,* or of the Greek, *phileo,* meaning "to love" (Fienberg: 133).

In her study of first-century portrayals of women in the Bible, *No Longer Be Silent,* Cheryl Anne Brown considers Pseudo-Philo's use of the story of Jephthah's daughter in *Biblical Antiquities.* Brown argues that Pseudo-Philo elevates Jephthah's daughter to the level of tragic heroine by seeing her death as fated and even necessary for Israelite nation-building. In *Biblical Antiquities,* Pseudo-Philo finds Jephthah's daughter, whom he names Seila, to be the central character of the drama. Paral-leling Seila's story with that of Abraham's near sacrifice of Isaac, Pseudo-Philo "finds in her an important symbol, a symbol of the destruction of Jerusalem, whose 'sacrifice' was decreed by God, yet ulti-mately for the good of the Jewish people" (C. A. Brown: 117). Pseudo-Philo's descriptions of Seila as tragic heroine is in keeping with traditional interpretations that cast "this nameless Israelite girl ... [as] a paradigm for later Jewish and Christian martyrology" because of her identification with the near sacrifice of Isaac in Gen 22:9 and the Suffer-ing Servant of Isa 53:7 (94, 101).[4]

---

4 See Brown's discussion of "Akedah," from the Hebrew "to bind," as it relates to Isaac's being bound to the altar. Also, see Brown's discussion of traditions that suggest that Isaac actually was sacrificed to atone for the sins of Israel.

How significant that Pseudo-Philo, in a practice typical of *Biblical Antiquities*, even names Jephthah's daughter, who is elsewhere nameless, by calling her Seila. The name perhaps derives from "the Hebrew root *s'l*, to ask, demand; thus, *se'ila* denotes 'she who was demanded'" (C. A. Brown: 100). Pseudo-Philo places in her mouth a lament in which Seila is able to state that she believes her death to be meaningful, even going so far to redeem the story as to see special virtue in the girl's virginity. "Seila emerges as a tragic heroine of the order of her Greek predecessors Antigone and Iphigenia at Aulis. She too goes to her doom lamenting her fate as a 'bride of death.' Seila goes to her death as to her marriage bed. She is a 'willing sacrifice' and thus 'acceptable' as a woman, as a daughter, as a victim" (Baker: 200–201; Day: 60–61).[5] Therefore, her death is not in vain; instead, it is upon her sacrifice that the nation-state is built.

HERMENEUTICAL IMPLICATIONS: THE DOUBLE DILEMMA OF BLACK WOMEN IN AMERICA

Jephthah was a marginalized man, rejected by his family because he was the son of a "prostitute" (Judg 11:1). Sent to live in Tob, "outside of Judah's sphere of influence," Jephthah grew up and was educated somewhat outside of the sphere of the centralized worship of Yahweh. Disinherited by virtue of obscure and unmerciful readings of the law (Mendelssohn: 116–19), Jephthah was locked out of the economic security and status that landholding afforded Israelite men. Eventually, he was surrounded by "outlaws" who accompanied him on raids (Judg 11:3).

Bat-Jephthah was the unmarried daughter of a marginalized man; she was, in fact, doubly marginalized. Patriarchal society afforded her no power as a single woman; Israelite society afforded her father no power as a disinherited man. The sacrifice of Jephthah's daughter represents the loss of life on several levels: she dies an only child without offspring, thereby ending the familial line, and her youth and potential are all sacrificed without procreative expression. Jephthah's guilt is plain: he has made a foolish vow. Society's guilt is less obvious but no less heinous: it allows him to sacrifice his daughter to this foolish vow.

But where else was Jephthah's daughter to go? Ancient Israel provided few if any socially sanctioned places for women outside of their fathers' or their husbands' homes. Even if she had chosen to flee, where

---

5 Baker goes on to note the work of other scholars such as Eva C. Keuls, Margaret Alexiou, and Peter Dronke, who have striven to document the links between virginity and death in Hellenistic ideology and practice.

could she have gone? Other social and economic options were nearly nonexistent for her.

I see in the tale of Jephthah's daughter analogies to the state of the Black woman in America.[6] She is doubly marginalized: still, today, she is excluded from the centers of power by virtue of her gender and by virtue of her race. Still, her ability to progress in society is intricately tied to that of the Black man—and, like Jephthah's daughter, she is strangely, even tragically obligated to the rash and foolish bargains Black men sometimes strike to solidify their place in the world.

For Jephthah's daughter, the choice was between death and dishonor. For Bat-Jephthah, to accept her father's words meant certain death, but to reject her father's rash vow meant to declare a fool the man all of Israel had once before rejected and then to run, with no place to hide. Bat-Jephthah held not only her own honor but her father's in her hands. For many Black women today, the same choices define their conduct as they barter their silence for the prestige of the men they love. They accept choices that may ultimately mean death to them, if it will "save face" for the men they love.

African American men are as marginalized and historically have been as securely locked out of economic and political power as Jephthah was. Once able to barter their strength for a place in American heavy industry, they have found less success in the technological and service economy that is now replacing it from the Rust Belt to the Sun Belt. According to Boston pastor Eugene Rivers, "The biggest culprit is an economy that has locked them out of the mainstream through a pattern of bias and a history of glass ceilings.... America has less use for black men today than it did during slavery" (Chideya, Ingrassia, Smith, and Wingert: 24).

Less likely than Black men to marry outside of their race, Black women are therefore left prey to every ill Black men suffer, even the ills of those who, like Jephthah, have befriended "outlaws" or turned to criminal enterprises to sustain themselves after legitimate businesses found no place for them. According to Howard University sociologist Joyce Ladner, "the combined factors of joblessness, low skill levels, a lack of education, the social problems of substance abuse, alcoholism, [and] imprisonment [affecting Black men] all lead to reducing the pool

---

6 The women's auxiliary of the Black Masons, the Eastern Stars, used to reenact the story of Jephthah's daughter regularly. Apparently, they identified with Bat-Jephthah on some level. My mother tells of the time she watched her grandmother (my great-grandmother) perform in the title role. When they got to the execution scene, the drama and seeming realism was all too much for my mother, who was not quite six years old at the time. She says she stopped the show with her screams.

of individuals who would be able to earn a living and support a family. The result is that a surprisingly high percentage of Black women may never marry" (Vobeja: A12). Knowing that their fathers and brothers have been dishonored and shut out by society, knowing that their own cries will not be heard, except by their sisters, and knowing that they have nowhere to run, Black women face the double dilemma of Bat-Jephthah. They must choose between that which will hurt the men they love and that which will hurt them.

Tied together by race, Black men and women nonetheless find their relationships and families pulled apart by the consequences of racism. Then, Black women are saddled with an additional burden—the consequences of sexism. So it is that even among a marginalized people, interlocking rings of oppressions divide Black families, just as cruelly as Jephthah and his daughter were parted.

So, some Black women barter with death, turning mutely away as their sons or boyfriends pursue illicit or illegal trades that offer them fleeting fame and economic stability rather than to deliver them over to [often White] legal authorities who would shame and incarcerate them. They would sacrifice themselves before they would humiliate the men they love.

So, some Black women, who represent the majority within the congregations of African American churches, deny themselves or other women any pastoral or leadership role or allow men to deny them the same, in part justifying their actions with the excuse that "they recognize the need for viable images of black males and support the church which keeps the men 'out front'" (Massey and McKinney: 43). Because African American churches are among the few places where Black men have provided unquestioned leadership, these women accept the death of silence in the very churches that they maintain by their participation, rather than to undermine the image of the Black men who would preach or pastor. Then, like Jephthah's daughter, having chosen the death of silence, they make a crying space for themselves in the many women's auxiliaries, clubs, and prayer circles that they have created.

So, some Black women barter with death; silently reasoning that Black men's misconduct is born of Black men's marginalization, they accept it as their fate. They are beaten, they are abused, they are disrespected, they are abandoned, they are left holding the baby, they are left standing alone.

Is Jephthah the only man who has ever tried to barter blood for blessing, or has he sons today whose lives model his? Isn't "Gangsta Rap" a product of outlaw ghetto culture and a kind of modern vow of Jephthah? When Black men destroy Black women with their words, calling them "bitch" or "ho" [whore], haven't they in fact traded women's reputations and lives for the money or fame such "art" buys them? Does the men's experience of oppression in the marketplace excuse their own oppression of their mothers, sisters, daughters, girlfriends, or wives? Does some women's willing participation in such "art" excuse it? It does not. Yet today's Black Jephthahs mistreat Black daughters as mute offerings to their own societal powerlessness, while the society that keeps Jephthah marginalized has some of his daughters' blood on its hands.

So, Black women who cannot find a voice or an advocate find only a place for tears and make flawed choices that represent their limited options. I do not justify these poor choices; I merely suggest that they fit within a flawed system not only of Black people's creation. And in America, it should be understood that Black men's tortured vows are often the product of the worldview of the Tob of their exile or of the Israel of their oppression.

There are those who find God's apparent silence in this narrative troubling—myself among them. However, I know that humanity is as much revealed by God's silences as by God's words. God's silence in Judg 11 uncovers and reveals the cold machinations of a heartless humanity; Israel shows little compassion for Jephthah and less for his daughter. Moreover, the Israelites knew better and should have done better. The silence from the heavens revealed that humanity had learned nothing from all that God had spoken to that point.

And what of Israel? Was there no one to speak out against the abominable blood sacrifice about to take place in the midst of the congregation? Perhaps Jephthah, raised far from Jerusalem, in Tob, had an excuse for being ignorant of God's ways. What excuse had Israel?

But would Jephthah barter blood for blessing? Not with God: this is a deal with the devil. Romans 12 provides a more excellent model: offer *yourself* to God as a living sacrifice. To offer *someone else* is to misunderstand sacrifice and to misunderstand God. However, in the silence we do not hear the people's protests against the injustice that characterizes the life of Jephthah and his daughter. We hear only the woman's tears as she and her friends gather to mourn her impending sacrifice.

Yet it is in the tears that I find comfort. (I am not condoning the daughter's silence or her passivity; I am appreciating that she took the time to cry.) In the midst of this hard, hard canyon of a text that is so spare and comfortless, I find a small refuge in the women who gather together to weep and to remember. The story of Jephthah's daughter can then speak to those who do not yet hear a reprieve from heaven as Isaac did, because it contains in it the hope that even those who forget their names will remember their tears.

Somehow it comforts me that, despite the horror and the lack of a real alternative in her situation, Jephthah's daughter manages to find dignity and solace in her tears and in her comrade's tears. In Bat-Jephthah's redemptive, proactive choice to share her sadness with her sisters, she sets the pattern for a long line of women who would follow her example, seeking "to make a way out of no way." This is the heritage, both bitter and beautiful, of those who, although nameless, nonetheless survive to be remembered.

Not everyone hears a reprieve from heaven; some die without ever having received the promise, as Heb 11:39 reminds us. At least sometimes remembrance is accorded to those to whom even life is denied. And although there was no place in all of Israel for her to live, there was some place for Bat-Jephthah to cry.

The plot of the novel *Beloved* (Morrison) also revolves around the aftermath of the tragic murder of a child by her parent. A mother who has escaped slavery with her children subsequently tries to kill them rather than allow them to be retaken into captivity. She does kill her child named Beloved. Presumably she was also about to kill herself but was prevented from killing herself and the other children by her own recapture. What some readers did not know was that in writing *Beloved*, author Toni Morrison based the story upon an actual historical event.

While the novel graphically details the sexual, physical, and psychic damage slavery wrecked upon Black folk, its main action takes place after Emancipation. Then the characters struggle under the weight of remembering the terror of slavery. Sethe, the mother, is haunted, quite literally, by the child whose life she took with her own hands. Unable either to bear or to banish those memories, Sethe is trapped. How, after all, is one to bear the unbearable? How is one to remember what is too painful to remember? How can one heart contain a history that bears such scars, that hides such terrible sacrifices?

Morrison proposes this answer: when memory is too much for any one heart to bear, it is best born in community. In *Beloved*, the women of the community gather with Sethe to sing and to pray and to be a presence until she is no longer haunted. So, Jephthah's daughter did a wise thing in gathering the women of her community to mourn with her. So it is that Black women do a wise thing when they gather to form enclaves of healing and solidarity against the forces that would sunder their families and their communities. Perhaps it is from such enclaves that the resolve will come that no more names be forgotten, that no more foolish vows be made, that no more lives be pointlessly sacrificed.

From the New Testament author of the Epistle to the Hebrews, who includes Jephthah in the hall of faith found in Heb 11:32, to biblical scholars of today, theologians have reinterpreted the text of Scripture to serve contemporary purposes. Heroine or dupe, Jephthah's daughter's worth seems tied to the value that individual writers, or their societies, place upon women. Again and again, her story is invoked to suit the ideologies of the time: she is one age's martyr, another's tragic heroine, today's battered woman. Yet she is most often a mirror, reflecting the interpreter's values and self—for what we see in Jephthah's daughter says much about who we are, what we believe about ourselves, what we believe about others, what we believe about society, and what we believe about God.

Daughter Zion:
Giving Birth to Redemption

Mary Donovan Turner
Pacific School of Religion

Introduction

Sometimes in strange and unexpected ways two seemingly unrelated worlds collide and new understandings are created and become the lens through which both worlds are seen. We may be shocked, surprised, unnerved, made to feel uncomfortable, self-conscious, comforted, or filled with insight—any of these. This happens with lectionary preachers who open the biblical text and read a story, a lament, a letter, a proverb, or a parable in light of a new context, place, and time. New meaning is created that reflects upon life. New questions are raised. There are new arenas for discernment and evaluation. This essay is the result of such a collision; it is a collision of metaphors, one ancient and one new: Daughter Zion and "voice." Over the centuries the female metaphor that is used almost exclusively in prophetic texts becomes more complex. Second Isaiah uses the metaphor to bring a hopeful word of redemption to the devastated woman/city. This word, spoken in response to the immeasurable suffering found in Lamentations, clearly names Yahweh as the redeemer of the city Yahweh has destroyed. A study of the woman from the perspective of the contemporary metaphor of voice, however, invites us to consider the woman herself as the agent of redemption. Through her expression of a resistant word, the words of apology, hope, and restoration from Yahweh pour forth.

Tracing the Growth of the Ancient Metaphor—Daughter Zion

Early in the eighth-century prophets (Amos, Micah, and First Isaiah) there are only brief glimpses of this female, short brush strokes, if you will, of her and her life. She is the female figure who represents Jerusalem. Most often she is called "daughter," sometimes "virgin daughter." She is sometimes designated Jerusalem, sometimes Zion, Israel, Judah or My People.[1]

From the first glimpses we get of her, we know that she is a devastated woman. She is introduced in lament. "Virgin Israel has fallen, she will never rise again. She is forsaken. There is none to raise her" (Amos 5:2). That is all we know about her. She does not speak; she is not addressed, and as quickly as she appears in the text, she disappears. The themes, however, that are related to her have already begun to emerge and in consequent prophetic generations remain squarely in place. There is associated with her presence the aura of death, premature death.

In Micah, as in Amos, the prophet names the devastation of the city through the personification of this female, Daughter Zion. In Micah she holds the transgressions of Israel (1:13). Disaster is coming to this woman, this city. The conqueror is coming upon her; there is a call to lament. Again, the woman is silent. In First Isaiah Daughter Zion is left isolated in the vineyard, like a besieged city (1:8). There is abandonment and destruction at the hand of Yahweh. With remarkable economy, each prophet is able to provide the audience with a graphic image of city or nation. The rhetoric is shocking. In this early cluster of images, the themes of reproach, judgment, and lament are interwoven in explicit and implicit ways. The prophet describes her and laments her condition. But the woman who personifies the city remains silent; she addresses no one.

From this sparse beginning, the portrait of this female becomes more complete as details about her existence and her life become more vivid in Jeremiah. The references to her become more numerous and concentrated. The beginning chapters of Jeremiah are permeated with allusions to the female Israel and Jerusalem. A simple cataloging of these uses demonstrates not only the pervasive use Jeremiah makes of the female

---

[1] See the following texts: **The Suffering, Lamented Daughter** (36)—Amos 5:2 (Virgin Israel); Mic 1:13 (Daughter Zion); Isa 1:8 (Daughter Zion); Isa 10:32 (Daughter Zion); Isa 22:4 (Daughter My People); Jer 4:11, 31 (Daughter My People, Daughter Zion); Jer 6:2, 23, 26 (Daughters Zion, Zion, My People); Jer 8:11, 19, 21, 22, 23; 9:6 (Daughter My People); Jer 14:17 (Virgin Daughter My People); Jer 18:13 (Virgin Israel); Lam 1:6, 15 (Daughter Zion, Virgin Daughter Judah); Lam 2:1, 2, 4, 5, 8, 10, 11, 13 (2x), 15, 18 (Daughters Zion, Judah, Jerusalem); Lam 3:48 (Daughter My People); Lam 4:3, 6, 10, 23 (Daughter My People [3x], Daughter Zion); **The Restored Daughter**—(14): Mic 4:8 (2x), 10, 13, 14 (Daughter Zion [3x], Daughter Jerusalem); Zeph 3:14 (2x) (Daughter Zion and Jerusalem); Jer 31:4, 21, 22 (Virgin Israel [2x], Faithless); Isa 52:2 (Daughter Zion); Isa 62:11 (Daughter Zion); Zech 2:14 (Daughter Zion); Zech 9:9 (2x) (Daughters Zion and Jerusalem); **Foreign Daughters**—Gallim (Isa 10:30); Dibon (Isa 15:2); Tarshish and Sidon (Isa 23:10, 12); Babylon, Chaldea (Isa 17:1, 5); Egypt (Jer 46:11, 19, 24); Dibon (Jer 48:18); Faithless (Jer 49:4); Babylon (Jer 50:42); Babylon 51:33); Lam 4:21, 22); Babylon (Zech 2:7).

metaphor but also the way he creatively expands its potential. The multi-valent dimensions of the metaphor are explored. The female is like a faithful bride who is bound to Yahweh in new covenant (2:32); harlot and unfaithful spouse who has sought out other lovers (3:1);[2] a mother whose terror is as great as her anguish in labor, as great as if she has lost a child that she has delivered (6:26); and a devastated one whose coming destruction is lamented by the prophet (8:23), by Yahweh (14:17), and by the female herself (6:26). The disaster is described as a hot wind or as a military onslaught from the evil foe of the north. She is near death.[3] In 4:31 the female is named. She is Daughter Zion, and she voices the agony of the community that is experiencing destruction. Her *silence is finally broken.* The prophet gives her voice and also hears her. "For I heard a cry as of a woman in labor, anguish as one bringing forth her first child, the cry of daughter Zion gasping for breath, stretching out her hands, 'Woe is me! I am fainting before killers.'" The vision of the lamented daughter, then, which had been used to accuse and to indict and which had been used to illustrate graphically the overwhelming desperation of the hopeless and powerless people in the face of the mighty and powerful Yahweh, here is also the source of the prophet's pain and the impetus for his grief. The daughter speaks again: "My joy is gone, grief is upon me, my heart is sick" (8:18). Jeremiah hears her cry.

> For the hurt of my poor people [Daughter My People] I am hurt. I mourn, and dismay has taken hold of me. Is there no balm in Gilead? Is there no physician there? Why then has the health of my poor people [Daughter My People] not been restored? O that my head were a spring of water, and my eyes a fountain of tears that I might weep day and night for the slain of my poor people [Daughter My People]. (Jer 8:21–9:1)

Whatever anger the prophet feels is subordinate to his grief. In the midst of the impending crisis, the voice of the daughter is begun to be heard. In cursory yet powerful ways she speaks of her pain but addresses the words to no one—and thus to everyone. The pain is unbearable.

---

2 Terse descriptions made by earlier prophets are now replaced with extended descriptions of the woman, her behaviors, and their consequences. The harlot of Isa 1:21 is enhanced by a graphic picture of the desolate one who dresses in scarlet, is adorned in gold, and paints her eyes for her lovers.

3 The explicit references to the virgin, daughter, or virgin daughter are clustered primarily in three sections of the text: (1) 4:11, 31; (2) 6:2, 23, 26; (3) 8:11, 19, 21, 22, 23; and 9:6. Two isolated uses are found in 14:17 and 18:13.

The use of the metaphor of the female becomes more concentrated and at the same time more complex in the book of Lamentations, where the dirge/complaint is used to give expression to grief in light of great calamity and to petition Yahweh's aid. The book of Lamentations describes the unimaginable suffering of Jerusalem in 587 B.C.E., and it does so through the metaphor of the desolate and destitute woman. Eighteen times in the five poems of Lamentations, the one who has experienced calamity is identified as "daughter." Most often she is called Daughter Zion (1:6; 2:1, 4, 8, 10, 18; 4:2), but she carries other designations as well: Daughter Judah (2:25); Daughter My People (2:11; 3:48; 4:3, 6, 10); Daughter Jerusalem (2:13, 15); and once virgin Daughter Zion (2:13). Here the metaphor used only sporadically in the eighth century and then more frequently in Jeremiah is used with an unsurpassed intensity. Here, not only does the daughter speak, but she speaks directly to Yahweh, imploring Yahweh to see the unparalleled destruction that has been wrought. In contrast to the distanced and undeveloped stock metaphor of the eighth century, the author of Lamentations (written after the destruction of Jerusalem) provides a detailed and complex description of her. The audience finds that the lonely city is like a widow, vassal, slave, trapped prey, yoked ox, and bereaved mother who has lost her children. This woman is disgraced by her enemy and abandoned. Passers-by look upon her and sneer; her friends and lovers have betrayed her. Her children have been torn from her; her suffering is astonishing and extensive. All suffer: babes, sucklings, children, boys, young men, young women, mothers, fathers, and old women and men are portrayed as suffering varying degrees of trauma. Slaves, priests, prophets, widows, orphans, princes, and kings are all there as well. Her suffering is unparalleled (M. Moore: 534–55). "Is there any suffering like my suffering?" she asks (1:12b).

As readers, we move imperceptively and unknowingly between the image of the grieving woman and that of the city. The personal is communal, and the communal is personal. As such, the woman comes to represent the community, the systemic dimension of suffering. The suffering that is concealed and haunts the city is broken when the observer gives voice to it. The observer in Lamentations looks and sees and recognizes the pain (A. Smith: 9). Through the careful watch of the observer, experience is given voice, and the door is opened for release from suffering. In poetic terms, the author of Lamentations describes the decimated Judahite community (Newsom: 73–78). Lamentations is Judah's religious response to the loss of relationship with their land, with their spiritual inheritance, and with God (Gous: 351).

While Lamentations unquestionably acknowledges the daughter's sin, it is not in wholehearted fashion. There is never any specificity as to the nature of the sin involved (Lam 1:5b, 8, 18; 5:7; Dobbs-Allsopp:

54–55). This is in marked contrast to the great detail given to the destruction of the city. Moreover, poems explicitly and implicitly question the appropriateness and the degree of punishment. The injustice of what she has experienced provides foundation for pathos (Dobbs-Allsopp: 54–55).

In limping meter reminiscent of a funeral song, the daughter's fate is described. Though there is the stench of death, she lives still. She speaks. While in Jeremiah she spoke of her terrifying fear; here she directly addresses and implores Yahweh in the style of the complaint to look upon her distress. In Lam 1, the female figure becomes the primary speaker. She describes the horror Yahweh has brought against her with twelve masculine singular verbs; Yahweh is the sole agent of her pain. In fierce anger, Yahweh has inflicted sorrow. Yahweh has sent fire, spread a net, turned her back, left her stunned and faint, bound her transgressions, handed her over, rejected her warriors, proclaimed a time against her, and trodden her as in a winepress. She responds, "A comforter is far from me." This "lack of comfort" is the recurring thematic element in the first chapter of Lamentations. Five times we hear that she is the one with no comfort (1:2b, 9b, 16b, 17a, 21a). In the midst of the tragedy, there is no word from Yahweh. Yahweh remains unyielding and silent. In Lamentations, we are left with an unresolved tension between the silence of God and epic human suffering; a response is required.

THE RESPONSE TO VIOLENCE

We have witnessed the growth of the female metaphor for Jerusalem from its sparse beginnings in the eighth-century prophets to its concentrated and complicated usage in Lamentations. Second Isaiah subsequently uses the language and motifs of Lamentations, the portrait of the woman (Zion) who is in distress, who has lost her children, who weeps bitterly, and who is nearing death (Willey: 57–84). Second Isaiah takes the language of Lamentations and uses it as the backdrop, the foundation for the new words of hope and comfort, the words of redemption that are spoken in the prophet's "Zion songs."[4] The Zion

---

4 In the Old Testament a person's brother, uncle, cousin, or some other kinsman who is responsible for standing up and maintaining the person's rights is called the redeemer. If, for instance, someone sells a house or a piece of property to pay a debt, there is a right of redemption, and the nearest relative at the time is bound to buy back that which was sold and restore it to the family. Boaz is the redeemer of Naomi and Ruth. Or if an Israelite sold himself to a foreigner as a slave, he could be redeemed by his relative. Murder is avenged by the redeemer. How these secular meanings influenced the theological understanding of redeemer in the Old Testament is not entirely clear, but we do know that

songs are clustered in the second half of Second Isaiah, chapters 49–54, and are introduced by 40:1–11. Specifically, they are found in 49:14–26; 50:1–3; 51:9–52:12; and 54:1–17. These songs are distinguished from the first major section in Second Isaiah, 40:12–49:12, which features Jacob and Israel as the primary symbols for the redeemed community.

The words of Lamentations are, in their new context, revised. We might say they are reversed, diminished, minimized or distilled, abolished or transformed. But the relationship between the two, Lamentations and Second Isaiah, is a tight one; thematically and linguistically the two are bound together. This close congruence between the two texts has been researched and articulated as intertextual methodologies have been formulated and utilized.[5] In Second Isaiah there are specific but unspecified traces of the poems in Lamentations—allusions and appropriations, echoes, if you will, of the book's five chapters. The reading of the Second Isaiah text is richer, of course, when the relationships, both explicit and implicit, are recognized and acknowledged. All five chapters in Lamentations are somehow present in Second Isaiah, particularly in the Zion songs, thematically and through the quotation of particular words and phrases. The density of references invites the reader to view text B (Second Isaiah) through the experience of reading text A (Willey: 57–84).

To illustrate this relationship between the two, we can begin with the recurring theme or motif of "comfort." In Lam 1 and 2 a controlling element is the affirmation and reaffirmation that the female has no one to "comfort" (נחם) her:

- She has no one to comfort her. (1:2)
- Her downfall was appalling, with none to comfort her. (1:9)

Yahweh is the *go'el* of the fatherless and the widow and pleads their cause (Prov 23:11; Jer 50:43). Yahweh took up the cause of a worshiper and redeemed his life (Lam 3:58). The psalmist pleads to Yahweh to redeem him and give him life (119:154). In the Old Testament people are redeemed from evil, violence, oppression, the hand of the enemy, the hand of those who are too strong, distress, danger, imprisonment, illness, death, and sin. In the exodus, God promises to bring the people out from under the burden of the Egyptians, to redeem them with outstretched arm. Redemption is deliverance; people are drawn from one world into another.

5 See in particular the work done by Patricia Tull Willey in *Remember the Former Things: The Recollection of Previous Texts in Second Isaiah*. In this work, Willey explores methods for examining the relationship between two texts and focuses her work on the many texts used by Second Isaiah. She indicates that the relationship between Lamentations and Isa 51:9–52:12 is particularly strong. Xuan Huong Thi Pham also recognized this relationship by his attempts to put Lamentations into the context of ancient Near Eastern mourning customs.

- For these things I weep; my eyes flow with tears; for a comforter is far from me. (1:16)
- Zion stretches her hands, but there is no one to comfort her. (1:17)
- They heard how I was groaning, with no one to comfort me. (1:21)
- What can I say for you, to what compare you, O daughter Jerusalem? To what can I liken you, that I may comfort you, O virgin daughter Zion? For vast as the sea is your ruin; who can heal you? (2:13)

One of the tasks of Second Isaiah is to overthrow this pain-filled language. The antidote must use language as powerful as that which described the demise. In this instance, Second Isaiah uses the same language. To the female in Lamentations who had "no comforter," the words of Second Isaiah loudly resound. "Comfort, O comfort my people, says your God. Speak tenderly to Jerusalem, and cry to her that she has served her term, that her penalty is paid, that she has received from Yahweh's hand double for all her sins" (Isa 40:1). Here in the introduction and later in the Zion songs themselves, the female Zion is being reassured that her lament has been heard and answered. Isaiah 49:13, the prelude to the first Zion song, reiterates the promise. "Sing for joy, O heavens, and exult, O earth; break forth, O mountains, into singing! For the LORD has comforted his people, and will have compassion on the suffering ones" (49:13). And again in 51:3, "For the LORD will comfort Zion; he will comfort all her waste places." Another call to exuberant rejoicing occurs in 52:9: "Break forth together into singing, you ruins of Jerusalem; for the LORD has comforted his people, he has redeemed Jerusalem."

The relationship between Lamentations and Second Isaiah can be understood in the following ways. First, within the "daughter" tradition these two works share a unique relationship in that they are shaped by the same themes and motifs. In particular, the motherhood of Zion is emphasized. There are in both texts numerous terms and phrases that speak of womb, mother, children, and bereavement.

There are also phrases used *solely* by Lamentations and Second Isaiah that demonstrate the literary dependence of the prophet on the songs of lament. This is witnessed in the repetition of the phrase "at the head of every street" (Lam 2:19; 4:1 and Isa 51:20), which both texts use to designate the place where the slain children of mother Zion lie. The double imperatives "Depart! Depart!" are used in both. In the first text, they are used to describe the situation of the priests who have become unclean and in the second to describe the departure from exile of those who bear the sacred vessels and who have been cleansed.

Finally, there are parallelisms between Lamentations and Second Isaiah that are not unique to these but that serve to complement the unique commonalities between the two. The author of Second Isaiah relies heavily on lament language to bring his message. Examples of words and phrases used by both are the uses of the word *comfort* and the reiteration of the cry that Yahweh has forsaken and forgotten. Repeated also are terms that describe the daughter and her condition. The daughter "sighs" (Lam 1:4, 8, 11, 21, 22 and Isa 51:11), is "swallowed up" (Lam 2:2, 5, 8, 16 and Isa 49:19), is "afflicted" (Lam 1:4, 5 and Isa 51:23), and "desolate" (Lam 1:4, 13, 16; 3:11; 4:5; 5:18 and Isa 49:19; 54:1,3). Zion is like a "widow" (Lam 1:1 and Isa 47:8; 54:8). Yahweh "hurls his fury" (Lam 2:4; 4:11 and Isa 51:13, 17, 20, 22). Zion must contend with the "foe" (Lam 1:5, 7, 10, 17; 2:4, 17; 4:12 and Isa 49:20) (M. D. Turner: 157–61).

THE DILEMMA

In understanding the development of the metaphor of Daughter Zion, its association with violence (causing damage or harm) and death, and in understanding the consequent relationship between her devastation in Lamentations and the words of hope in Second Isaiah—the theological dilemma emerges.

In Lamentations, clearly it is Yahweh who has brought the violent devastation to Zion. Yahweh has become the enemy.

> He has sent his bow like an enemy,
>   with his right hand set like a foe;
> he has killed all in whom we took pride
>   in the tent of daughter Zion. (1:4)
> The Lord has become like an enemy;
>   he has destroyed Israel. (1:5)

There are other references to the enemy in Lamentations. Sometimes they clearly refer to the human agencies of war who have come to Jerusalem and destroyed it. Sometimes they clearly refer to Yahweh, as in the above quotations. Sometimes they are ambiguous: "For these things I weep, my eyes flow with tears; for a comforter is far from me, one to revive my courage; my children are desolate for the enemy has prevailed" (1:16). These references to Yawheh as enemy and the host of violent verbs attributed to him stand in "close relationship" to the Yahweh of Second Isaiah, where Yahweh is consistently identified as the one who redeems (41:14; 43:14; 44:6, 24; 47:4; 49:7, 26; 54:5, 8).The designation is used in the Zion songs and other sections of Second Isaiah as well. In the Old Testament the redeemer is the one who delivers a person or community from slavery or from that which oppresses, confines, frightens, or destroys. Thus, the relationship between Lamentations and Second Isaiah invites the following questions: What is the relationship between Yahweh who is the enemy in Lamentations and the one who delivers Zion from devastation in Second Isaiah? Can the one who is the perpetrator of violence against Daughter Zion also be the one who redeems her from it? What or who calls forth the word of redemption?

These are the enduring questions that arise from the intertextual reading of Lamentations and Second Isaiah. How tempting to allow contemporary understandings of cyclical, domestic violence to inform our readings of Second Isaiah and Yahweh's words of apology and promise that come to the devastated "daughter." This is true particularly because the text engages familial, spousal imagery to define the relationship between Yahweh and Zion. In the analysis of the female's words themselves, using the metaphor of voice, perhaps we can come to some understanding.

The Contemporary Metaphor—Voice

In her volume entitled *Suffering,* Dorothee Soelle discusses the experience of mute suffering. She analyzes three dimensions of suffering: physical pain, psychological pain, and the fear of social degradation. She concludes that there is a kind of suffering that reduces one to silence. The person no longer has a sense of personal agency; she has no sense of a potential course of action, nor can she make changes in her circumstances. Unbearable suffering excludes learning and change. *Suffering that can find no language expresses itself in brooding or sudden explosion.*

The first step toward overcoming suffering is, then, to find a *language* that leads one out of silence. One must find the language of lament, of crying, of pain. One must find the language that *names* the situation one is in. Finding the language of lament facilitates the movement from muteness to expression, from isolation to communication, from powerlessness and submissiveness to change (Soelle: 64–86). Soelle was claiming the importance of voice.

The metaphor of "voice" is alive and well in most every theological and academic discipline. "Voice" has become a metaphor of choice for theologians, ethicists, literary critics, biblical scholars, pastoral care providers, and the like. Scholars talk about finding voice and claiming voice. Moreover, when persons previously denied or discounted have made contributions to a field of study they have been dubbed "voices from the margin." The "voices of the silenced" began to be heard. Since the 1970s the metaphor of voice has inundated public and private discourse. The emergence of its use coincided with the cultural changes that followed the civil rights and women's liberation movements. "Voice" as a metaphor corresponds to basic principles in feminist, womanist, liberationist thought that recognize the issues of power and oppression in relationships. The polyvalent dimensions of "voice" have allowed those considered "other" to adopt it as a means of symbolizing and depicting their value in our pluralistic, postmodern world. In analyzing its use, it is possible to discern at least five different categories of meaning for this metaphor. "Voice" is used to represent distinctiveness, authenticity, resistance, authoritativeness, and relationality (Turner and Hudson: xi–xiii).

Globally, women use various images and expressions to describe what it is like to speak in the face of resistance, abuse, and oppression. Redemption is sometimes used to identify and describe that moment when words once repressed because of fear, shame, confusion, or unimaginable suffering are at least being spoken. It is a movement from one world of experience to another, a being drawn forth; it is deliverance from that which oppresses, limits, or binds. "The internal movement is from fear to faith, shame to acceptance, guilt to forgiveness, denial to affirmation.... Moving from silence into speech for any oppressed, colonized or exploited being is healing. At the same time, this gesture of defiance makes new life possible" (ibid.: 93–94).

The female Zion in Lamentations began her journey toward redemption by naming her realities (Lam 1, 2, 4). She is a victim; the text is punctuated with words that have to do with her physical and emotional distress. Yahweh has "sent fire," spread a net for her feet, left her stunned, destroyed without mercy, broken down, bent his bow, and poured out fury. These are only a few of the vivid verbs ascribed to Yahweh that depict the violence done to Daughter Zion. The emotional and psychological pain is replete. Zion feels isolated. She sits lonely, like a widow. Does anyone see her? Her eyes are spent with weeping. She experiences physical pain, psychological pain, and also social degradation.

- All her friends have dealt treacherously with her; they have become her enemies. (1:2)
- Her foes have become the masters, her enemies prosper. (1:5)
- From daughter Zion has departed all her majesty. (1:6)
- She has become a mockery; all who honored her despise her. (1:8)
- Her downfall was appalling. (1:9)
- Jerusalem has become a filthy thing. (1:17)
- All my enemies heard of my trouble; they are glad that you have done it. (1:21)
- All who pass along the way clap their hands at you; they hiss and wag their heads at daughter Jerusalem. (2:15)
- Yahweh ... has made the enemy rejoice over you, and exalted the might of your foes. (2:17)

It is the other speaker in Lamentations, the onlooker, who encourages the female Zion to keep crying out against the one who has devastated her and who has brought to her the pain and degradation. She encourages her to cry out for her children, to cry out until she receives some kind of response. The gender of the onlooker is unidentified, but it is tempting to consider the possibility that the onlooker, the one who helps bring forth Zion's lament, is female. There is in ancient Israel a strong association between lament and professional women who mourn. See, for instance, Jer 9:16–21, where the skilled mourning women come and sing the dirge so that the eyes run down with tears and the eyelids overflow with water, imagery and langauge consistent with Lam 2:16. Professional mourning was a trade women taught to their daughters (de Vaux: 61). Female or male, it is the onlooker in Lamentations who spurs Zion not only to lament but also to direct her cries to Yahweh.

> Cry aloud to the LORD!
>> O Wall of daughter Zion!
> Let tears stream down like a torrent
>> day and night!
> Give yourself no rest,
>> your eyes to respite!
> Arise, cry out in the night,
>> at the beginning of the watches!
> Pour out your heart like water
>> before the presence of the Lord!
> Lift your hands to him
>> for the lives of your children
> who faint for hunger
>> at the head of every street! (2:18–19)

The onlooker plays the role of one who in Nelle Morton's words "hears another into speech" (Morton: 55). The onlooker is the one who helps Daughter Zion find the language with which she then names the realities of her own experience. Immediately she speaks, "Look, O LORD, and consider! To whom have you done this?" (2:20). On the "day of the anger of the LORD" all the children she has born and reared her enemy has destroyed.

Not only the words of lament but also the spirit of this lamenting Zion, once victim and now woman with resistant voice, is brought into the text of Second Isaiah. The words of announcement are given in Isa 40 that the female Jerusalem will be comforted (40:1). And again in 49:13 there is the announcement of a grand celebration and festivity because comfort has come.

The words come too easily. This one who has suffered unjustly and whose punishment has been doubled *speaks* using words from the communal lament in Lam 5:20, where the community has been forgotten (שכח), forsaken (עזב). "But Zion said, "The LORD has forsaken me, my

Lord has forgotten me" (49:14). She will not allow easy reconciliation. The resistant voice of the female immediately brings forth a rush of assurance, of evidence, and of promise from Yahweh. In the first Zion song Yahweh answers the complaint that he has forgotten ("Can a woman forget her nursing child, or show no compassion for the child of her womb? Even these may forget, yet I will not forget you" [Isa 49:14]). The final Zion song answers the second complaint that Yahweh has forsaken. "For a moment I abandoned [have forsaken] you, but with great compassion I will gather you. In overflowing wrath for a moment I hid my face from you, but with everlasting love I will have compassion on you, says the LORD, your Redeemer" (54:7–8). Responses to the two concerns voiced by Zion bracket the songs; they provide the beginning and ending to Yahweh's words. But the balance in the relationship shifts. Zion, who has been accused of wrongdoing, is now the accuser. Following her accusation Yahweh is given new names; no longer is Yahweh the enemy. Yahweh is the comforter. Yahweh redeems.

Our contemporary minds are left thinking that Yahweh's words are too facile; they come too quickly. Yahweh claims to be the one who brings forth deliverance for the female. At the bidding of the onlooker, however, and through her own resistant voice, Zion has begun to usher in her own redemption. She is drawn out of the world of the silent and the powerless into the world of future, a world of agency. Yahweh offers not only apology but also a promise of everlasting commitment; even a cursory read of the Zion songs demonstrates that the words of Yahweh are profuse and extravagant. Zion is encouraged to rouse herself (51:17), to stand (51:17), to awaken (52:1), and to sing (54:1) in response to them. Yahweh anticipates a questioning response from her (49:21), but there is none. Daughter Zion becomes, once again, *silent*. Her few brief words in Second Isaiah ("The LORD has forsaken me, my Lord has forgotten me" [49:14]) are words of resistance, and since they are her last, they linger. And so, we are invited to wonder if she finds it difficult to understand how the perpetrator of the violence can be the one who redeems her from it. Is she unconvinced? The prophet, by leaving Zion silent, invites us also to ask the enduring questions about silence, epic suffering, violence, redemption, and God.

THE POWER AND PROBLEM OF REVELATION 18: THE RHETORICAL FUNCTION OF GENDER

Susan E. Hylen
Emory University

INTRODUCTION

The fall of the whore/Babylon in Rev 18 invites a discussion of gender, sex, violence, and the Bible. The writer presents the image of a woman, a whore, also identified as the city of Babylon in Rev 17, as an embodiment of the political power and violence of the Roman Empire. In Rev 18 there is a prophetic announcement of her downfall and the prediction of laments by the kings, merchants, and sailors who based their wealth and power upon her own. The sexual nature of the destruction of the whore is depicted in 17:16: "And the ten horns that you saw, they and the beast will hate the whore; they will make her desolate and naked; they will devour her flesh and burn her up with fire." In some interpretations, the violence of Rev 17–18 is the culmination of the destructive power of Revelation;[1] that the force of this violence is directed toward one who is imaged in female and sexual terms is worthy of exploration.

A question then arises as to what sort of exploration this might be, for Rev 18 also serves as an example of a tension biblical scholars face when trying to determine what to do with images of sex, gender, and violence. The tendency of recent scholarship is to read the text as either all about gender or not about gender at all, leading the interpreter to see it as entirely oppressive or liberating. In either extreme, this tendency seeks to explain away the difficulties of the text—either to discard or redeem it.

One beauty of the book of Revelation is that it is not easily explained, let alone explained away. While scholars may resist the gender stereotypes and violence of the book, the text also resists our simplified readings of it. In this essay, I seek to hold on to the tension that the text

---

[1] See for example the interpretations of Boesak; Fernandez; Schüssler Fiorenza 1991.

creates—both liberating and oppressing, hopeful and destructive, violent yet eschewing violence—to offer a reading of Rev 18 that allows the symbol to remain multivalent. In opposition to scholars who advocate for the liberating message of the passage or against its sexist imagery, I argue that these features are intertwined. Both the violence and the gender of the image are troubling, yet both are an integral part of the liberating function of the metaphor.

After addressing the dominant opinions on the interpretation of gender regarding the woman/whore/Babylon/Rome,[2] I explore this image as a blended metaphor. By combining information from different input sources (woman, whore, Babylon, Rome, Israel), the author creates a complex image. In the new image, different aspects of the sources are blended together in such a way that they can no longer be separated from one another. Through this blending, the metaphor achieves its effect: it implicates the reader as a participant in the very evils that the passage condemns. Thus, the combination of the whore and city imagery actually helps to bring out the purpose of Rev 18: the author seeks to convict the reader of participation in systemic evil. Since this is a goal that can be helpful for both feminist and liberationist interpreters, it seems worthwhile to take a step back from the either-or approach and toward the multivalent metaphor.

1. Gender or Idolatry

Two opinions dominate in the discussion of the gender of the woman/whore/Babylon/Rome: those of Tina Pippin and Elisabeth Schüssler Fiorenza. While each of these scholars recognizes in some way the multivalency of imagery in Revelation, her reading of this symbol reifies the language and allows only one reading. I will argue that it is precisely because of the way the metaphor of the whore/Babylon functions in Rev 18 that we cannot and should not limit the reading of the metaphor to one meaning.

In Tina Pippin's reading of Revelation, the image of the woman/whore/Babylon is irredeemable. While she admits—at least in theory—to

---

2 In this essay, I alternate the designation of references to the woman/whore/Babylon/Rome, sometimes referring to the whore, harlot, Babylon, Babylon/Rome, etc. This is both for convenience and because the author of Rev also switches between the designations while evoking the same collection of images. I refer to this complex image as a metaphor because I take it to be one multivalent metaphor rather than a group of distinct and separate metaphors. Contemporary conceptual metaphor theorists such as George Lakoff and Mark Johnson, Mark Turner, and Raymond Gibbs shape my understanding of metaphor.

the possibility of more than one reading (1992: 87), Pippin's writing leaves no room for outside interpretations on this matter. She sees the use of the whore image as fatally flawed due to its implicit sanctioning of violence against women. "Women in the Apocalypse are victims—victims of war and patriarchy. The Apocalypse is not a safe space for women" (1992: 80). Pippin translates the violence she perceives against the female image in the text into violence against modern women: "The Apocalypse is cathartic on many levels, but in terms of an ideology of gender, both women characters in the narrative and women readers are victimized." Pippin condemns the book with such vehemence—"the Apocalypse means death to women" (1992: 86)—that it is difficult to see any room left for a different interpretation of the metaphors.

Schüssler Fiorenza sees Pippin as "overinterpreting the text in gender terms" (1998a: 217). This, she argues, "negates the possibility of readers' ethical decision and resistance insofar as it does not leave a rhetorical space for wo/men who desire to read Revelation 'otherwise'" (1998a: 217). Schüssler Fiorenza has picked up on a problem in Pippin's analysis, namely, that although Pippin intends her work to "reveal the focus of fundamentalist and conservative Christian readings of the Apocalypse" (Pippin 1999: 98), in her criticism she essentially accepts their interpretation of Revelation and deconstructs what it means for women. Instead of asserting that the fundamentalist reading is a sexist one, Revelation itself is seen as a sexist text. "By establishing a one-to-one relationship between female/feminine language and symbol on the one hand and actual wo/men on the other, Pippin's reading does not destabilize but rather literalizes the gender inscriptions of the Apocalypse" (Schüssler Fiorenza 1998b:100).

Schüssler Fiorenza, in turn, asserts that the harlot image has one meaning—that of its reference to idolatry. Her interpretation confirms what I will argue below, that the whore metaphor uses imagery from the Hebrew Bible "that indicts Jerusalem and the people of Israel for idolatry" (Schüssler Fiorenza 1998a: 220). However, in order to read the text in this way, Schüssler Fiorenza also limits the whore/Babylon to refer only to idolatry and not to gender: "the sexual metaphor of 'whoring' does not speak about a female person and actual historical wo/man but must be read as a conventional metaphor for idolatry" (1998b: 101). Contrary to this view, I argue below that the gender of the whore metaphor and the multiple options for its interpretation are crucial aspects of its function in Revelation.

In limiting the metaphor of the whore/Babylon, both Pippin and Schüssler Fiorenza are trying to weed out destructive uses of the image. Pippin's perspective is a corrective for readings of Revelation that have ignored and/or confirmed the negative and binary images of women, reinscribing these readings in their own context.[3] Pippin points out how the image of the whore can have a powerful, negative effect on women. Schüssler Fiorenza's interpretation illustrates how the book of Revelation sides with the poor and oppressed. She sees the book not as vengeful but as hopeful (1998a: 100). This makes room for a liberating reading of the text that Pippin excludes. Schüssler Fiorenza sees the importance of reading the gendered language for messages other than the sexist coding of language. This opens the possibility that Revelation is not irredeemable but may still be useful for modern readers.

At the same time, these readings are unhelpful in that they limit the reading of the image of Babylon. Pippin's interpretation denies that some women might find a liberating reading in the text. She sees the dualistic image of women set up by the opposition of the whore and the bride (19:7–8) as necessarily negative for women, for it reasserts false cultural assumptions about women and sexual norms. Clearly, however, there are women who read Revelation differently, including Schüssler Fiorenza. But the liberating interpretation proposed by Schüssler Fiorenza is no less problematic. While she accuses Pippin of binary thinking, she also forces an either-or scenario onto the language of the text. The metaphor of the whore is not only about gender; however, neither is it valid to say that "the vision of Babylon does not tell us anything about the author's understanding of actual wo/men" (Schüssler Fiorenza 1998a: 221) and to make the metaphor speak only of idolatry.

The disagreement expressed by Pippin and Schüssler Fiorenza is also emblematic of a conflict that is often encountered when comparing feminist and liberationist perspectives. Concerns about gender often conflict with concerns about race and/or class. In this case, Pippin's reading leaves no room for other liberating interpretations; she claims the text does violence to women. Schüssler Fiorenza ignores the important functions of the gendered symbolism in order to read the text as liberating.

The tendency for one set of concerns to block an author's consideration of others is certainly not limited to these two feminist interpreters. Other studies of Revelation have read the whore/Babylon in a one-sided fashion—usually without any reference to gender. Bauckham, Fernandez, Rossing, and Christopher Smith all read the metaphor of Babylon as only economic. In doing so, their analyses implicitly render concerns about gender unimportant. For example, Bauckham states that "Rome is a harlot because her associations with the peoples of her empire are for her

---

3 A recent example of this type of interpretation is that of G.K. Beale, who attributes the destruction of Babylon to her "idolatrous seduction of people" (892).

own economic benefit" (347). Such a statement pays no attention to the problematic assumption that prostitutes really benefit from their activities or undertake them because of the economic benefits. Christopher Smith reads a message of economic liberation in the text, ignoring the possibility that the text sanctions violence against women. The analysis of the imagery that Pippin provides never enters into the conversation for most scholars.

Such authors work to limit ideas and behaviors that are destructive to a particular group; in the process, the interpreter may become blind to the ways his or her interpretation is a part of behaviors and attitudes that are destructive of others. (In the examples above, attention to economic concerns leads the author to ignore the impact of the imagery depicting violence against a woman.) Womanist scholars have been pointing out this process for some time. A helpful parallel is bell hooks's analysis of a well-publicized, interracial rape incident in Central Park in which hooks points out the tendency of commentators to choose sides, seeing the interpretive lens for the case as *either* sexism *or* racism. Both must be considered, hooks argues:

> If one reads *The Demon Lover* and thinks again about this crime, one can see it as part of a continuum of male violence against women, of rape and terror as weapons of male domination—yet another horrific and brutal expression of patriarchal socialization. And if one considers this case by combining a feminist analysis of race and masculinity, one sees that since male power within patriarchy is relative, men from poorer groups and men of color are not able to reap the material and social rewards for their participation in patriarchy. In fact they often suffer from blindly and passively acting out a myth of masculinity that is life-threatening. Sexist thinking blinds them to this reality. They become victims of the patriarchy. No one can truly believe that the young black males involved in the Central Park incident were not engaged in a suicidal ritual enactment of a dangerous masculinity that will ultimately threaten their lives, their well-being. (63)

In hooks's description, patriarchy blinds people to consideration of racism and sexism that would ultimately be useful in dismantling both simultaneously. In the case of Rev 18, focusing on only one aspect of the whore metaphor blinds interpreters to the metaphor's full potential. Feminist and liberationist interpretations end up being pitted against one another.

2. Babylon As a Blended Metaphor

Revelation 18 follows the initial vision of the woman/whore/Babylon/Rome of Rev 17. Building on some of the themes of 17, this chapter takes the image of Babylon in a new direction. In Rev 18, Babylon/Rome is condemned for sins such as idolatry, violence, self-glorification, and wealth. Drawing on Hebrew Bible uses of the whore metaphor to refer to both foreign cities and to Israel, Rev 18 points out to the hearer both the evils of the political and economic world of the Roman Empire and their own complicity in this system. The language of the chapter functions to convince the hearer that God's power is greater than Babylon's and to convict hearers of the ways in which they have fallen under Babylon's power.

In the terminology of conceptual metaphor theorists, the woman/Rome/Babylon is a "blended metaphor" (M. Turner: 57–84). A blended metaphor uses information and logic from more than one source (called an "input source"). In the case of Rev 18, the multiple input sources include woman, whore, Babylon, Rome, Israel. Both abstract and specific information from the sources is projected into the blended space of the metaphor. One of the creative features of a blended metaphor is the ability to construct the inference of the metaphor according to the logic of a different frame of reference. In the case of the whore/Babylon, the blended space allows the reading community (which likely does not normally identify itself with the evils of Rome) to become embroiled in the sins of Rome.

There are multiple ways to describe the blending of the whore/Babylon metaphor. The metaphor itself is multiple. In Rev 17 an angel introduces the "great whore" (17:1), and when the Seer looks, he sees a "woman" (17:3) on whose forehead is written "Babylon the great" (17:5). The angel then explains this metaphor in 17:18: "The woman you saw is the great city that rules over the kings of the earth." Whore, woman, Babylon, Rome: this is neither one simple metaphor nor one in which the elements of the metaphor can easily be separated from one another. In the sections that follow I describe two specific aspects of the blending of this metaphor. First, the Babylon metaphor has multiple referents: Rome, for example, as well as Israel. The blending of Rome and Israel and the sins attributed to them is one crucial aspect of the metaphor's ability to implicate the reader in the sins of Babylon. Second, the fornication metaphor is blended with Babylon. This additional blending supplies the logic by which the whore/Babylon will be destroyed. Although I discuss these aspects of the metaphor separately, they are at times indistinguishable and have the same ultimate effect: to implicate the reading community in the sins of Rome/Babylon and to call the reader to "come out."

2.1. Blending Babylon: Rome and Israel

In Rev 17 the woman/whore/Babylon has been set up as a metaphor for Rome. While this remains the case in Rev 18, the image is used here to implicate the reading community in the sins of Babylon/Rome. In the prophetic literature, the image of the whore has been applied not only to foreign cities but also to God's own people; thus, the metaphor easily takes on a blended character. This is especially useful in Rev 18; it convicts the reader of participation in Babylon's sin and thus encourages the reader to heed the call to "come out."

There are many indications in Rev 18 that the primary input source for the metaphor of Babylon is Rome. The author uses the language from prophetic literature dealing specifically with Babylon, although other cities (Tyre) or kingdoms (Edom) are also in the background.[4]

The connection of Babylon and Rome, already present in Jewish circles and implied in Rev 17, is reinforced by images here that paint a picture of Babylon in a way that looks strikingly like the contemporary power of the Roman Empire. Additionally, the plagues Babylon will receive are typical acts of retribution following the capture of a foreign city (Aune: 996). The description of the power and wealth of Rome expressed in 18:5–19 also expresses features of Roman life that were well known in the first century (Bauckham: 338–83). The whore/Babylon would thus have been recognizable to the first-century reader as Rome.

Conversely, some scholars have argued that the primary input source for Babylon is not Rome but Jerusalem (Ford: 285–86, 296–307; Provan: 91–97). The above references to Babylon as a foreign city work against this reading. What does happen in Rev 18 is that the input sources of Rome and Israel are blended in the metaphor Babylon. Because of this, Babylon is not a simple tool for the condemnation of Rome but becomes one that is used to implicate the reading community in the sins attributed to Rome. Some aspects of the text that have been used as evidence for identifying Babylon as Jerusalem may be seen in this light.

A few of the arguments have stemmed from features of the text that seem incongruous if Babylon is read simply as Rome. To say that Rome "has become a house of demons and a refuge of every unclean spirit" would imply that Rome was previously viewed as clean. This would make no sense from the Jewish-Christian milieu of Revelation. Likewise, the accusations of idolatry in the fornication theme are not sensibly applied to a foreign power that was never understood to worship the God of Israel.

---

4 A list of the most obvious references to the prophets' condemnation of foreign cities would include: v. 2 (Isa 21:9; Jer 51:8; Isa 13:21; Jer 51:37); v. 3 (Isa 13:21–22; Jer 51:7; 25:15); v. 4 (Jer 51:45, 6, 9); v. 5 (Jer 51:9); v. 6 (Jer 50:15, 29; 16:18; Isa 40:2); v. 7 (Isa 47:8; Exod 28:2); v. 8 (Isa 47:9).

In addition to these facets of the text, there are Hebrew Bible references that show that the language of Rev 18 could also apply to Israel.
While some of the prophetic language points to a parallel between Babylon and foreign cities, some connects Babylon and Israel. The strange
inhabitants of the city in 18:2 resemble statements in Amos 5:2 and Jer
9:11 that refer to Israel and Jerusalem. While less explicit, the wine
imagery of 18:3 may also evoke the images of Israel as God's vineyard
(Isa 5; 27:1–5; Jer 12:10). Verse 6 becomes especially interesting because of
the language of doubling punishment. This more extreme punishment is
an idea in the Hebrew Bible applied only to Israel/Jerusalem (Jer 16:18;
Isa 40:2), while foreigners were depicted as receiving a punishment equal
to their crime (Jer 50:29).

The harlot image itself is most commonly a reference to the faithless-
ness of God's people.[5] Although foreign cities are described in the
Hebrew Bible using the metaphor of the whore, the prophetic image of
Israel as harlot is especially relevant in Rev 18, because here fornication is
attributed not to Babylon but to her consorts. Revelation 18:3 contains
three references to fornication using slightly different vocabulary. In all
three of these, the subject of the verb is not Babylon but the nations,
kings, and merchants who, in their various ways, fornicated with her.
The implication is that these sins belong not only to Babylon but also to
those who have participated with her in fornication.

Rather than shifting the weight of the evidence toward Babylon as
Jerusalem, these factors point to a function of Rev 18, to implicate the
reading community in the sins of Rome. While the metaphor of the
whore/Babylon is initially identified as Rome, the blending of the image
allows the additional assertion that the reading community participates
in the sins of the empire. As part of a Jewish-Christian community, the
reader is expected to identify with Israel as a character evoked through
the prophetic texts. The readers thereby understand their participation in
these sins and can see themselves as those who are called to "come out."

The metaphor also helps to indict the reading community because of
the multiplicity of sins that are implied through the blended metaphor.
The sins of Babylon/Rome—and the reading community—are numerous. There is a blanket condemnation of Babylon's sin in 18:5: "her sins
have reached up to heaven and God has remembered her wrongs." Specific sins are somewhat difficult to identify. This is partly because they are

---

5 References to Israel/Judah as harlot include Lev 17:7; 20:5–6; Num 14:33; 15:39; Deut
1:16; Judg 2:17; 8:27; 1 Chr 5:25; 2 Chr 21:11; Ps 73:27; Hos 1:2; 2:4; 4:15; 9:1; Jer 2:20; 3:2, 9, 13;
5:7,11; 13:27; Ezek 6:9; 16; 23; 43:7, 9.

not listed but are spread throughout Rev 17 and 18. Some of these sins are explicit and directly attributed to the whore/Babylon: fornication (πορνεία, 17:4–5; 18:3), sorcery (φαρμακεία, 18:23), and the slaughter of the saints (17:6; 18:24). Other sins are implied through the language of the chapter. Arrogance is implied through the speech attributed to Babylon in 18:7, idolatry through the language of Babylon's self-glorification (18:7) and the harlot image, and wealth through its attribution to the merchants (18:3), listed as one of the reasons for Babylon's downfall.

The ample space allotted to economic sins in the lament portion of the chapter gives them special emphasis. The subjects of the laments—kings, merchants, and sailors—as well as their content (especially in the exhaustive list of goods of 18:11–13) point to the prominence of the economic critique. Adding to this is the nuance of meaning of the word στρῆνος (luxury) and its cognates in 18:1–10. While usually translated "luxury" (NRSV), this word can also be translated as "sensuality," which retains its relationship to the idea of fornication. Thus the reference to luxury is not only present in more places than is readily apparent from many translations, but it is integrally tied to the fornication image.

The dual definition of στρῆνος is important to remember in interpreting the meaning of wealth in the rest of Rev 18. Living sensually/luxuriously is indicated twice as reason for Babylon's condemnation (18:3, 6). Wealth, then, is probably not viewed ambiguously in this chapter, as Adela Yarbro Collins suggests (129). Equally unlikely is Provan's assertion that wealth is only important for what it symbolizes about religious commitment (88–89). The lengthy descriptions of finery (18:12–13, 16) not only suggest the gravity of the sin in the extent of wealth that is represented but also tie the criticism to actual practice familiar within the Roman Empire (Bauckham: 350–66). While a spiritual critique of wealth is possible (as seems to be present in 3:17), the concrete nature of the wealth described in this chapter seems to exclude a purely spiritual analysis. As a whole, Rev 18 depicts real criticism of the economic practices of the Roman Empire. However, it is not necessary to choose between economic and other types of sins. The multiplicity of sins is important to the interpretation of the chapter. As Bauckham notes,

> John sees a connection between Rome's economic affluence, Rome's idolatrous self-deification, and Rome's military and political brutality. The power of his critique of Rome—perhaps the most thorough-going critique from the period of the early empire—lies in the connection it portrays between these various facets of Rome's evil. (349)

The connection between the sins heightens the awareness of Babylon's evils.

The interrelatedness of various sins means that "coming out" of Babylon has more than one meaning, depending on the sin the reader has in view. The options in reading numerous sins give readers more opportunities to identify themselves as the recipients of this call. Bauckham has identified merchants as one component of John's audience for whom the author "has set a kind of hermeneutical trap. Any reader who finds himself [sic] sharing the perspective of Rome's mourners ... should thereby discover, with a shock, where he stands, and the peril in which he stands" (376). While Bauckham has pointed to one of the important functions of Rev 18—that of the self-identification of the reader with the sins of the Roman system—it is not necessary for the reader to be a merchant in order for this identification to take place. The multiplicity and interconnectedness of the sins involved allow for anyone who participates in the Roman economy or cultic system to see himself or herself as implicated in the downfall of Babylon.

Revelation 18 convinces readers of Babylon's sins at the same time it convicts them of participation in that sin. If readers do not heed the call to "come out," they will "receive from her plagues" (18:4). The metaphor of Babylon is an important part of this function because of the way it allows the author to draw upon language that evokes the evils of an oppressive empire as well as the sins of God's own people. Through this blended metaphor, the agency of the readers becomes intertwined with that of the Roman Empire. The call to "come out" is not one for the reader to sit idly by and witness the destruction of evil but is a call to act.

The blending of Babylon, Rome, and Israel is a key to the metaphor's ability to implicate the reader in this multitude of sins. The gender of the metaphor is another key. This was implicit in the discussion of the whore and Israel above; I now turn to a more explicit discussion of this feature of the metaphor.

2.2. Gender Blending: The Whore/Babylon

The Babylon metaphor is also blended with the image of the woman/whore of Rev 17. This additional step of blending forms one complex metaphor. In the blending of the metaphor, the inference of the metaphor is created: the reading community is associated with the sins of Rome, whose immanent destruction is deserved. The inclusion of the woman/whore is crucial to the function of the metaphor.

The gender of the whore/Babylon plays an important role in the way the metaphor functions. Numerous features of the text point to the careful use of a gendered metaphor to achieve its effect. The fact that Rome is pictured as a woman is relevant in and of itself. There were certainly other possibilities available to the author, even though cities were conventionally imaged as women. Consider, for example, the coin that Aune cites as an item that the author might have had in mind in creating the metaphor (920). The coin depicts the goddess Roma seated on seven hills. Yet in the image of the coin, the "goddess" is depicted as a *male* warrior. Even if this coin were not known to the author of Revelation, its image reminds us that the goddess Roma does not necessarily have to be imaged as a woman. This is a choice made by the author.

In Rev 18 Babylon is no longer pictured directly as a woman or a whore; the imagery is that of a city. However, the input source of the whore and the logic associated with fornication are blended with the city imagery of the Babylon metaphor in Rev 18. As I explain in the following paragraphs, the fornication theme establishes the logic through which it is understood that the hearer participates in the sins of Babylon/Rome and brings about her destruction. The gender of the whore/Babylon and the social conventions she evokes are an integral part of this logic.

One can see the usefulness of the whore image clearly in 18:2–3, where human responsibility for Babylon's downfall becomes apparent. Here Babylon is described as fallen, and the reason for her falling is given in 18:3: "Because all the nations have fallen down from the wine of the anger of her fornication, and the kings of the earth have fornicated with her, and the merchants of the earth have grown rich from the power of her sensuality." From this statement, it is not Babylon's actions, but those of others, that are responsible for the city's destruction. The metaphor of fornication functions to associate the activities of the people with Babylon's sin and destruction. The fall of Babylon is described here as a result of the activity of humans who have fallen down, fornicated, and gotten rich.

The gender of the whore/Babylon is a critical aspect of its utility. The whore is an input source that contributes the logic that undergirds the destruction of Babylon. As Aune notes, a list of what others have done hardly qualifies as reason for destroying Babylon:

> Who is to blame for committing fornication, the kings of the earth or Babylon? This can only be construed as a reason for Babylon's fall given the ancient and modern double standard that holds the woman rather that the man responsible for violating sexual mores. (988)

The metaphor functions as it does in part because of the background assumption of a double standard for women and men in their responsibility for sexual norms. This assumption is present in Rev 18 when the whore is described as fallen because others have fornicated with her. She is seen as being held responsible for their sins. This is possible because of cultural norms regarding gender, which were present at the time of the writing and are still largely active today. Were Babylon imaged as a man, it would not make sense to the reader that Babylon is blamed for what others have done. The sexual nature of the actions would seem disconnected because men are generally not harshly judged for having multiple sexual partners. Since it is a woman who is blamed—and one who has already violated sexual mores, at that—her condemnation is not incongruous with what the reader already believes.

The image of the whore is useful to the author because of the social conventions it evokes. This point seems similar to what Schüssler Fiorenza has said of her own hermeneutic, which "understands language as a convention or tool that enables writers and readers to negotiate linguistic tensions and inscribed ambiguities and thereby to create meaning in specific contexts and sociopolitical locations" (1998b: 96). Because of the conventions associated with female prostitutes, the whore metaphor functions to imply that the actions of the nations contribute to the fall of Babylon. Thus the gender of the whore—and the unjust cultural assumptions that it implies—are not at all incidental to the vision of Rev 18. Rather than being an aspect of the passage that is easily treated separately, the gender of the metaphor must be considered as an aspect of its ability to convict the reader of participation in the sins of Babylon/Rome.

3. A READING OF THE BLENDED METAPHOR

Ironically, from a present-day feminist perspective the image of the whore not only functions to convince the reader of sin but also enacts the very dynamic it seeks to represent. As I have argued, one power of the whore/Babylon metaphor is in its ability to convince the reader of participation in systemic evil while at the same time convicting the reader of that activity. A feminist reading of Revelation would see the division of women into virgin/whore stereotypes and the blame and punishment of women for sexual acts as systemic evils themselves. The text, however, relies on this particular form of evil in its construction of the blended metaphor. Part of the metaphor rests on the logic of "whore" as an input source; the logic of this source includes the notion that the whore deserves punishment because of the actions of others. In order to understand and utilize the image of the whore, the reader buys into the logic of the metaphor and in so doing accepts the unjust social norms on which it rests.

In grasping this image, the reader reinforces harmful stereotypes of women and thus participates in human sin. The metaphor of fornication convinces the reader that humans are entangled in evil; the way the metaphor functions becomes an additional example of the reader's participation in this evil. The text does not itself reveal sexist stereotypes as a systemic evil; however, the message of the text and its rhetoric invites a feminist interpretation that allows the text to critique its own perspective on gender norms.

In the metaphor of the whore/Babylon, the message of liberation is intertwined with the stereotyping and violence of the image. The feminist critique of the above paragraph depends upon the liberating message of the downfall of oppressive powers; this message in turn rests upon the use of the female as a symbol of evil. Rather than acting as a deterrent for feminist interpreters, this aspect of the text may invite further reflection upon the larger patterns of feminist response to texts like Rev 18.

CONCLUSION

Going back to the many meanings of the metaphor is helpful in analyzing the conversation between Pippin and Schüssler Fiorenza, because each author attempts to limit the metaphor to one of its aspects. Pippin focuses on the whore as woman, Schüssler Fiorenza on the description of the sins of Rome and their implications. One might say Pippin limits the metaphor to the whore, Schüssler Fiorenza to Babylon. But the metaphor of Rev 18 blends both these concepts into one creative image. Keeping the blended nature of the metaphor in view reminds us of the function of the passage, to implicate human action in the many sins of the powerful Roman Empire. Focusing on only one aspect of sin should alert the reader to the possibility that the interpretation will be limited in important ways.

This is not an argument that the text has no limits. Rather, it is that the interpreter should try to discern the possibilities of the metaphor based on the language of the text and what is known of the culture in which it was formed. In this case, Greco-Roman and Jewish traditions regarding Babylon, Rome, and the whore may be explored as primary sources for the metaphor. The openness of the text comes in the blending of a variety of sources into a complex metaphor. Limitation of the metaphor to only one referent reads against the construction of the image as a blended metaphor.

The very openness of the metaphor is perhaps what leads interpreters to try to set such limits. Eugene Boring has noted the prevalence of indirect communication in the description of Babylon's destruction, which he says "has two advantages: (1) the hearer-readers cannot be passive but must in their imaginations construct the scene themselves from the spectators' laments; and, (2) it gives them the freedom to choose whether to identify with the speakers in the drama. John does not tell his congregations how they should respond" (186). The problem becomes that interpreters seem to *want* to know how to respond. Or at least, we want to limit the possible ways that others will respond. The potential use of the metaphors of Revelation for promoting violence against other humans is one of the problems recognized by both Pippin and Schüssler Fiorenza. Limiting the openness of the whore/Babylon metaphor, however, also limits the reader's ability to stand convicted of the multitude of Babylon's sins.

Feminist interpretations often present an either-or scenario through which a biblical text is either redeemed (seen as nonsexist) or denied (seen as entirely sexist and, therefore, not "scripture"). Schüssler Fiorenza and Pippin's analyses of Rev 18 are examples of this tendency. The reasons for this are understandable; after centuries of interpretations that have caused harm to women both individually and corporately, there has been a perceived need to gain clarity about whether a text is for or against the interests of women.

This approach creates its own problems, however. One problem, noted above, is that the structure and language of this passage resists such an approach. The liberating message of the text—the destruction of the forces of oppression—cannot be separated from its use of female metaphors, which reinforce the stereotypes of a patriarchal society. At the same time this liberating message is a powerful one, calling attention to economic and social forces that are both detrimental to people and widespread. The either-or approach flattens the language of the text by denying the blending of images and subsequently reducing the importance of the inferences accomplished through that blending.

Another problem is that the approach does not recognize fully that women have various interests. The reduction of the text to one reading bears with it the assumption that such a reading can speak for all women (and all people). This is not the case; even in the exchange between Pippin and Schüssler Fiorenza it is clear that these two women have divergent interests and appreciate different aspects of the passage. Although the exchange is not unfriendly, there nevertheless remains little possibility that the two interests might be seen as compatible. The options that seem to be available in the Pippin–Schüssler Fiorenza debate are for one side to capitulate to the other or for the two interests to remain in opposition to one another. Yet it is such opposition between feminist and liberationist concerns—or between concerns of racism and sexism or classism and sexism—that have frequently been recognized as harmful to both positions. The possibility of affirming the importance of liberation for both economic and gender concerns is lost in the assertion that the metaphor bears only one meaning.

For scholars concerned to address both sexism and economic or other forms of oppression, the either-or approach fails because it requires that these interests become separated. The approach of this essay has been to recognize that gender oppression that is culturally embedded in a biblical text can be harmful, without denying that the text may still be useful.

Some texts that rely on negative stereotypes or violence against women may also bear a liberating message. This approach recognizes that the willingness to give up part of the text—either its liberating message or its gender coding—means that the interpreter must forfeit something important. If the interpreter emphasizes the gender stereotyping, then the text is only oppressive and sexist. If the interpreter emphasizes the message of liberation from economic oppression, then she loses the ability to say anything critical of the violence against the whore.

By embracing both the message of liberation and the sexist norms it employs, the interpretation is not fully satisfying; it is liberating and oppressive at the same time. Yet this complexity is helpful because it reflects the realities that forms of oppression are often intertwined and that humans can be blind to the way our own participation maintains these forms. The reader of Rev 18 is called to recognize complicity in systemic evils and to "come out." Even though the text itself is complicit in sexist stereotyping, the vision of the passage is one in which the sins of Babylon are always multifaceted and with which the reader is always involved. In a complex world, this way of seeing may be the most important message that Rev 18 offers.

Pregnant Passion: Gender, Sex, and Violence in the Bible—A Response to Part 3: Types, Stereotypes, and Archetypes

Barbara Green
Dominican School of Philosophy and Theology, Graduate Theological Union

The task of the volume as articulated by editor Cheryl Kirk-Duggan is to pose and explore the topic of how gender, sex(uality), and violence meet in biblical texts, how they intersect also in the lives of those who generated the texts and consequently in the lives of all who have received them, ourselves included. The texts are claimed to be heavy with fertile implications that call for hopeful exploration and heavy with the potential for being badly read, misread, or ignored. The challenge offered in this volume is that we, exploring the dynamics of these texts, are to embrace their passion and energy, or perhaps also feel more deeply our own. Pregnant passion encodes the scholars engaging the gender, sex, and violence of the texts as well, Kirk-Duggan claims. To examine the dynamic of intersection in the texts studied here (the ones chosen being a good entry to a wider topic) and to show how, specifically, certain readers appropriate the narratives for their own reasons and purposes, be they bitter or sweet, is a promise made in the introduction to the volume to its readers. The specific section to which I will respond, subtitled by reference to types, stereotypes, and archetypes, promises implicitly to rehearse and explicitly to define the gender, sex, and violence issues in these more precise categories.

It will come as a surprise to no reader that proposals-become-introductions are not always exactly matched by completed essays and that authorial plans and hopes are difficult to write presciently while essays are still on the drawing board (if they are there). In fact, it is a good sign that a volume under construction outgrows to some extent its early articulations. So I will not spend time exegeting the somewhat general and allusive language of the introductory claim of the volume or even the triplet of terms that purports to describe the section but rather reframe what I think the three articles in this section have set out to do, what they have accomplished, what I think lacks in the endeavor, and what goes still pregnant within the work and promises to develop fruitfully. In so doing, I will try to make my own questions, interests, and viewpoints adequately clear. But as an overarching question, let me name this one: What is it we are doing when we read and appropriate biblical texts? Since "we" vary considerably, as do our texts, the question will need refinement in every aspect. To explore how we, and each of us in greater company, reads is at least part of the topic on the table, perhaps simultaneously both a larger and a smaller question than this volume and its authors, including the three to whom I am responding, have asked.

Aims of the Three Essays

"Some Place to Cry: Jephthah's Daughter and the Double Dilemma of Black Women in America" by Valerie C. Cooper samples from the long line of interpreters of the portion of the Jephthah narrative where the father and daughter interact (Judg 11) and proposes that the combination of political and economic deficiency that characterizes the father endangers the young woman in the Judges story. Cooper suggests as well that a blend of racism and sexism that hobbles so many black males increases the danger for contemporary African American women. Not simply racism is the problem and not simply sexism, but their interaction. And black women are not only tied together with black men but split apart from them as well, when sexism and racism wreak their havoc in the political and economic, in the social and religious lives of African Americans. The danger, especially to women, increases if only part of the problem is seen and the other not. Cooper places before her readers modern scholarship on a number of issues raised by the biblical narrative she is dealing with: its genre, the ambiguity of the Jephthah vow itself, certain sociological particularities of the plausible state of the daughter's virginity, the female characters' presumed demeanor, the story's uncertain ending. The outcome of Cooper's reading is not so much to negotiate the various factors of each subtopic in relation to each other but simply to name into conversation various issues similar to those of the contemporary group she is speaking about. Cooper raises as well the question of how Jephthah's daughter can be seen in relation to Abraham's not-sacrificed son, and she samples from Pseudo-Philo, Shakespeare, and Toni Morrison to imply analogy among the situations posed by those later narratives. Cooper concludes by developing further the double bind for black women: when their men are racistly marginalized both economically and socially, women not only tend to be excluded from their own opportunities but also find themselves compensating variously to black males. Black women are both tied to the problems of black men and suffer their own special editions of those problems while coping. They may condone illicit or illegal moves of their kin or allow themselves to be denied appropriate roles in black churches; they exchange their own best interests to stand by their men, who may choose less than well for all concerned. A place for tears is what remains, an option made visible in the Jephthah text, where women gather to com- memorate a grief. It is a small comfort, Cooper maintains, referencing both the story and her maternal forbears' experience, but a welcome one. As have many other readers of the story, Cooper reads to serve particular interests and urgent purposes but calls attention to the dynamic as well (not true of all readers). Interpretation makes visible the viewpoint and situation of the interpreter.

"Daughter Zion: Giving Birth to Redemption" is Mary Donovan Turner's occasion to examine a chain of sex- and gender-linked metaphor components (e.g., virgin, daughter, virgin daughter, widow, bride, people, city) that runs from the early preexilic prophets through Lamen- tations and into Second Isaiah, cutting new channels as well as widening an old one en route. As the metaphoric language grows and shifts, it is clear that the symbol depicts its referent as faithless and displeasing to God, though also as capable of becoming hopeful and consoled. When the female character(ization) voices her own pain, and when it moves into dialogue with the deity, a complexity for the divine referent is engaged: Can he be both perpetrator of her suffering and redeemer of it as well? Is the female/feminine character's own capacity to speak forth part of the redemptive process? Turner's piece offers specific observa- tions about the female voice in the various texts: in Amos, Micah, Isaiah of Jerusalem, Lamentations, and in exilic Isaiah the language enters as well into internal conversation, when texts of one speaker are picked up and reused in the mouth of another, all with rich and complexifying result. Though focusing most overtly on the personified Zion and the explicit female/feminine referent, Turner also draws attention to the peculiar problems for the male/masculine partner, whose language risks minimizing the experience and even silencing the voice of its dialogue partner by covering over too hastily and cosmically the experience she is articulating so carefully. Turner's concluding question raises the nature of redemption for our contemporaries.

Susan E. Hylen's "The Power and Problem of Revelation 18" focuses as well on a central sex- and gender-based metaphor steeped in violence: the whore. Hylen questions how it has and is to be read: harmfully, surely, and how, why? She maintains that it has a liberating potential as well and can thus be read healthily; but how and why? She offers the insight of two scholars whose positions differ. (Tina Pippin sees the whore as a sex-linked trope and finds it fatally flawed and too dangerous for use; Elisabeth Schüssler Fiorenza construes it as offering access to the phenomenon of civic idolatry and thus as helpful to understanding the nature of betrayal of the poor and powerless.) Hylen finds each of these positions too reductive in practice if not in theory and urges what she calls the blended metaphor, whose multiple facets are able to be appropriated quite variously by the many readers of Revelation. Hylen goes on to explain how such readers—engaging the complex figure who is Babylon, Rome, and Jerusalem by turns, who can offer access to various constructions of participatory infidelity—are implicated as guilty and offered as well a way out of their situation. Thus the language that shares in the realms of sex, gender, and violence as well as economics, politics, and religion challenges the reader to insight about others and to self-knowledge and makes clear the need to act decisively as the world of "the whore" is about to collapse. The reader, unless he or she disregards the valence of the metaphor and reads simplistically and self-righteously blind, has no illusion of innocence, thanks to the blended metaphor and the strategy of reading it prompts. But neither is he or she condemned to go down with the ship. The complexity of the metaphor, correctly navigated, is what works successfully.

ACCOMPLISHMENTS OF THE THREE ESSAYS

Each essay places before us the intersection of sex, gender, and violence in a particular biblical text or set of them. Each writer senses, names, understands, or articulates the dynamic of their linkage. For Cooper, social and economic marginalization leads to class-linked and gender-specific violence. When race is a factor as well, the violence is intensified. Though Cooper does not draw out the ethnic struggles that seem clear in Judges and that debauch constantly into the violence of warfare (both "international" and ultimately domestic), she would have ample cause to do so. Her article seems grounded on a basic similarity or analogy between the circumstances visible or retrievable in the ancient biblical narrative and their capacity to shed light on similarities in the experience of later and in fact contemporary readers. She does not quite say, but I sense understands, that the reverberation is mutual: the double binds experienced by readers make prominent the various dynamics articulated within the narrative: sex, gender, violence, and many others. Cooper's naming of the multiple relationalities that can prompt women to go complicit in the Hobson's choices of their various males throws valuable light onto the less well known circumstances that may lie beneath the Judges story.

Turner brings into a dense colloquy voices we are perhaps more prone to hear one at a time, or at best dyadically. Her attention to the timbre of the woman's voice—more faint and indirect in the eighth-century prophets and emerging with greater intensity and directness in the (perhaps) more dramatic circumstances of the sixth-century crisis—maintains the urgency of the sex- and gender-linked figure and the violations and violences she is given to articulate. How various readers appraise the subtle effect evoked when Zion is primarily spoken about, as well as when the speaker takes responsibility for her own situation (appropriately? not so?), receive a jolt when the one consistently articulated as the source or occasion of her troubles speaks up to brush them away, minimizing them or silencing her, as Turner suggests may be the effect on readers constructing Zion so attentively. Turner raises more briefly and inconclusively the question of the male figure or masculine voice that is given such a role in the violence bruited in the text. But the nuance she exercises for the one gender is made available, implicitly, for the other as well. How does the sex- and gender-linked male figure participate in violence, both to urge it and to suffer from it as well? What case can be made for the deity by attending with careful ear to his voicing of his experience? As Turner so well outlines, the various levels of violence that may attend the literary treatment of the female character, her actual flesh and blood sisters of mid-first millennium Judah/Israel, and surely the many other actual women whose lives have been made wretched by those who claim the metaphor as justification, may go the other way as well. God is not perhaps well-served by these metaphoric figures and their discourse, nor are we who struggle to imagine and approach the divine.

Hylen works to move us beyond the reductive, however right it may be so far as it goes. That is, her willingness to risk the complexity and potential confusion of both/and does us, reading, a great favor. Though the whore metaphor is undoubtedly sex/gender-and-violence-laden, it is not simply equivalent to that linkage. And though it undoubtedly borrows from the realms of improper political, economic, and social dalliance with violence (hence with idolatry), to say that is not to say all. Carefully owning that both Pippin and Schüssler Fiorenza know well that metaphor is complex by its nature and resists reduction, Hylen challenges them and us to act on what they know. Rather than simply dismiss the metaphor or excuse it, she urges that we allow it to offer multiple possibilities, some of which we will approve and engage, others not. The dynamic of Hylen's piece aims, I think, to push readers off the too-comfortable rock of self-righteousness, where we can rest too confident that we have got it clear and are correct. The gain from the rich texture where violent situations are constructed of sex- and gender-linked images and from the sketching of those partaking also in economic and political realities stops us, perhaps, from claiming an innocent or justified position. How we choose to read, particularly insofar as we make explicit what we are aiming to do, eliminates clear rights and wrongs. Pippin's dismissal of the metaphor looks now to me too simplistic; Schüssler Fiorenza's insistence upon the more political (as distinct from gender-linked) valence seems naïve. Each is right, to a point. Hylen's discriminating both/and, her calling attention to the braided quality of the figure, looks wiser. Recognizing, acknowledging the fear that to allow for complexity can deteriorate into "anything goes," she nonetheless encourages us to stay complex, hence remaining more likely to find something to critique not only in the egregious other but in ourselves as well. And such self-knowledge can lead to compunction, to conversion, to a way out.

Aporiai in the Three Essays

Mindful of the hazards and potential unfairness of criticizing scholars for what they failed to do, I think nevertheless there is a place to highlight some of what might have been picked up and developed well but that did not leave the runway. I will suggest a few possibilities here.

First, and perhaps most lamentable, the writers all fail to make the careful distinctions in terms and to provide definitions for the slippery if technical language they use. It is not so much that they disregard "type," "stereotype," and "archetype," since the essays they have produced are not so clearly participating in that realm of discourse as might have seemed likely when the volume was conceived. But these three writers do use the language of analogy and metaphor without any explicit clarification of what precisely they understand by these easy-to-misconstrue terms. Is the rough similarity between certain features of the story world of Jephthah and daughter really analogous for the circumstances of African Americans, as Cooper suggests? It seems that, if a general and in fact quite selective resemblance is able to be simply alleged and not discussed with some precision, we are too close to the sort of precritical allegorical reading whose pitfalls have been made clear in modern criticism. The hazards of such interpretation have been pointed out in the writings of South African biblical scholar Gerald O. West (ch. 3). West's sustained and basically sympathetic analysis of the differing methodologies of Allan Boesak and Itumeleng Mosala have shown how easy it is to allegorize when the historical factors are substantially ignored. Cooper's own suggestion that Judg 11 may be a cautionary tale would take the piece in another direction, it seems. I have a similar question and concern about metaphor. Turner is on familiar terrain when she makes the female a figure for the city and people Israel and sees the overlord in the relationship as male. But as she develops the concept of voice, and breaks apart usefully the various strategies by which a subject can be made articulate and be construed by a reader, I am not sure "metaphor" any longer does the job. We may need a more complex anthropology to negotiate the content of the voiced language. How are the various speech utterances metonymically able to represent the various phases of the experience of the suffering figure? Hylen's use of blended metaphor seems useful, but unless lifted out of context and placed abstractly on a list, is there any metaphor that is not born and must not go blended in context? "Blended metaphor" seems tautologous, and the task would seem to be to begin to map the various possibilities of intersection, not only in a given piece (which Hylen does), but in theory. That is, if every metaphor is in fact a complex braid, how can an author or a reader make sensible and discriminating use of such tropes without being stymied by the simultaneous clamorings of too many referent realms?

Second, and perhaps quite excusably in short papers, there is little reference to the current challenge facing every academic biblical interpreter to explain what she is doing methodologically. By that I do not mean that Cooper, Turner, and Hylen do not explain their moves. They do, up to a point. But it strikes me that volumes of Semeia Studies, which claim to be "experimental [and] devoted to the exploration of new and emergent areas and methods of biblical criticism" owe the guild (and its own readership as well) a brief discussion of how their effort contributes to the vast repositioning of the interpretation exercise that has dominated the second half of the twentieth century without yet being satisfactorily articulated. As Claudia Camp challenges, how will each of us "find the methodological means to understand both the period and its literature by means of each other: that is, to overcome the breach between literary and historical methodologies" (Camp: 8)? Specifically, is it legitimate and any longer defensible to discuss a narrative with virtually no historical-critical work on its relevant circumstances? The vast complexities and inevitable frustrations encountered in the book of Judges do not, in my view, excuse the effort to situate the narrative somewhere, "somewhen." We are likely to be inadequate in what we say of it, but to avoid the whole issue of what factors lie behind the book seems inevitably to underwrite misuse of it. Cooper's sense that the hero of Judg 11 is marginalized needs sociological amplification, not likely to come from the sources she cites. Turner as well skirts the various historical issues that underlie her texts. If I were she, I would immediately rejoin, "But you can't do everything in a short essay!"—a contention with which I would have great sympathy. But notes can assist, and they need to refer readers to portions of scholarship that cannot be discussed in detail but that can serve to undergird and amplify one's own work. Is there any sense in which changing circumstances between the early eighth and late sixth centuries influenced the articulation of both the male and female speakers? It seems a possibility at least to name. Hylen has perhaps the easier task of making use of historical-critical work on the book of Revelation, and her work with an image that participates in multiple realms makes it difficult to ignore completely. But her notes seem also an inadequate guide for any who want more detail on the actual social worlds implied by the metaphor in Revelation of the city as whore.

Third, and related to that same large topic—perhaps another way of naming it—is to miss in all of the articles explicit discussion and development of how a literary text continues to shelter the circumstances and worldview of its origins and hence what a reader is legitimately able to do. Camp is succinctly pertinent again: "God only knows whether the joke is sitting 'in' the text waiting for my eye, or whether it is the product only of my own skewed view of things" (Camp: 8). Each essay hints about the various possibilities envisioned when a reader engages an ancient text. Cooper is rightly clear *that* the experience of a reader influences insight into a text; but specifically, *how?* Turner is a highly sensitive reader of the phases of discourse pursued by the figure Zion, yet she seems to deny the implications of her own theory when she asserts that "In Lamentations, clearly it is Yahweh who has brought the violent devastation to Zion. Yahweh has become the enemy" (200). It seems to be the case that at least some contemporary theory is backing away a bit from the insistence on the death of the author, a move that still leaves us plenty of room for resistant readings (Lodge: 92).[1] If the metaphor works one way for Zion, are there not similar possibilities for the deity? Is it so axiomatic that the patriarchal god of the Hebrew Bible is a villain that there is no alternative possible? Can contemporary critical analysis lend a hand here or not? Can a feminist reading save Yahweh from total brutishness? I think so and would love to hear it attempted or at least discussed. Hylen, again, comes closer with her analysis of the reading strategies set forth by Pippin and Schüssler Fiorenza, eschewing the particularities of why they each read as they do but making plain that they read quite differently. Hylen's ability to name the place where assumptions differ fundamentally helps readers

---

1 Lodge's article usefully analyzes Jane Smiley's *Charles Dickens,* a recent addition to the Penguin Lives series. For an author/critic (as Lodge is) to write about a writer writing about a writer provides wonderful scope for rethinking some of the possibilities. Lodge says, quoting Smiley: "'Writing is an act of artistic and moral agency,' she asserts firmly, 'where choices are made that the author understands, full of implications and revelations that the author also understands.' If this attitude somewhat underestimates the contribution of a writer's unconscious to the creative process, it also enables Smiley to make us see Dickens' immense creative achievement afresh" (92), without too complex a critical apparatus but also, I think, without preventing other constructions, so named.

(herself and others) to be able to track their qualified use of the excellent work of those two scholars with some precision.

Another quite starting omission (a fourth) shared by these three works is the anonymity of them. Again, perhaps there is some editorial reason for it that remains hidden from at least this reader (and from all, I fear). I am not wishing for the rather clumsy and artificial way in which writers used to self-identify, giving race, caste, citizenship, and gender as though they were name, rank, and serial number. What I think would work in a volume on passion is to be told directly at the appropriately contextualized moment what generated each piece. There are hints, to be sure, and no authoring voice should be or feel forced to ante up what she does not wish to say. Yet Cooper's analysis would stand stronger, I think, were it to rise explicitly from actual context and thence to reading rather than to work somewhat artificially from application of the biblical text to life. Shawn Copeland has recently put into conversation the whole issue of how all of us are serving in "the Master's" house, and she raises a similar collusion to Cooper's: "To win protection and affirmation in this house, white women resign themselves to the definitions and designs of white men. Our sisters learn and practice the ways of the fox and the ways of the lion, or they take up ornamental poses from the sidelines" (Copeland: 20). Turner hints at the problems that arise when the deity who hastens (if that is the word) to console is the same character who inflicted the pain. That point is so well named but remains somewhat underdeveloped in the article. For whom, specifically, can this be an urgent matter? Cooper makes a similar point when she registers feeling troubled at the silence of God in the Jephthah narrative. How does each of the women writing these insightful articles situate the problem of the narrative divine character and the "real" deity? Why, in fact, does each bother to read her text? I am well aware of the complexities of mixing academic and pastoral or "personal" concerns, especially in an academic volume, but when three women write under the rubric of pregnant passion, I think a space is created for a bit more immediacy and candor. Is the canonical aspect of the biblical texts the elephant in the living room? If so, it needs to be named, appropriately. But perhaps that is not why any of these women are reading these texts. I miss knowing what has driven their readings.

I can say as well that I miss a precise articulation, even if abstractly, of how the sex/gender/violence equation goes in each article. That it does is surely well-discussed. How is not so clear. The introduction to the volume defines violence (though not sex and gender) as follows:

> Violence is that which violates, destroys, manipulates, corrupts, defiles, and robs us of dignity and of true personhood. Violence is the use of thought and deed within a continuum of the physical, the philosophical,

and the psychological that oppresses and robs an individual or community of their gift of freedom and the sacredness of their person. Violence is a practice of idolatry: that which defames God's created order. (3)

Does that rather general, almost too full, and nonfactored definition work adequately for all of these essays? I doubt it, but there is no mention of it. The nature of violence, especially in worlds of competing goods, begs for discussion in our communities, large and small. Of course it is discussed, in our world and in these three essays. The complex violence of racism and sexism, the implicitly shocking violence of a male deity and a female partner, the potential of woman-bashing so often made to seem legitimate in the prophets' language and in the encouragement of the narrating voice of Revelation all present themselves. But all present themselves. Though each essay seems poised to carry things a step further, each disappoints me, ultimately. How can those caught in a double bind (which in the real world is likely all of us) begin to negotiate the conflicting goods and harms that we may encounter? How do we begin to deconstruct the violence that seems stock to the God of the prophets? If part of relief and liberation come as the woman speaks her grief and pain, then how does she undertake to do it responsibly and we to read it answerably? Do we want a biblical text in which the rightness and wrongness are less clearly polarized than they sometimes emerge in some feminist studies? Is Jephthah wholly wrong, and are his daughter and friends only blameless victims when we read? Does the text of prophetic tradition invite us to negotiate the complexity of the voices of God and Zion locked in dialogue, and are we willing to see violence and weakness on both parts, hence marking a challenging path for ourselves as readers? Does Revelation do well to suggest, if that is what it does, that some situations are so impacted that only violence can address them? Is the whore so bad that all that any can do is run for their (our) lives? Is that an ethic we endorse, on occasion? Is some violence necessary? These are difficult issues crying out for careful, nuanced, situated, dialogical discussion. Regina Schwartz has raised recently and provocatively the link between monotheism and violence, a topic surely hinted at in all the texts under consideration here and fitting well within the strictures of gender and sex (Schwartz 1997).

PROMISE IN THE THREE ESSAYS

But finally, let me express my fundamental appreciation for what each contributor has not only expressed but in fact planted. Or, to shift the image, each article remains pregnant with insight offered for negotiation by future readers and in conversations that have not yet begun—but that can do so, thanks to the efforts of these three scholars.

Valerie Cooper has set up the context to explore in detail and with precision some of the relationships between how interpreters see and the cultures and worldviews from which they speak. She has asserted that the link is present and might follow up her reading of criticism on Jephthah and daughter and the circumstances that attend them, attentive to the complex contexts of interpreters. The question of analogy is also a good one. Cooper might ask exactly what similarities various interpreters choose to pick up on, what seems legitimate and what less so, and by what criteria. Her own womanist interpretation, which is rich in detail of the sociocultural factors of African American life, might push her to investigate the same factors in the story from Judges. What can we know and how can we know it, and what is the impact of our (lack of) sociological and historical knowledge on our reading. The links among Judg 11 and Gen 22, among the biblical stories and their extrabiblical cognates (such as *Hamlet* and *Beloved*) are promising and deserve more sustained attention, if that is where Cooper would like to spend her energies. Finally, Cooper raises the excellent question of options: What choices does Jephthah seem to have? does his daughter? do contemporaries of ours caught in various double binds? How, in more detail, does she recommend that we—or she and those women and men she knows well—might best proceed? Her essay has a great deal in it for fruitful development.

Mary Donovan Turner is one of several scholars (former students of Carol Newsom) working these days on the world of language and culture shared among those with whom Daughter Zion interacts. Turner has named a wonderful agenda for such studies as she moves past the keen observations she has made about how the language works to deal more fully with its significance, from whatever point of view she might choose as her place to stand. She herself has called attention to the issues of the complexity of the deity-voice with its apparent double roles of perpetrator and redeemer. But as she attends in more detail to that voice, are the choices she sees inevitably polarized, or can they resist such dichotomy? How is the male voice constructed by the female voice but as well by the narrator? The role of the onlooker, however defined, is another angle that seems likely to pay rich dividends when looked at carefully. Should Turner choose to bring more explicitly to bear some of the historical and social research that is making the circumstances of the sixth century clearer, her readings will only be enhanced. Turner's interest in and commitment to the preaching of biblical texts offers her another way to angle this material. How can "voice" be well preached? Finally, her suggestive remarks about the work of Dorothee Soelle want development, especially if combined with other careful and interdisciplinary work on the biblical text. Turner's sensitivity wants a greater scope, and we all need her to reach toward it.

Susan Hylen has been the most incisive in working at the growing edge of the questions that seems to have prompted the present volume. How, in what many ways, does human sexuality in all its complexity, does gender and its various facets, mesh with violence in its many aspects? That it does is not news; how it can be shown to do so, whether as cautionary or suasive, is a conversation that we need to have, particularly around religious texts. The question of the relationship between violence and liberation, between violation and remediation could not be more urgent than at the present time. The study of even one complex image from Revelation will not answer every question we have, nor should it need to do. But a careful and multilayered study of one text will make a contribution to issues that go beyond one narrative but to which it can contribute usefully. Hylen seems interested as well in the question of readerly choices of texts, the impact made when scholars choose to render a complex metaphor reductively, even when they concede theoretically that it has a more nuanced realm. Her article engages the questions of the implications of reading strategy for the address to the reader. How we choose to read, especially if we try to be articulate about what we are doing, may eliminate the option of "right reading," reading in which we can take the comport of knowing we are on the side of the angels, whoever they may be at the moment. It is possible for feminist readings to seem self-righteous and smug, to sound as if they claim the rock of righteousness as their ground. (Of course, they are far from the only group scrabbling to get to that place!) Hylen goes a good length toward demonstrating that the very texts we read, depending on our choices, make such a goal undesirable. It is a wonderful contribution to the field of hermeneutics, should Hylen choose to follow up in more detail. As any reader begins to come to grips with the multiple choices offered by an embedded metaphor that will have blended in many ways with many other textual features, no one can make every choice; some will be left undone. None of us can stand in every position and see everything, nor should that be a goal for us, it seems. If one reader can do it all, why do we read with each other? Our blindspots are not simply places where those smarter than we are can ambush us; they are genuine places of chaos where we may choose to dwell and come to understand better, if that is one of our reading goals. Hylen's work on Rev 18, a controversial text from which she does not shy away, promises much more to her colleagues.

My remarks indicate, I hope, that I think the urgent challenge for any or all of us, one that I struggle myself to begin to do, is to seek to show how we reintegrate, freshly integrate, the aspects of biblical studies that have seemed at war with each other over the centuries and certainly in the last one. What is the suitable if chastened and challenged role for historiographic work? The more we learn about how to proceed, the less confident are we likely to be of the correctness of our results. Though it could and does seem tempting to simply throw up our hands agnostically, that would be the riskier path by far. The literary work, long neglected, comes off best in these articles, but there is more precision needed as we constantly ask ourselves to make clear our assumptions and our moves. The work of literary theorists, flaws and all, must be part of our language as we deal with analogy and metaphor and even with type, stereotype, and archetype, which have been staples of biblical criticism for longer than any of us has been working! As we appropriate and refuse to do, and as we converse with those who proceed differently, we need to be able to name our moves so that others can articulate selectively in reference to our work. Finally, the position of the interpreter needs to be brought into greater clarity, the multiple, various, and complex ways in which we proceed. If we are reading as advocates, we need to say for what positions. Those who comment on biblical texts need, as appropriate, to bring in the question of whether or not—or how—its aspect of Scripture in their lives affects their reading. If it does, and that whole conversation stays mute, I think the reading has not been frank. I think we do best when we speak from what we know best, which will be only a small part of the conversation. But that is why we collaborate on projects such as this volume, so that the voices and insights can intersect and offer to ourselves, our colleagues, our students—and to many we never meet—something of value. I know I will not be the only one to find this volume very promising and am grateful to those who have contributed to it.

WORKS CONSULTED

Amit, Yairah. 1987. "The Dual Causality Principle and Its Effects on Biblical Literature." *VT* 37:385–400.

Anderson, Arnold A. 1989. *2 Samuel.* WBC. Dallas: Word.

Ashcroft, Bill, Gareth Griffiths, and Helen Tiffin. 1989. *The Empire Writes Back: Theory and Practice in Post-Colonial Literatures.* New York: Routledge.

Aschkenasy, Nehama. 1998. *Woman at the Window: Biblical Tales of Oppression and Escape.* Detroit: Wayne State University Press.

Aune, David E. 1998. *Revelation 17–22.* WBC 52C. Dallas: Word.

Bach, Alice. 1997. *Women, Seduction, and Betrayal in Biblical Narrative.* Cambridge: Cambridge University Press.

Bailey, Randall C. 1990. *David in Love and War: The Pursuit of Power in 2 Samuel 10–12.* JSOTSup 75. Sheffield: JSOT Press.

———. 1995. "The Redemption of YHWH: A Literary Critical Function of the Songs of Hannah and David." *BibInt* 3.2:213–31.

———. 1998. "The Danger of Ignoring One's Own Cultural Bias in Interpreting the Text." Pages 66–90 in *The Post-Colonial Bible.* Edited by R. S. Sugirtharajah. Sheffield: Sheffield Academic Press.

Baker, Cynthia 1989. "Pseudo-Philo and the Transformation of Jephthah's Daughter." Pages 195–209 in *Anti-covenant: Counter-Reading Women's Lives in the Hebrew Bible.* Edited by Mieke Bal. Sheffield: Almond.

Bal, Mieke. 1987. *Lethal Love: Feminist Literary Readings of Biblical Love Stories.* Bloomington: Indiana University Press.

———. 1988. *Death and Dissymetry: The Politics of Coherence in the Book of Judges.* Chicago: University of Chicago Press.

———. 1989. "Between Altar and Wondering Rock: Toward a Feminist Philology." Pages 211–31 in *Anti-covenant: Counter-Reading Women's Lives in the Hebrew Bible.* Edited by Mieke Bal. Sheffield: Almond.

Bal, Mieke, and Bryan Gonzales, eds. 1999. *The Practice of Cultural Analysis: Exposing Interdisciplinary Interpretation.* Stanford, Calif.: Stanford University Press.

Barkley Brown, Elsa. 1995. "'What Has Happened Here': The Politics of Difference in Women's History and Feminist Politics." Pages 39–56 in *"We Specialize in the Wholly Impossible": A Reader in Black Women's History.* Edited by Darlene Clark Hine, Wilma King, and Linda Reed. Brooklyn, N.Y.: Carlson.

Barry, Jonathan, Marianne Hester, and Gareth Roberts, eds. 1996. *Witchcraft in Early Modern Europe.* Cambridge: Cambridge University Press.

Bassler, Jouette M. 1996. *1 Timothy, 2 Timothy, Titus.* Nashville: Abingdon.

Bauckham, Richard. 1993. "The Economic Critique of Rome in Revelation 18." Pages 338–83 in *The Climax of Prophecy: Studies on the Book of Revelation.* Edinburgh: T&T Clark.

Baylis, Charles P. 1989. "The Woman Caught in Adultery: A Test of Jesus as the Greater Prophet." *Bibliotheca Sacra* 146:171–84.

Beal, Timothy K. 1995. "Tracing Esther's Beginnings." Pp. 87–110 in *A Feminist Companion to Esther, Judith and Susanna*. Edited by Athalya Brenner. FCB 7. Sheffield: Sheffield Academic Press.

Beale, G. K. 1999. *The Book of Revelation: A Commentary on the Greek Text*. Grand Rapids: Eerdmans.

Bechtel, Lyn M. 1994. "What If Dinah Is Not Raped? (Genesis 34)." *JSOT* 62:19–36.

Bergant, Dianne. 1992. "Power: A Blessing or a Curse?" *TBT* 30:260–66.

Berlin, Adele. 1982. "Characterization in Biblical Narrative: David's Wives." *JSOT* 23:69–85.

Birch, Bruce C. 1998. "The First and Second Books of Samuel." *NIB* 2:947–1383.

Bledstein, Adrien Janis. 2000. "Tamar and the 'Coat of Many Colors.'" Pages 65–83 in *Samuel and Kings*. Edited by Athalya Brenner. FCB 2/7. Sheffield: Sheffield Academic Press.

Boaz, Cohn, 1966. *Jewish and Roman Law: A Comparative Study*. New York: Jewish Theological Seminary of America.

Boesak, Allan A. 1987. *Comfort and Protest: The Apocalypse from a South African Perspective*. Philadelphia: Westminster.

Boring, M. E. 1989. *Revelation*. Louisville: John Knox.

Bostridge, Ian. 1997. *Witchcraft and Its Transformations c. 1650–c. 1750*. Oxford: Clarendon.

Boudreaux, Paul. 1980. "Booth v Maryland and the Individual Vengeance Rationale for Criminal Punishment." *Journal of Criminal Law and Criminology* 80:177.

Bowman, George, III. 1998. *Dying, Grieving, Faith and Family: A Pastoral Care Approach*. New York: Haworth Pastoral Press.

Braulik, Georg. 1986–92. *Deuteronomium*. 2 vols. NEchtB. Würzburg: Echter.

Brenner, Athalya. 1985. *The Israelite Woman: Social Role and Literary Type in Biblical Narrative*. Biblical Seminar 2. Sheffield: JSOT Press.

Brown, Cheryl Anne. 1992. *No Longer Be Silent: First Century Jewish Portraits of Biblical Women Studies in Pseudo-Philo's Biblical Antiquities and Josephus' Jewish Antiquities*. Louisville: Westminster John Knox.

Brown, Lucinda. 2000. "1 Tim 2:9–15: Women Who Profess Reverence for God." Pages 487–89 in *Women in Scripture: A Dictionary of Named and Unnamed Women the Hebrew Bible, the Aprocryphal/Deuterocanonical Books, and the New Testament*. Edited by Carol Meyers, Toni Craven, and Ross S. Kraemer. Boston: Houghton Mifflin.

Brueggemann, Walter. 1985. *David's Truth in Israel's Imagination and Memory*. Minneapolis: Fortress.

———. 1996. *The Threat of Life: Sermons on Pain, Power, and Weakness*. Edited by Charles L. Campbell. Minneapolis: Fortress.

Burge, Gary M. 1984. "A Specific Problem in The New Testament Text and Canon: The Woman Caught in Adultery (John 7:53–8:11) *JETS* 27:141–48.

Burr, George L. 1914. *Narratives of the Witchcraft Cases 1648–1706*. New York: Barnes & Noble.

Cairns, Ian. 1992. *Word and Presence: A Commentary on the Book of Deuteronomy*. Grand Rapids: Eerdmans.

Camp, Claudia V. 2000. *Wise, Strange and Holy: The Strange Woman and the Making of the Bible*. JSOTSup 320; Gender, Culture, Theory 9. Sheffield: Sheffield Academic Press.

Campos, Paul. 1992. "The Paradox of Punishment." *Wisconsin Law Review* 1992:1931–35.

Carman, John. 2000. "Millionaire's Final Answer—I Do." *San Francisco Chronicle*. February 15.

Carter, P. Kyle, Jr. 1980. "The Apology of David" *JBL* 99:489–504.

Cervo, Diane M. 1983. *Witchcraft in Europe and America: Guide to the Microfilm Collection*. Woodbridge: Research Publications.

Chideya, Farai, Michelle Ingrassia, Vern E. Smith, and Pat Wingert. 1993. "Endangered Family." *Newsweek* 122(9):17–27.

Choi, Rai Ok. 1981. "Gwantal minnyo hyong solhwa ui yongu." Pp. 91–112 in *Hanguk gojun sanmun yongu*. Seoul: Donghwa munhwasa. [Korean]

Clark, Beverly. 1999a. "Aristotle." Pp. 30–45 in *Misogyny in the Western Philosophical Tradition*. New York: Routledge.

———. 1999b. "Augustine." Pp. 59–74 in *Misogyny in the Western Philosophical Tradition*. New York: Routledge.

Clines, David J. A., Stephen E. Fowl, and Stanley E. Porter, eds. 1990. *The Bible in Three Dimensions: Essays in Celebration of Forty Years of Biblical Studies in the University of Sheffield*. JSOTSup 87. Sheffield: JSOT Press.

Cohn, Norman. 1970. "The Myth of Satan and Fis Human Servants." Pages 3–16 in *Witchcraft Confessions and Accusations*. Edited by Mary Douglas. New York: Tavistock.

Coker, Donna K. 1992. "Heat of Passion and Wife Killing: Men Who Batter/Men Who Kill." *Southern California Review of Law and Women's Studies* 2.1:71–130.

Collins, Adela Yarbro. 1979. *The Apocalypse*. Wilmington, Del.: Michael Glazier.

Collins, Patricia Hill. 1991. *Black Feminist Thought: Knowledge, Consciousness, and the Politics of Empowerment*. New York: Routledge.

Cooper-White, Pamela. 1995. *The Cry of Tamar: Violence against Women and the Church's Response*. Minneapolis: Fortress.

Copeland, M. Shawn. 2002. "Racism and the Vocation of the Christian Theologian." *Spiritus* 2:20.

Coursen, Herbert R. 1986. *The Compensatory Psyche: A Jungian Approach to Shakespeare*. Lanham, Md.: University Press of American.

Craigie Peter C. 1976. *The Book of Deuteronomy*. NICOT. Grand Rapids: Eerdmans.

Croatto, J. Severino. 1995. "Exegesis of Second Isaiah from the Perspective of the Oppressed: Paths for Reflection." Pages 219–36 in vol. 2 of *Reading from This Place*. Edited by Fernando F. Segovia and Mary Ann Tolbert. Minneapolis: Fortress.

Crompton, Rosemary. 1998. "Explaining Inequality." Pages 1–20 in idem, *Class and Stratification: :An Introduction to the Current Debate*. Malden: Blackwell.

Cross, Tom Peete. 1919. "Witchcraft in North Carolina." *Studies in Philology* 16.3: 217–87.

Davidoff, Steven. 1996. "A Comparative Study of the Jewish and the United States Constitutional Law of Capital Punishment." 3 *ILSA Journal of International and Comparative Law* 93.

Day, Peggy L. 1989. "From the Child Is Born the Woman: The Story of Jephthah's Daughter." Pages 58–74 in idem, *Gender and Difference in Ancient Israel*. Minneapolis: Fortress.

Dershowitz, Alan M. 2000. *The Genesis of Justice*. New York: Warner.

Dewey, Joanna. 1992. "1 Timothy." Pages 353–58 in *The Women's Bible Commentary*. Edited by C. A. Newsome and S. H. Ringe. Louisville: Westminster John Knox.

Dobbs-Allsopp, F. W. 1993. *Weep, O Daughter of Zion: A Study of the City-Lament Genre in the Hebrew Bible*. Roma: Editrice Pontificio Istituto Biblico.

Douglas, Kelly Brown. 1995. "To Reflect the Image of God." Pages 67–77 in *Living the Intersection: Womanism and Afrocentrism in Theology*. Edited by Cheryl J. Sanders. Minneapolis: Fortress.

Douglas, Mary. 1991. "Witchcraft and Leprosy: Two Strategies of Exclusion." *Man* NS 26:723–36.

Dube, Musa W. 2002. "Postcoloniality, Feminist Spaces, and Religion." Pages 100–120 in *Postcolonialism, Feminism and Religious Discourse*. Edited by Laura E. Donaldson and Kwok Pui-Lan. New York: Routledge.

Dworkin, Andrea. 1983. *Right-Wing Women*. New York: Perigee.

———. 1989. *Letters from a War Zone*. Boston: Dutton.

Eagleton, Terry. 1983. *Literary Theory: An Introduction*. Minneapolis: University of Minnesota Press.

Eisenstein, Zillah. 1988. *The Female Body and the Law*. Berkeley and Los Angeles: University of California Press.

Encyclopedia Judaica. 1997. CD-ROM edition. Shaker Heights, Ohio: Judaica Multimedia.

Exum, J. Cheryl. 1989. "Murder They Wrote: Ideology and the Manipulation of Female Presence in Biblical Narrative." *USQR* 43:19–39.

———. 1993. *Fragmented Women: Feminist (Sub)versions of Biblical Narratives*. Valley Forge, Pa.: Trinity Press International.

———. 1996. "Bathsheba Plotted, Shot, and Painted." *Semeia* 74:47–73.

Faith, Karlene. 1994. "Resistance: Lessons from Foucault and Feminism." Pages 36–66 in *Power/Gender: Social Relations in Theory and Practice*. Edited by H. Lorraine Radtke and Henderikus J. Stam. London: Sage.

Fernandez, Dagoberto Ramirez. 1997. "The Judgment of God on the Multinationals: Revelation 18." Pages 75–100 in *Subversive Scriptures: Revolutionary Readings of the Christian Bible in Latin America*. Edited by Leif E. Vaage. Valley Forge, Pa.: Trinity Press International.

Ferreiro, Alberto, ed. 1998. *The Devil, Heresy and Witchcraft in the Middle Ages: Essays in Honor of Jeffrey B. Russell*. Boston: Brill.

Fewell, Danna Nolan, and David M. Gunn. 1991. "Tipping the Balance: Sternberg's Reader and the Rape of Dinah." *JBL* 110:193–211.

———. 1992. *Gender, Power, and Promise: The Subject of the Bible's First Story*. Nashville: Abingdon.

Fienberg, Nona. 1991. "Jephthah's Daughter: The Parts Ophelia Plays." Pages 128–43 in *Old Testament Women in Western Literature*. Edited by Raymond-Jean Frontain and Jan Wojcik. Conway, Ark.: UCA Press.

Fischer, Alexander. 1989. "David und Batseba: Ein literarkritischer und motivgeschichtlicher Beitrag zu II Sam 11." *ZAW* 101:50–59.

Fokkelman, J. P. 1981. *Narrative Art and Poetry in the Books of Samuel: A Full Interpretation Based on Stylistic and Structural Analyses.* Vol. 1. Assen: Van Gorcum.

Fontaine, Carole R. 1986. "The Bearing of Wisdom on the Shape of 2 Samuel 11–12 and 1 Kings 3." *JSOT* 34:61–77.

———. 1994. "A Response to 'The Bearing of Widom.'" Pp. 161–67 in *A Feminist Companion to Samuel and Kings.* Edited by Athalya Brenner. FCB 5. Sheffield: Sheffield Academic Press.

Ford, J. M. 1975. *Revelation.* AB 38. Garden City, N.Y.: Doubleday.

Frazer, J. G. 1914. *The Dying God.* London: Macmillan.

Fretheim, Stephen. 1984. *The Suffering of God.* Philadelphia: Fortress.

Freud, Sigmund. 1938. "Totem and Taboo." Pages 807–33 in *The Basic Writings of Sigmund Freud.* Edited by A. A. Brill. New York: Random House.

Frug, Mary Joe. 1992. *Postmodern Legal Feminism.* New York: Routledge.

Fuchs, Esther. 1989. "Marginalization, Ambiguity, Silencing: The Story of Jephthah's Daughter." *JFSR* 5:35–45.

———. 2000. *Sexual Politics in the Biblical Narrative: Reading the Hebrew Bible As a Woman.* JSOTSup 310. Sheffield: Sheffield Academic Press.

Garcia, J. L. A. 1998. "Lies and the Vices of Deception." *Faith and Philosophy* 15: 514–37.

Gardiner, Tom. 1981. *Broomstick over Essex and East Anglia: An Introduction to Witchcraft in the Eastern Counties during the Seventeenth Century.* Hornchurch: Ian Henry.

Garland, David. 1991. "Book Review: Rehabilitating Theories of Punishment. Punishment And Modern Society." *Harvard Law Review* 104:1126.

Garsiel, Moshe. 1993. "The Story of David and Bathsheba: A Different Approach." *CBQ* 55:244–62.

Gerstein, Beth. 1989. "A Ritual Processed: A Look at Judges 11.40." Pages 175–93 in *Anti-covenant: Counter-Reading Women's Lives in the Hebrew Bible.* Edited by Mieke Bal. Sheffield: Almond.

Gibbs, Raymond W. 1994. *The Poetics of Mind: Figurative Thought, Language, and Understanding.* Cambridge: Cambridge University Press.

Gibson, Marion. 2000. *Early Modern Witches: Witchcraft Cases in Contemporary Writing.* New York: Routledge.

Gilligan, Carol. 1982. *In a Different Voice: Psychological Theory and Women's Development.* Cambridge, Mass.: Harvard University Press.

Girard, René. 1977. *Violence and the Sacred.* Translated by Patrick Gregory. Baltimore: Johns Hopkins University Press.

Gleicher, Jules. 1998 "Three Biblical Studies on Politics And Law." *Oklahoma City University Law Review* 23:869, 890–99.

Goldingay, John. 1986. "The Bible and Sexuality." *SJT* 39:175–88.

Gottwald, Norman K. 1954. *Studies in the Book of Lamentations.* SBT 14. Chicago: Allenson.

Gous, I. G. P. 1993. "Exiles and the Dynamics of Experience of Loss: The Reaction of Lamentations 2 on the Loss of Land." *OTE* 6:351–63.

Graczyk, Michael. 1998. "Tucker 'Face to Face with Jesus." *Arizona Republic,* 4 February, A.1.

Graetz, Naomi. 1993. "Dinah the Daughter." Pages 306–17 in *A Feminist Companion to Genesis.* Edited by Athalya Brenner. FCB 2. Sheffield: Sheffield Academic Press.

Gunn, David M. 1978. *The Story of King David: Genre and Interpretation.* JSOTSup 6. Sheffield: JSOT Press.

———. 1996. "Bathsheba Goes Bathing in Hollywood: Words, Images, and Social Locations." *Semeia* 74:75–101.

Hackett, Jo Ann. 1992. "1 and 2 Samuel." Pages 85–95 in *The Women's Bible Commentary.* Edited by C. A. Newsome and S. H. Ringe. Louisville: Westminster John Knox.

Halpern, Baruch. 2001. *David's Secret Demons: Messiah, Murderer, Traitor, King.* Grand Rapids: Eerdmans.

Hanson, A. T. 1989. "Origen's Treatment of the Sacrifice of Jephthah's Daughter." Pages 298–300 in *Papers Presented to the Tenth International Conference on Patristic Studies held in Oxford 1987 (Second Century, Tertullian to Nicaea in the West, Clement of Alexandria and Origen, Athanasius).* Edited by Elizabeth A. Livingstone. StPatr 21. Leuven: Peeters.

Haraway, Donna J. 1997. *Modest-Witness, Second-Millennium: Femaleman Meets Oncomouse: Feminism and Technoscience.* New York: Routledge.

Harland, P. J. 1998. "Menswear and Womenswear: A Study of Deuteronomy 22:5." *ExpTim* 110.3:73–76.

Hayes, Diana L. 1989. "And When We Speak: To Be Black, Catholic, and Womanist." Pages 102–19 in *Taking Down Our Harps.* Edited by Diana L Hayes and Cyprian Davis. Maryknoll, N.Y.: Orbis.

Hazou, Winnie. 1990. *The Social and Legal Status of Women: A Global Perspective.* New York: Praeger.

Hertzberg, Hans Wilhelm. 1964. *I and II Samuel.* Translated by J. S. Bowden. OTL. Philadelphia: Westminster.

Higganbotham, Evelyn Brooks. 1993. "The Black Church: A Gender Perspective." Pages 1–18 in idem, *Righteous Discontent: The Women's Movement in the Black Baptist Church, 1880–1920.* Cambridge: Harvard University Press.

———. 1995. "African-American Women's History and the Metalanguage of Race." Pages 3–24 in *"We Specialize in the Wholly Impossible": A Reader in Black Women's History.* Edited by Darlene Clark Hine, Wilma King, and Linda Reed. Brooklyn, N.Y.: Carlson.

Hill, Frances. 2000. *The Salem Witch Trials Reader.* New York: Da Capo.

Hirsh, James. 1991. "Othello and Perception." Pages 135–59 in *Othello: New Perspectives.* Edited by Virginia Mason Vaughan and Kent Cartwright. London: Associated University Press.

hooks, bell. 1990. *Yearning: Race, Gender and Cultural Politics.* Boston: South End.

Humphreys, W. L. 1976. "Esther." Pp. 279–81 in *IDBSupp.*

Isasi-Diaz, Ada Maria. 1994. "The Task of Hispanic Women's Liberation Theology—Mujeristas: Who We Are and What We Are About." Pages 88–102 in *Feminist Theology from the Third World.* Edited by Ursula King. Maryknoll, N.Y.: Orbis.

———. 1999. *Mujerista Theology.* Maryknoll, N.Y.: Orbis.

James, E. O. 1961. *Seasonal Feasts and Festivals.* New York: Barnes & Noble.

Jennings, Theodore W., Jr. 2001. "YHWH As Erastes." Pages 36–74 in *Queer Commentary and the Hebrew Bible.* Edited by Ken Stone. Cleveland: Pilgrim.

Jensen, Hans J. L. 1992. "Desire, Rivalry and Collective Violence in the 'Succession Narrative.'" *JSOT* 55:39–59.

Johnson, Claudia Durst, and V. Johnson. 1998. *Understanding the Crucible: A Student Casebook to Issues, Sources, and Historical Documents.* Westport, Conn.: Greenwood.

Jones, Jill. 1999. "The Christian Executioner; Reconciling 'An Eye for an Eye' with 'Turn the Other Cheek.'" *Pepperdine Law Review* 27:139.

Kaiser, Barbara Bakke. 1987. "Poet As Female Impersonator: Poems of Suffering." *JR* 67:164–82.

Karmen, Andrew. 1995. "Women Victims of Crime: Introduction." Pages 181–96 in *The Criminal Justice System and Women.* Edited by Barbara Price and Natalie Sokoloff. 2d ed. New York: McGraw-Hill.

Kassindja, Fauziya, and Layli Mill Bashir. 1998. *Do They Hear You When You Cry.* New York: Delacorte.

Keefe, Alice A. 1993. "Rape of Women/Wars of Men." *Semeia* 61:79–97.

Keener, Craig S. 1992. *Paul, Women and Wives: Marriage and Women's Ministry in the Letters of Paul.* Peabody, Mass.: Hendrickson.

Kille, D. Andrew. 2001. *Psychological Biblical Criticism.* Minneapolis: Fortress.

Kim, Hyun Chul Paul. 2000. "Gender Complementarity in the Hebrew Bible." Pages 263–91 in vol. 1 of *Reading the Hebrew Bible for a New Millennium.* Edited by Wonil Kim et al. Harrisburg, Pa.: Trinity Press International.

———. 2001. "Interpretative Modes of Yin-Yang Dynamics As an Asian Hermeneutics." *BibInt* 9:287–308.

Kirk-Duggan, Cheryl. 2001a. *Misbegotten Anguish: Theology and Ethics of Violence.* St. Louis: Chalice.

———. 2001b. *Refiner's Fire: A Religious Engagement with Violence.* Minneapolis: Fortress.

Klein, Lillian R. 2000. "Bathsheba Revealed." Pages 47–64 in *Samuel and Kings.* Edited by Athalya Brenner. FCB 2/7. Sheffield: Sheffield Academic Press.

Kors, Alan, and E. Peeters. 2001. *Witchcraft in Europe 400–1700: A Documentary History.* Philadelphia: University of Pennsylvania Press.

Kostielney, Monica. 1996. "Death Penalty Symposium: Understanding Justice with Clarity, Civility, and Compassion by Reflecting on Selected Biblical Passages and Catholic Church Teachings on the Death Penalty." *Thomas M. Cooley Law Review* 13:967–76.

Lagassé, Paul, ed. 2000. *The Columbia Encyclopedia.* 6th ed. New York: Columbia University Press.

Lakoff, George, and Mark Johnson. 1980. *Metaphors We Live By.* Chicago: University of Chicago Press.

Lakoff, George, and Mark Turner. 1989. *More Than Cool Reason: A Field Guide to Poetic Metaphor.* Chicago: University of Chicago Press.

Lamb, Sydney, ed. 2000. *Shakespeare's Othello.* Foster City, Ga.: IDG Books.

Landes, Solomon. 1991. "Did Jephthah Kill His Daughter?" *BRev* 7.4:28–42.

Lanahan, William F. 1974. "The Speaking Voice in the Book of Lamentations." *JBL* 93:41–49.

Lea, Thomas, and Hayne P. Griffin Jr. 1993. *1, 2 Timothy, Titus*. NAC. Nashville: Broadman.

Levenson, Jon D., and Baruch Halpern. 1980. "The Political Import of David's Marriages." *JBL* 99:507–18.

Lewis, C. S. 1977. *Mere Christianity*. New York: Macmillan.

Lodge, David. 2002. "Dickens Our Contemporary." *Atlantic Monthly* 289: 92–101.

Lorde, Audre. 1984. *Sister Outsider*. Trumansberg, N.Y.: Crossing.

Lyotard, Jean François. 1984. *The Postmodern Condition: A Report on Knowledge*. Minneapolis: University of Minnesota Press.

MacKinnon, Catharine. 1987. *Feminism Unmodified: Discourses in Life and Laws*. Cambridge: Harvard University Press.

Makiya, Kanan. 1993. "State Rape: Violation of Iraqi Women." *New Statesman and Society* 6.251: 16–17.

Maly, Eugene H. 1966. *The World of David and Solomon*. Englewood Cliffs, N.J.: Prentice-Hall.

Marcus, David, 1986. *Jephthah and His Vow*. Lubbock: Texas Tech Press.

Marshall, Howard I. 1999. *A Critical and Exegetical Commentary on the Pastoral Epistles*. Edinburgh: T&T Clark.

Massey, Floyd, Jr., and Samuel Berry McKinney. 1976 . *Church Administration in the Black Perspective*. Valley Forge, Pa.: Judson.

Matthews, Victor H. 1994. "Female Voices: Upholding the Honor of the Household." *BTB* 24:8–15.

Matthews, Victor H., Bernard M. Levinson, and Tikva Frymer-Kensky, eds. 1998. *Gender and Law in the Hebrew Bible and the Ancient Near East*. JSOTSup 262. Sheffield: Sheffield Academic Press.

Mazor, Yair. 1995. "Scolding Aesthetics in Biblical Literature." *SJOT* 9:297–313.

McCarter, P. Kyle. 1984. II Samuel. AB 9. Garden City, N.Y.: Doubleday.

McCord, James N., Jr. 2000. "Politics and Honor on Early-Nineteenth-Century England: The Dukes' Duel." *Huntington Library Quarterly* 62:88–114.

Mendelsohn, I. 1953. "The Disinheritance of Jephthah in the Light of Paragraph 27 of the Lipit-Ishtar Code." *IEJ* 4:116–19.

Metzger, Bruce. 1975. *A Textual Commentary on the Greek New Testament*. London: United Bible Societies.

Miller, Jean Baker. 1976. *Toward a New Psychology of Women*. Boston: Beacon.

———. 1984. "The Development of Women's Sense of Self." Pages 1–15 in *Work in Progress, No. 12*. Wellesley, Mass.: Stone Center Working Papers Series.

Mintz, Alan. 1983. "The Rhetoric of Lamentations and the Representation of Catastrophe." *Prooftexts* 2:1–17.

Mitchell, Kenneth R., and Herbert Anderson. 1983. *All Our Losses, All Our Griefs: Resources for Pastoral Care*. Philadelphia: Westminster.

Moessner, Jeanne Stevenson. 1996. *Though the Eyes of Women: Insights for Pastoral Care*. Minneapolis: Fortress.

Monter, William E. 1987. *Enforcing Morality in Early Modern Europe*. London: Variorum Reprints.

Moore, Carey A. 1971. *Esther*. AB 7B. Garden City, N.Y.: Doubleday.

Moore, Michael. 1983. "Human Suffering in Lamentations." *RB* 90:534–55.

Morrison, Toni. 1988. *Beloved.* New York: Penguin.

Morriss, Peter. 1987. "What Power Is and What Power Is Not." Pages 7–36 in idem, *Power: A Philosophical Analysis.* New York: St. Martin's.

Morton, Nelle. 1985. *The Journey Is Home.* Boston: Beacon.

Mosala, Itumeleng. 1992. "The Implications of the Text of Esther for African Women's Struggle for Liberation in South Africa." *Semeia* 59:129–37.

Müllner, Ilse. 1998. "Blickwechsel: Batseba und David in Romanen des 20. Jahrhunderts." *BibInt* 6:348–66.

Newsom, Carol A. 1992. "Response to Norman K. Gottwald, 'Social Class and Ideology in Isaiah 40–55.'" *Semeia* 59:73:–78.

Nicol, George G. 1987. "Bathsheba, a Clever Woman?" *ExpTim* 99:360–63.

———. 1997. "The Alleged Rape of Bathsheba: Some Observations on Ambiguity in Biblical Narrative." *JSOT* 73:43–54.

———. 1998. "David, Abigail and Bathsheba, Nabal and Uriah: Transformations within a Triangle." *SJOT* 12:130–45.

Niditch, Susan. 1993a. *War in the Hebrew Bible: A Study in the Ethics of Violence.* New York: Oxford University Press.

———. 1993b. "War, Woman, and Defilement in Numbers 31." *Semeia* 61:39–57.

———. 1995. "Esther: Folklore, Wisdom, Feminism and Authority." Pp. 26–46 in *A Feminist Companion to Esther, Judith and Susanna.* Edited by Athalya Brenner. FCB 7. Sheffield: Sheffield Academic Press.

Noll, Kurt L. 1997. "The Faces of David." Pages 43–69 in idem, *The Faces of David.* JSOTSup 242. Sheffield: Sheffield Academic Press.

North, Robert. 1982. David's Rise: Sacral, Military, or Psychiatric?" *Bib* 63:524–44.

Nygaard, Richard Lowell. 1996. "On the Philosophy of Sentencing: Or, Why Punish?" *Widener Journal of Public Law* 5:237, 265–66.

Ochshorn, Judith. 1994. "Woman As Witch: The Renaissance and Reformations Revisited" Pages 91–107 in *Feminist Pedagogy and Politics.* Edited by Sara Munson Deats and L. Tallent Lenker. Lanham, Md.: Rowman & Littlefield.

O'Day, Gail R. 1992. "John." Pages 293–304 in *The Women's Bible Commentary.* Edited by C. A. Newsom and S. H. Ringe. Louisville: Westminster John Knox.

O'Kane, Martin. 1998. "The Biblical King David and His Artistic and Literary Afterlives." *BibInt* 6:313–47.

Perry, Menahem, and Meir Sternberg. 1986. "The King through Ironic Eyes: Biblical Narrative and the Literary Reading Process." *Poetics Today* 7:275–322.

Peterson, Eugene H. 1999. *First and Second Samuel.* Westminster Bible Companion. Louisville: Westminster John Knox.

Pham, Xuan Huong Thi. 1999. *Mourning in the Ancient Near East and the Hebrew Bible.* JSOTSup 302. Sheffield: Sheffield Academic Press.

Pippin, Tina. 1992. *Death and Desire.* Edited by Danna Nolan Fewell and David M. Gunn. LCBI. Louisville: Westminster John Knox.

———. 1999. *Apocalyptic Bodies: The Biblical End of the World in Text and Image.* New York: Routledge.

Pitt-Rivers, Jullian. 1977. "The Fate of Shechem or the Politics of Sex." Pages 126–71, 182–86 in *The Fate of Shechem or the Politics of Sex: Essays on the Anthropology of the Mediterranean.* Edited by Jullian Pitt-Rivers. Cambridge Studies in Social Anthropology 19. Cambridge: Cambridge University Press.

Poling, James Newton. 1991. *The Abuse of Power: A Theological Problem.* Nashville: Abingdon.

Pressler, Carolyn. 1993. *The View of Women Found in the Deuteronomic Family Laws.* Berlin: de Gruyter.

Prouser, O. Horn. 1994. "The Truth about Women and Lying." *JSOT* 61:15–28.

Provan, Iain. 1996. "Foul Spirits, Fornication and Finance: Revelation 18 from an Old Testament Perspective." *JSNT* 64:81–100.

Rahman, Anika, and Nahid Toubia, eds., *Female Genital Mutilaltion: A Guide to Laws and 2000 Policies Worldwide.* New York: St. Martins.

Rand, Herbert. 1996. "David and Ahab: A Study of Crime and Punishment." *JBQ* 24:90–97.

Rapaport, Elizabeth. 1996. "Capital Murder and the Domestic Discount: A Study of Capital Domestic Murder in the Post-Furman Era." *Southern Methodist University Law Review* 49:1507.

Redditt, Paul L. 1992. "Tob." *ABD* 6:583.

Riggs, Marcia Y. 1994. *Awake, Arise and Act: A Womanist Call for Black Liberation.* Cleveland: Pilgrim.

Rose, Margaret Jaster. 1994. " 'Fashioninge the Minde and Condicions': The Uses and Abuses of Apparel in Early Modern England." Dissertation, University of Maryland.

Rossing, Barbara R. 1999. *The Choice between Two Cities.* Harrisburg, Pa.: Trinity Press International.

Rudolph, Daniel A. 1996. "The Misguided Reliance in American Jurisprudence on Jewish Law to Support the Moral Legitimacy of Capital Punishment." *American Criminal Law Review* 33:437.

Sanders Nancy K., ed. 1972. *Epic of Gilgamesh.* Baltimore: Penguin. [Orig. 1960]

Schneider, Matthew. 1997 "Writing in the Dust: Irony and Lynch-Law in the Gospel of John." *Anthropoetics* 3.1:1–8.

———. 1999 "Writing in the Dust and Lynch-Law in the Gospel of John." *Legal Studies Forum* 23:21–35.

Scholz, Susanne. 1999. "Was It Really Rape in Genesis 34? Biblical Scholarship As a Reflection of Cultural Assumptions." Pages 182–98 in *Escaping Eden: New Feminist Perspectives on the Bible.* Edited by Harold C. Washington, Susan Lochrie Graham, and Pamela Thimmes. New York: New York University Press.

Schüssler Fiorenza, Elisabeth. 1991. *Revelation: Vision of a Just World.* Minneapolis: Fortress.

———. 1998a. *The Book of Revelation: Justice and Judgment.* 2d ed. Minneapolis: Fortress.

———. 1998b. *Sharing Her Word.* Boston: Beacon.

Schwartz, Regina M. 1992. "Adultery in the House of David: The Metanarrative of Biblical Scholarship and the Narratives of the Bible." *Semeia* 54:35–55.

———. 1997. *The Curse of Cain: The Violent Legacy of Monotheism.* Chicago: University of Chicago Press.

Shakespeare, William. 2001. *Othello.* Edited by John Russell Brown. New York: Applause.

Sheres, Ita. 1990. *Dinah's Rebellion: A Biblical Parable for Our Time.* New York: Crossroad.

Sigal, Lillian. 1990. "Models of Love and Hate." *Daughters of Sarah* 16:8–10.

Skaine, Rosemarie. 1996. *Power and Gender: Issues in Sexual Dominance and Harassment.* Jefferson, N.C.: McFarland.

Smith, Archie, Jr. 2001. "'Look and See If There Is Any Sorrow Like My Sorrow?' Systemic Metaphors for Pastoral Theology and Care." *WW* 21:5–15.

Smith, Christopher R. 1989. "Another Look at Babylon: Revelation 18 and Contemporary Social Justice." *Other Side* 25:24–26.

———. 1990. "Reclaiming the Social Justice Message of Revelation: Materialism, Imperialism and Divine Judgment in Revelation 18." *Transformation* 7:28–33.

Smith, H. Shelton. 1972. *In His Image, But ... Racism in Southern Religion, 1780–1910.* Durham, N.C.: Duke University Press.

Soelle, Dorothee. 1975. *Suffering.* Translated by Everett R. Kalin. Philadelphia: Fortress.

Somerville, Henry. 1929. *Madness in Shakespearian Tragedy.* London: Richards.

Sternberg, Meir. 1992. "Biblical Poetics and Sexual Politics: From Reading to Counter-Reading." *JBL* 111:463–88.

Stoebe, Hans Joachim. 1986. "David und Uria: Überlegungen zur Überlieferung von 2 Sam 11." *Bib* 67:388–96.

Streete, Gail Corrington. 1997. *The Strange Woman: Power and Sex in the Bible.* Louisville: Westminster John Knox.

Surrey, Janet L. 1985. "The 'Self-in-Relation': A Theory of Women's Development." Pages 1–17 in *Work in Progress, No. 13.* Wellesley, Mass.: Stone Center Working Papers Series.

Tapp, Anne Michele. 1989. "An Ideology of Expendability: Virgin Daughter Sacrifice in Genesis 9:1–11, Judges 11:30–39 and 19:22–26." Pages 157–74 in *Anti-Covenant: Counter-Reading Women's Lives in the Hebrew Bible.* Edited by Mieke Bal. Sheffield: Almond.

Tertullian. 1959. "The Apparel of Women." Pages 117–33 in *Disciplinary, Moral and Ascetical Works.* Translated by Rudolph Arbesmann. New York: Fathers of the Church.

Thistlethwaite, Susan Brooks. 1993. "'You May Enjoy the Spoil of Your Enemies': Rape As a Biblical Metaphor for War." *Semeia* 61:59–75.

Thomas, Keith. 1970. "The Relevance of Social Anthropology to the Historical Study of English Witchcraft." Pages 47–79 in *Witchcraft Confessions and Accusations.* Edited by Mary Douglas. New York: Tavistock.

Thompson, Berryl Gordon. 1999. "The Justification, Purposes and Functions of Punishment in Our Domestic Society." *Southern University Law Review* 26:265.

Time, Victoria M. 1999. *Shakespeare's Criminals: Criminology, Fiction, and Drama.* Westport, Conn.: Greenwood.

Toensing, Holly Joan. 1998. "The Politics of Insertion: The Pericope of the Adulterous Woman and its Textual History." Dissertation, Vanderbilt University.

Trask, Richard B. 1997. *"The Devil Hath Been Raised": A Documentary History of the Salem Village Witchcraft Outbreak of March 1692.* Danvers: Yeoman.

Trible, Phyllis. 1981. "A Meditation in Mourning: The Sacrifice of the Daughter of Jephthah." *USQR* 36:59–74.

———. 1984. *Texts of Terror: Literary-Feminist Readings of Biblical Narratives.* Philadelphia: Fortress.

Turner, Mark. 1996. *The Literary Mind.* New York: Oxford University Press.

Turner, Mary Donovan. 1993. "Daughter Zion: Lament and Restoration." Ph.D. diss., Emory University.

Turner, Mary Donovan, and Mary Lin Hudson. 1999. *Saved from Silence: Finding Women's Voice in Preaching.* St. Louis: Chalice.

Valler, Shulamit. 1994. "King David and 'His' Women: Biblical Stories and Talmudic Discussions." Pages 129–42 in *A Feminist Companion to Samuel and Kings.* Edited by Athalya Brenner. FCB 5. Sheffield: Sheffield Academic Press.

Vaux, Roland de. 1965. *Social Institutions.* Vol. 1 of *Ancient Israel.* New York: McGraw-Hill.

Vobeja, Barbara. 1991. "25 Percent of Black Women May Never Marry." *Washington Post,* 11 November, A1, A12.

Walker, Alice. 1983. *In Search of our Mother's Gardens: Womanist Prose.* New York: Harcourt Brace Jovanovich.

Walker, Alice, Pratibha Parmar, and Vicki Austin-Smith, eds., 1993. *Warrior Marks: Female Genital Mutilation and the Sexual Binding of Women.* New York: Harcourt Brace.

Walker, Barbara G. 1987. *The Skeptical Feminist: Discovering the Virgin, Mother and Crone.* New York: Harper Collins.

Walsh, Thomas J. 1996. "On the Abolition of Man: A Discussion of the Moral and Legal Issues Surrounding the Death Penalty." Clev. St. L. Rev. 44:23.

Wartenberg, Thomas E. 1990. *The Forms of Power: From Domination to Transformation.* Philadelphia: Temple University Press.

Washington, Harold C. 1997. "Violence and the Construction of Gender in the Hebrew Bible: A New Historical Approach. *BibInt* 5:324–63.

Webb, Barry. 1986. "The Theme of the Jephthah Story (Judges 10:6–12:7)." *RTR* 45:34–43.

Weinfeld, Moshe. 1972. *Deuteronomy and the Deuteronomistic School.* Oxford: Clarendon.

Weems, Renita J. 1988. *Just a Sister Away: A Womanist Vision of Women's Relationships in the Bible.* San Diego: LuraMedia.

———. 1995. *Battered Love: Marriage, Sex, and Violence in the Hebrew Prophets.* OBT. Minneapolis: Fortress.

Wegner, Judith. 1988. *Chattel or Persons? The Status of Women in the Mishna.* New York: Oxford University Press.

Wenham, G. J. 1983. "Why Does Sexual Intercourse Defile (Lev 15:18)?" *ZAW* 95:432–34.

Wesselius, J. W. 1990. "Joab's Death and the Central Theme of the Succession Narrative (2 Samuel IX–1 Kings II)." *VT* 40:336–51.

West, Gerald O. 1995. *Biblical Hermeneutics of Liberation: Modes of Reading the Bible in the South African Context.* 2d ed. Maryknoll, N.Y.: Orbis.

Westermann, Claus. 1994. *Lamentations: Issues and Interpretation.* Translated by Charles Muenchow. Minneapolis: Fortress.

White, Sidnie Ann. 1989. "Esther: A Feminine Model for Jewish Diaspora." Pages 161–77 in *Gender and Difference in Ancient Israel.* Edited by Peggy L. Day. Minneapolis: Fortress.

———. 1992. "Esther." Pages 124–29 in *The Women's Bible Commentary*. Edited by C. A. Newsome and S. H. Ringe. Louisville: Westminster John Knox.

Wikipedia, the Free Encyclopedia. September 2002. "Sex." Online: http://www.wikipedia.com/wiki/Sex.

Willey, Patricia Tull. 1997. *Remember the Former Things: The Recollection of Previous Texts in Second Isaiah*. SBLDS 161. Atlanta: Scholars Press.

William and Mary College Quarterly Historical Magazine. 3–4 (1894–95).

Willis, Deborah. 1995. *Malevolent Nurture: Witch-Hunting and Maternal Power in Early Modern England*. Ithaca, N.Y.: Cornell University Press.

Wink, Walter. 1984. *Naming the Powers: The Language of Power in the New Testament*. Philadelphia: Fortress.

———. 1986. *Unmasking the Powers: The Invisible Forces That Determine Human Existence*. Philadelphia: Fortress.

———. 1992. *Engaging the Powers: Discernment and Resistance in a World of Domination*. Minneapolis: Fortress.

———. 1998. *When the Powers Fall: Reconciliation in the Healing of Nations*. Minneapolis: Fortress.

———. 1999. *The Powers That Be: Theology for a New Millennium*. New York: Doubleday.

Wittig, Monique. 1992. *The Straight Mind and Other Essays*. Boston: Beacon.

Wolde, Ellen von. 1997. "Texts in Dialogue with Texts: Intertextuality in the Ruth and Tamar Narratives." *BibInt* 5: 1–28.

Worden, J. William. 1991. *Grief Counseling and Grief Therapy: A Handbook for the Mental Health*. 2d ed. New York: Springer.

Women's Caucus for Gender Justice. September 2002. "Clarification of Term Gender." Online: http://www.iccwomen.org/resources/gender.htm.

Yee, Gale A. 1988. "'Fraught with Background': Literary Ambiguity in II Samuel 11." *Int* 42:240–53.

Young, Brad. 1995. "Save the Adulteress! Ancient Jewish Responsa in the Gospels?" NTS 41:59–70.

CONTRIBUTORS

Randall C. Bailey is the Andrew W. Mellon Professor of Hebrew Bible at the Interdenominational Theological Center in Atlanta, Georgia. He is an ideological critic and the author of *David in Love and War: The Pursuit of Power in 2 Samuel 10–12* (Sheffield, 1990), co-editor with Jacquelyn Grant of *The Recovery of Black Presence: An Interdisciplinary Exploration* (Abingdon, 1995) co-editor with Tina Pippin of the *Semeia* volume, *Race, Class and the Politics of Bible Translation* (1996) and editor of *Yet with a Steady Beat: Contemporary U.S. Afrocentric Biblical Interpretation* (Society of Biblical Literature, 2003). He may be reached at rcbailey@itc.edu.

Valerie Cooper is ABD from Harvard Divinity School and is an instructor in Religion at Wake Forest University. Her interests include American and African American religious history, Pentecostalism, and the roles of women in religious institutions. She can be reached at coopervc@wfu.edu.

Nicole Duran, after receiving the Ph.D. in New Testament from Vanderbilt in 1997, has taught in a variety of contexts, from Ankara, Turkey, to Clinton, South Carolina. Currently she serves on the editorial board of the Global Bible Commentary and teaches courses at Rosemont College and Villanova University. Her interests include the interplay of ritual, gender, and ethnicity with the biblical text, from a combination of literary and cultural approaches. She may be reached at nicole.duran@villanova.edu.

Barbara Green is Professor of Biblical Studies at the Dominican School of Philosophy and Theology at the Graduate Theological Union, Berkeley. She is series editor of Liturgical Press Interfaces series on biblical characters, presented via particular methodologies. She has written several books and articles on various topics in Hebrew Bible and in Christian spirituality. She may be reached at bgreen@dspt.edu.

Gina Hens-Piazza is Professor of Biblical Studies at the Jesuit School of Theology at the Graduate Theological Union in Berkeley, where she teaches and writes in the area of the historical books and prophets in the Hebrew Bible. She may be reached at ghenspia@jstb.edu.

Barbara A. Holmes, J.D., Ph.D., is an Associate Professor of Ethics and African American Religious Studies at Memphis Theological Seminary. She is a public theologian, attorney, activist, and scholar. Her writing interests include race, science, law, and cultural critique. Holmes also collaborates with her sister, the Hon. Susan Holmes Winfield, on issues of law and religion. Holmes is the author of *A*

Private Woman in Public Spaces: Barbara Jordan's Ethics, Public Religion and Law, and *Race and the Cosmos: An Invitation to View the World Differently.* Both volumes were published by Trinity Press International. Holmes has practiced law in Georgia, Texas, and Florida and is ordained in the Holiness-Pentecostal tradition. She may be reached at bah9@earthlink.net.

Susan Hylen is a Ph.D. candidate in New Testament at Emory University. She received an M.Div. from Princeton Theological Seminary. During the period between her degrees, she served as Director of the Rape Crisis Service of the Finger Lakes and Program Director of Congregations Preventing Family Violence. She is an elder at Oakhurst Presbyterian Church in Decatur, Georgia. She may be reached at shylen@emory.edu.

Mignon R. Jacobs, Ph.D., is an Assistant Professor of Hebrew Bible at Fuller Theological Seminary. She is author of the book *Conceptual Coherence of the Book of Micah* and articles, including "Conceptual Dynamics of Good and Evil in the Joseph Story" and "Toward a Theology of the Underprivileged." Her current book projects include a commentary on Haggai and Malachi and *Gender, Power and Persuasion.* She may be reached at jacobs@fuller.edu.

Hyun Chul Paul Kim is Assistant Professor of Hebrew Bible in the Williams Chair of Biblical Studies at Methodist Theological School in Ohio, Delaware, Ohio. He is the author of *Ambiguity, Tension, and Multiplicity in Deutero-Isaiah* (Lang, 2003); "Form Criticism in Dialogue with Other Criticisms: Building the Multidimensional Structures of Texts and Concepts," in *The Changing Face of Form Criticism for the Twenty-First Century* (ed. Marvin A. Sweeney and Ehud Ben Zvi; Eerdmans, 2003); and "Interpretative Modes of Yin-Yang Dynamics As an Asian Hermeneutics," *Biblical Interpretation* 9 (2001): 287–308. He may be reached at pkim@mtso.edu.

Cheryl A. Kirk-Duggan, Ph.D., M.M., is the Director of the Center for Women and Religion; In Residence and Core Doctoral Faculty in Theology, Ethics, and Womanist Studies, the Graduate Theological Union, Berkeley, California; and an ordained minister in the Christian Methodist Episcopal Church. Other areas of teaching, research, and writing include pedagogy; rage, grief, and transformation; gender theory; sexuality; faith, health, and spirituality; and the milieu of popular media as a praxeology for constructive and narrative theology. She may reached at kirkdugg@comcast.net.

Madeline McClenney-Sadler holds the Ph.D in Hebrew Bible from Duke University (2001). Her dissertation, "Re-covering the Daughter's Nakedness: Ancient Israelite Terminology and the Internal Logic of Leviticus 18," is forthcoming (Sheffield Academic Press). She is the founder and President of Exodus Foundation.org, a nonprofit working to provide aftercare to African Americans who have been incarcerated. Her research and teaching interests include Hebrew Bible, women's studies, and Islamic law. She may be reached at mms100@earthlink.net.

M. Fulgence Nyengele is Associate Professor of Pastoral Care and Counseling in the William A. Chryst Chair of Pastoral Theology at Methodist Theological School in Ohio, Delaware, Ohio. His research interests include gender and cross-cultural studies, grief, and forgiveness. He is the author of *African Women's Theology, Gender Relations, and Family Systems Theory: Pastoral Theological Reflections and Guidelines for Care and Counseling* (Lang, forthcoming), and "Perichoresis As an Evocative Theological Image for Gender-Sensitive Pastoral Caregiving in African Context," *Africa Theological Journal* 25 (2002): 59–82. He may be reached at fnyengele@mtso.edu.

Dr. Mary Donovan Turner is the Associate Professor of Preaching at Pacific School of Religion in Berkeley, California, where she has taught for twelve years. She completed her graduate studies in Old Testament at Emory University. She is the author with Dr. Mary Lin Hudson of *Saved from Silence: Finding Women's Voice in Preaching* (1999) and also *Old Testament Words*, recently released by Chalice Press. She may be reached at mdturner@psr.edu.

Judge Susan R. Holmes Winfield, Associate Judge for the District of Columbia Superior Court, Washington, D.C., since 1984, is assigned to the Civil, Criminal, and Family Divisions of the Court, where she has presided over homicide, sexual offense crimes, medical malpractice, and other complex civil cases. Judge Winfield has assisted the governments of Tanzania, Uganda, Zambia, and Malawi in developing Civil Delay Reduction, Case Management Systems, and Alternative Dispute Resolution (ADR) programs within their judicial systems since 1994. A mentor, guest lecturer, Judge Winfield has served on the teaching faculties of George Washington University, Columbia School of Law, Harvard University Law School Trial Advocacy Program, and Georgetown Medical School Department of Psychiatry. She may be reached at winfield@dcsc.gov.

Printed in the United States
27175LVS00005B/238-252

9 781589 830745